Ty Cobb

THE MCFARLAND HISTORICAL BASEBALL LIBRARY

1. Cobb, Ty. *Busting 'Em and Other Big League Stories* (1914). 2003

2. Axelson, G.W. *"Commy": The Life Story of Charles A. Comiskey* (1919). 2003

3. Ellard, Harry. *Base Ball in Cincinnati: A History* (1907). 2004

4. Richter, Francis C. *Richter's History and Records of Base Ball, the American Nation's Chief Sport* (1914). 2005

5. Lanigan, Ernest J. *Baseball Cyclopedia* (1922). 2005

6. Evers, John J., and Hugh S. Fullerton. *Touching Second* (1910). 2005

7. Rice, Grantland. *Base-Ball Ballads* (1910). 2005

8. Claudy, C.H. *The Battle of Base-Ball* (1912). 2005

9. Kelly, Mike "King." *"Play Ball": Stories from the Diamond Field and Other Historical Writings about the 19th Century Hall of Famer* (1888). 2006.

10. Anonymous and Noah Brooks. *The Great Match* [1877] *and Our Base Ball Club* [1884]*: Two Novels from the Early Days of Base Ball,* volume editors Trey Strecker *and* Geri Strecker. 2010

11. Green, Guy W. *The Nebraska Indians* [1900] *and Fun and Frolic with an Indian Ball Team* [1907]*: Two Accounts of Baseball Barnstorming at the Turn of the Twentieth Century,* volume editor Jeffrey P. Beck. 2010

12. Salsinger, H.G. *Ty Cobb: Two Biographies—"Our Ty: Ty Cobb's Life Story" (1924) and "Which Was Greatest: Ty Cobb or Babe Ruth?" (1951),* volume editor William R. Cobb. 2012

13. Joss, Addie. *Addie Joss on Baseball: Collected Newspaper Columns and World Series Reports, 1907–1909,* compiled and annotated by Rich Blevins. 2012

Ty Cobb

Two Biographies — "Our Ty: Ty Cobb's Life Story" (1924) and "Which Was Greatest: Ty Cobb or Babe Ruth?" (1951)

by H.G. SALSINGER

volume editor WILLIAM R. COBB

The McFarland Historical Baseball Library, 12
Gary Mitchem *and* Mark Durr, *Series Editors*

McFarland & Company, Inc., Publishers
Jefferson, North Carolina, and London

"Our Ty: Ty Cobb's Life Story" by H.G. Salsinger (copyright 1924 & 1925, the North American Newspaper Alliance).

"Which Was Greatest: Ty Cobb or Babe Ruth?" by H.G. Salsinger (copyright 1951, *The Sporting News*, reprinted with permission).

LIBRARY OF CONGRESS CATALOGUING-IN-PUBLICATION DATA

Salsinger, H.G., 1885–1958.
Ty Cobb : two biographies — : "Our Ty, Ty Cobb's life story" (1924) and "Which was greatest, Ty Cobb or Babe Ruth?" (1951) / by H.G. Salsinger.
p. cm. — (The McFarland historical baseball library ; 12)
Includes index.

ISBN 978-0-7864-6546-0
softcover : acid free paper ∞

1. Cobb, Ty, 1886–1961. 2. Baseball players — United States — Biography. I. Salsinger, Harry G., 1885–1958. Our Ty. II. Salsinger, Harry G., 1885–1958. Which was greatest, Ty Cobb or Babe Ruth? III. Title.
GV865.C6S35 2012
796.357092 — dc23
[B] 2012012941

BRITISH LIBRARY CATALOGUING DATA ARE AVAILABLE

On the cover: Ty Cobb, 1915 (Photograph by Louis Van Oeyen)

Manufactured in the United States of America

McFarland & Company, Inc., Publishers
Box 611, Jefferson, North Carolina 28640
www.mcfarlandpub.com

Table of Contents

Part Two. "Which Was Greatest—Ty Cobb or Babe Ruth?" (1951)

Editor's Note

On September 30, 1907, 20-year-old Tyrus Raymond Cobb approached the batter's box at Philadelphia's Columbia Avenue Park in the top of the ninth inning, his first-place Tigers trailing Connie Mack's Athletics 8 to 6. A loss in this outing would drop the Tigers to second place in the championship race, one-half game behind Philadelphia. The Tigers had come from a 7–1 deficit that day with rallies in the seventh, eighth and ninth innings. With Sam Crawford on first base after a clean single, Cobb belted a home run high over the right-field wall to tie the game. In the next eight innings before the tied game was called for darkness, the Tigers and the Athletics would trade the lead several times as Cobb smacked a single and ground-rule double, stole a base, and was stranded on third in the 17th inning. This tie game was never completed, as Detroit went on to win its first American League title and make its first World Series appearance. In his later years, Cobb would describe playing this game as his greatest thrill in a 24-year baseball career.

That day, back in Detroit, a recently hired young copyreader at the telegraph desk of the *Detroit News* watched the ticker with ever-increasing excitement. Twenty-year-old H.G. Salsinger, an aspiring sportswriter, must have felt a real connection with the equally young Ty Cobb, who saved the game and the first-place standing for the Tigers. So moved was Salsinger by Cobb's performance, and by his batting average of .613 for the remaining five games of the 1907 season, that he immortalized the player's ninth-inning homer in a poem titled "Ty Cobb at the Bat," which the *Detroit News* published on October 6, 1907, the day after the 1907 season ended.

H.G. Salsinger rose quickly to become sports editor of the *Detroit News* in 1909, a position he would hold for 49 years, until his death in 1958. In his distinguished sportswriting career, he served as president of the Baseball Writers Association of America (BBWA) and covered every World Series for

50 years. Salsinger also wrote on football, golf, tennis and major boxing matches, and he covered the 1932 and 1936 Olympic Games. He has received posthumous recognition from the BBWA, which named him the 1968 J.G. Taylor Spink Award recipient; the Michigan Media Hall of Fame, in 1971; and the Michigan Sports Hall of Fame, where he was enshrined in 2002.

From 1907, Salsinger's connection to Cobb would grow into a deep personal friendship that would last more than 50 years. They hunted together, played cards, corresponded often on baseball and other subjects, and visited at each other's homes and at the ball parks. They also shared a deep and enduring love of dogs — Salsinger as a nationally acclaimed breeder of wire fox terriers, and Cobb as a proud owner, hunter and exhibitor of champion English setters.

To say that Salsinger became the foremost contemporary authority on the life, career and legend of Ty Cobb would be an understatement. No one, friend or foe, had anything near the level of interaction with Cobb, or the understanding of him, that Salsinger had. By the close of the 1923 season, Salsinger had watched, analyzed, written about, edited, or discussed the details of Ty Cobb's exploits in almost 2,200 games with Detroit. No one even came close to this level of familiarity with Ty Cobb's baseball career, and it was well recognized in the press, and throughout the sport, that Salsinger was *the* leading expert on Ty Cobb.

At the close of the 1923 season, Salsinger anticipated, as did many others, that Ty Cobb might soon retire. There were musings in the press of Cobb's age catching up with him, and from as early as 1910 he had talked about his plan to retire at the top of his game. With this in mind, Salsinger sought permission to write the first official biography of the great player. There were a few biographical magazine articles about Ty Cobb up to that point, but no comprehensive biography had yet been written. In a November 14, 1923, letter replying to Salsinger's request to do the biography, Ty wrote, "In regards to doing the story, I think the best time to start on it would be in the Spring — take plenty of time and do the thing right." Salsinger did take his time, completing the biography titled *Ty Cobb's Life Story* after the close of the 1924 season and publishing it as a syndicated series of 58 chapters beginning in November 1924.

Part One of this volume presents this, the first complete and authorized biography of Ty Cobb, in book form. There is uncertainty as to whether

Salsinger's serialized biography was ever published in book form before, however. Marc Okkonen, respected baseball historian and author, recounts in his 2002 *Ty Cobb Scrapbook* that on the eve of the twentieth anniversary of Ty Cobb's first major league game in August 1925, the *Detroit News* advertised a biographical book on Ty Cobb titled *Our Ty*. Cobb objected, however, because he had not authorized the book, and he insisted that it be withdrawn from distribution, which it apparently was. A diligent search for copies of this book has not uncovered a single existing copy. No other advertisement, reference or information about this book in any Detroit or Michigan newspaper has been located. Okkonen did uncover Salsinger's 58-chapter biographical series in the *Detroit News*, however, and because of Salsinger's long term affiliation with the *News*, Okkonen has speculated that *Our Ty* was actually Salsinger's serialized biography printed in book form. For this reason, Part One of this volume is titled *Our Ty* and subtitled *Ty Cobb's Life Story*.

Part Two is a second biography of Ty Cobb written by Salsinger 25 years later. This biography was serialized in 22 chapters appearing in *The Sporting News* in 1950, and later printed as a single article in the 1951 *Sporting News Baseball Register*. Salsinger titled this biography *Which Was Greater: Ty Cobb or Babe Ruth?* responding to a controversy then brewing over who was the greatest player of all time. A 1950 sportswriters poll to determine baseball's greatest player had recently given Babe Ruth the honors with twice as many votes as second-place Ty Cobb. Salsinger took exception, agreeing instead with the 102 major league players, managers and baseball executives polled by *The Sporting News* in 1942, who gave the accolade to Ty Cobb by a margin of six to one over third-place Ruth. As the acknowledged national expert on Ty Cobb, Salsinger presented his arguments that Cobb was greater than Ruth in the first two chapters, and provided another excellent biographical description of Cobb in the remaining twenty. The biography is reprinted in this volume with the kind permission of *The Sporting News*.

Each of these biographies is unique. Written by someone who had spent his entire career covering Ty Cobb, analyzing and writing about him in detail, they were also written from the perspective of someone who knew Ty Cobb personally as well. This is in striking contrast to the twelve other Cobb biographies written since 1961, all by authors who never saw Cobb play, only two of whom had ever actually spoken with him.

Another important characteristic worth noting is that this volume represents the first Ty Cobb biography published since the recent revelation of astounding deceit and fraud perpetrated by Al Stump, collaborator on Cobb's 1961 autobiography. The editor's article in the summer 2010 issue of *The National Pastime* presents irrefutable proof that Stump forged literally hundreds of letters that he claimed were written by Ty Cobb, and foisted them off at considerable profit on unsuspecting memorabilia collectors and historians. Stump also forged and sold at least two complete personal diaries, supposedly written by Ty Cobb, that found their way into the most respected baseball museums in the country, including the National Baseball Hall of Fame. These diaries contained completely fabricated facts and statements that have been widely accepted by historians and biographers. Given that almost all of the outrageous and near-unbelievable stories about Ty Cobb came from the post–1960 writings of Al Stump, revelation of Stump's massive deceit casts doubt on all that he has written.

Though Salsinger was Ty Cobb's personal friend, and certainly an ardent admirer, he was nevertheless an objective biographer. Salsinger presents in these two works not only the positive but the negative aspects of his friend. Cobb himself acknowledged the evenhandedness of Salsinger's 1924 biography in a comment he made after Salsinger's death in 1958: "I read every word of it. No man could have been fairer. Some of his comments hurt—but all of it was honest writing. That's what we always got from Sal."

A Word About the Text

Various Ty Cobb statistics that appear in this volume are as printed in the original work. In recent years, historians have proposed changes to the official record, but Major League Baseball does not acknowledge these revisions. The reader interested in statistics should refer to Baseball Reference (www.baseball-reference.com) for up-to-date (although not always officially sanctioned) numbers.

Within the text, the original capitalization and punctuation have been preserved. Archaic word usage, such as the use of "not alone" rather than the familiar "not only," has been retained as well. Words combined in modern usage, such as "worthwhile," are retained as separate words when they appeared so in the original.

There was some regionalization of the text itself by the newspapers that printed the original series in 1924. For example, the *Atlanta Constitution* omitted the phrase "the camera did not lie" in describing the famous Baker spiking photo. In 1924, use of the word "lie" was considered offensive to the polite Southern reader, not unlike a curse word, and hence it was avoided. The original text was retained for this edition: "the camera did not lie."

Salsinger sometimes refers to teams by city and league, a practice common at the time, but not so in modern writings. Thus, for example, the Pittsburgh Pirates are referred to in places as the Pittsburgh Nationals and the Browns as the St. Louis Americans. This convention is retained. Also, players are sometimes referred to by their last name only. In cases where clarification is needed, first names have been inserted in brackets.

Finally, the chapter numbering and arrangement differed slightly among the newspapers that printed the serialized text. In this volume, chapters have been arranged and numbered in the sequence that provides the best flow within the overall work.

Part Two, written only sixty years ago, did not require any editorial change or explanation for the modern reader. There is some duplication of the anecdotes and accounts from Part One, Salsinger having obviously used his earlier writing as a basis for the later biography. In the 26-year period between the biographies, Ty Cobb completed his career with a two-year stay at Philadelphia and became an outspoken analyst and critic of the game. Part Two shows that the passage of time had only deepened his conviction that Ty Cobb was the greatest baseball player that ever lived.

William R. Cobb, Editor
April 2012

"Ty Cobb at the Bat"

by H. G. Salsinger

It looked extremely rocky for the Tiger nine that day:
The score stood eight to six, with an inning left to play.
But Sam Crawford lined a single and brought suspense once more.
For Cobb, the mighty Tiger, was doping out the score.

There was ease in Ty Cobb's manner as he stepped into his place.
There was pride in Ty Cobb's bearing and a smile on Ty Cobb's face.
And, when responding to the silence, he tightly pulled his hat.
No stranger in the crowd could doubt 'twas Ty Cobb at the bat.

Eighty thousand eyes were on him as he rubbed his hands with dirt;
Forty thousand bit their lips when he wiped them on this shirt;
Then, when the writhing Waddell ground the ball into his hip,
Defiance glared in Ty Cobb's eye, a sneer curled Ty Cobb's lip.

But fame is fleeting as the wind and glory fades away;
There were no wild and wooly cheers, no glad acclaim that day
They hissed and groaned and hooted as they clamored, "Strike him out!"
But Ty Cobb gave no outward sign that he had heard their shout.

Then Reuben smiled and cut one loose;
Another hiss, another groan — "Strike one!" the umpire said.
No roasting for the umpire now — his was an easy lot.
But when Rube whirled 'round again — was that a rifle shot?
A whack! A crack! Through space the leather pellet flew.
A blot against the distant sky, a speck against the blue.

Above the fence in far right field, in rapid whirling flight,
The sphere sailed on; the blot grew dim and then was lost to sight.
Then forty thousand hearts were crushed, forty thousand threw a fit.
But none will ever find the ball that mighty Ty Cobb hit.

Oh, somewhere in this favored land the sun is shining bright.
The band is playing somewhere, and somewhere hearts are light;
And somewhere men are laughing where there never hangs a pall,
But there is no joy in Phillie since mighty Tyrus hit that ball.

Part One

"Our Ty: Ty Cobb's Life Story" (1924)

Preface

Leaving, He Leaves His Imprint
Has Broken All Records—Has Revolutionized the Game

A garrulous old gentleman named Socrates remade the mental processes of the world by his incessant questioning. Galileo got an idea the earth was running around the sun and not the sun around the world and remade the story of the heavens. Napoleon believed in the red star of destiny he saw shining for him at night in the heavens; and he remade the art of warfare and for his brilliant hour dominated the earth. And so it has ever been in the history of man; men spring up from obscure places, flash their genius upon their stage, drive, inspire, dominate—and fade away, but they leave their imprint on a remade world.

An Edison arises to dominate with dynamos, a Ford ordains a new industrial era, a Wilson dictates the world political thought of his time, a Pasteur remakes the field of medicine, and a Bach changes the course of music—they live their lives, these men, and pass on while a world of endless generations, fascinated by their deeds, seeks a key to the riddle of their baffling personalities. And there is no answer, for of the world's great each in his chosen way has been a law unto himself, refusing always to conform and daring always to sail out on uncharted seas.

There Are No Seconds

There is but one Shakespeare, one Lincoln, one Twain; there are no seconds. Grand opera will never know another Caruso and the prize ring will never know another Dempsey. And baseball also has its lonely figure sitting on the Olympian (or shall we say myopian) heights of hero worship.

There is but one, and the baseball world will never know his like again, Tyrus Raymond Cobb, the inspiration of the boyhood of America.

For 20 years he has dominated the thought of a sport-loving public. That boy who years ago was the star batter in the sand-lot team known as the Ty Cobb Juniors now has a son who stars on a team of the same name. For 20 years he has vied with the Roosevelts, the Fords, the Edisons for the newspaper space of the republic, because the people wanted to know about him and his deeds, his daring, ruthless, rushing, fiery, fighting; to get the thrill of his personality.

He Remade His Sport

And in their hearts he has won his place, for while others have changed the destinies of peoples, the ways of living and the means of life, Ty Cobb revolutionized and remade the sport of a nation.

What cares the erstwhile weary but now frantic business man in his box seat at the ball park for the fate of kings or the riddles of life? What cares the lowly worker, now king for a day in his bleacher seat? The game's the thing! And this strangely baffling, strangely contradictory genius of the ball field remade that game, so that, in leaving it, there will be left always his imprint. He was a law unto himself.

The career of Tyrus Raymond Cobb as a player is now drawing to a close. He has broken all the records there are in baseball to break and he has laughed at Father Time ten years beyond his allotted span, and so there is to be told in these pages, the story of his most restless life, of his deeds, and perchance here and there a misdeed or two. For the hero of our tale is human.

It is the story of how a mighty brain and the driving force of genius made him great when other men far superior in physical strength, natural ability and speed, remained mediocre.

Brain power made Ty Cobb.

CHAPTER 1

Brains

Secret of His Success—
A Thinker Who Acted—Physically Excelled.

Ty Cobb was the greatest ball player in history. He achieved that distinction not because he was the fastest base runner, nor the best base stealer, nor the fleetest fielder, nor the greatest hitter. He became baseball's greatest player because he had the best baseball brain ever developed, the fastest thinking brain in the realm of baseball. Because he had the ability to conceive a situation and take full advantage of it before his opponents awakened to it. He was a keener student of the game than they and he understood the game better than they. What is more he understood them—the other players—better than they understood themselves. He knew their strength and their weakness. He knew their virtues and their faults as far as playing ball was concerned. He was the greatest player because he thought ahead of them at all times. The play directly in front of him was not his aim, but the play of the moment, until he scored, was merely the foundation for the play that was to come.

He was not the greatest fielder, for a dozen men in baseball towered over him as outfielders. He was not the greatest place hitter, for "Wee Willie" Keeler was a bit better in placing hits. He was not the greatest slugger, for a few dozen men have been able to hit a ball harder than Cobb ever could. He was not the fastest man in the game for several others were just as fast, a few even faster.

Not the Body

The difference between Cobb and all the other stars of baseball did not rest in the body but in the head. He thought quicker than anyone else and he knew how to put his mechanical skill to more advantages than any of the others.

They said that he made many of his hits because he was so fast. He hurried the play and compelled in-fielders to make fumbles and bad throws by overhurrying.

Cobb had speed, yes. But baseball's dozen other men just as fast did not make infielders hurry so they fumbled and threw badly, enabling the runner to beat the play the way Cobb did.

One of the greatest sprinters of all time was Bernie Wefers.* Baseball men who saw him run decided he would star in professional baseball because of his speed. So they tried to make a ball player out of Wefers. They failed. Wefers was fast. He was faster than any man of his time. But he did not know what to do with his speed. In baseball, having speed and knowing how to apply it are different things. Cobb knew better how to apply it than other men just as fast. Cobb could have been trained to run straightaway and would have made a remarkable sprinter. But the biggest asset as a sprinter in him would have been his break from the mark. He would have had the jump on all competitors.

Did the Unexpected

In base-running his brain work was as conspicuous as his speed. He started before they expected him to start. He went when they did not expect him to go and he made no attempt to advance when he was expected to. He always crossed them up.

Nearing a bag, Cobb's next move was always figured out. He knew exactly what he wanted to do. More than that, he was certain of what the other fellow would do. That made it easy for him to act. He knew how to escape the fielder.

Cobb was not the hitter that the sluggers of the old school were, not in the strict sense of the word. He was never a natural hitter; they were. But Cobb made more hits than the men naturally fitted for hitting, again because of his brain. As he knew the workings of an infielder, or an outfielder, so

*Bernie Wefers (1873–1957) was the most dominant sprinter of the 1890s, winning the National 100 and 220 yard championships three times and the World 100 and 200 yard championships twice. He coached the New York Athletic Club from 1904 to 1947.

did Cobb know the system of the pitcher he was opposing. He batted accordingly.

Scientific Baseball

He did not use mystic powers. He had no occult gifts. He simply reduced baseball to a scientific basis and figured it out accordingly. Cobb's plays may appear mystifying, but in that they resemble a conjuror's tricks. The feats of a magician are astounding and beyond comprehension until they are explained. Then they become extremely simple. Cobb's play was always just as simple. Once explained by him, once he gave the reason for making the play the way he did, it became clear and simple. Analyzed, most great achievements become reduced to the same simple, comprehensive level.

He thought faster than any man that ever wore spiked shoes. And he thought more thoroughly. He saw the little things that the others missed and he took advantage of them. Nothing escaped his observation. The mechanical performances of a fielder, the minute physical characteristics of a pitcher, were studied by Cobb, analyzed by him and then used as the basis of his attack. He built his offense against the weak points of their defense.

There has been but one Cobb. There is likely never to be another. In him were strangely combined all those qualities that were needed to make the perfect competitor, a man with playing faults but with the most highly developed competitive spirit and the finest developed brain that the national pastime of the United States has produced.

CHAPTER 2

Cobb's Secret Ambition

A hope he cherished—
How pride was hurt—What it cost him.

Ty Cobb was never a perfect player. There has never been a perfect one. Cobb is recognized as the greatest because he came nearer perfection than any of the other leaders of baseball. Cobb had one outstanding mechanical fault and that was a weak throwing arm. This weakness could have been avoided. Cobb has only himself to blame for it. Cobb wanted to become a pitcher. As a boy he played on the infield, at short. But the ambition of every boy who likes baseball is to be a great pitcher. That was the secret ambition of Cobb.

Never during his long years in baseball has Cobb become fully convinced that, had he concentrated upon pitching, he could not have become one of the great moundsmen of the game. He brought his ambition with him to the majors and nursed it through all these years. Whenever he could enlist the services of a catcher Cobb practiced pitching. He would work with the catcher for half an hour or more, generally more. And while he worked Cobb pitched twice as many balls as any regular pitcher would in the same length of time, for Cobb pitched as he played, with a nervous speed.

Cobb's Pride Hurt

He managed to develop what players described as a "dinky hook," meaning an amateurish curve-ball delivery, he never was able to pitch a real fast ball, and what he called his slow ball was ineffective because of faulty delivery.

Players who looked over Cobb's pitching were never impressed by it and this hurt Cobb's pride. The result was that he tried all the harder.

We remember one brilliant spring day in San Antonio, Texas. It was in the spring of 1909 and the Detroit team was training there. Cobb had recruited a catcher and was having his morning workout, pitching.

The late Herman Schaefer, then a veteran and wise in the way of baseball, walked over to Cobb and said to him:

"Listen! Take a piece of advice from me and cut out this monkey business. Forget that you are a pitcher. You ain't. You can never be one. You've been pitching for four years that I know of an' you ain't got no more stuff than a high-school boy. There's a lot of good pitchers and there's a couple of thousand that's better than you'll ever be, but there ain't a lot of outfielders with good throwin' arms, and my advice to you is — quit tryin' to be a pitcher an' save your arm for the outfield."

Didn't Take Advice

Cobb did not take the advice. Instead he tried harder to prove that Schaefer and the others were wrong. He never proved them otherwise than right, but while he continued pitching, Cobb wore out his arm. It gradually weakened and baserunners, quick to observe the weakness, took advantage of it.

As a fielder Cobb never compared with Tris Speaker, Harry Hooper and a number of others in his league. His weak arm was his greatest handicap, but he had another fault in fielding and that was failure to play position for batters.

Cobb, during the days when he was climbing to the peak and after he held the heights, rarely ever changed his position in the outfield. He stood rooted to nearly the same spot in each game, playing a "dead" center position. Other outfielders moved according to the batter and the catcher's signal to the pitcher. An outfielder's position should depend upon the position of the batter, right or left-handed, and upon the pitcher's delivery. A right-handed batter, for instance, will not hit a high fast ball on the outside to the same spot that he will hit a low curve ball, pitched on the inside. When the catcher signals the pitcher the outfielder starts moving with the pitch, having taken up what is known as the natural position for that batter when he came to the plate.

Relied on His Speed

Cobb never did this. He played every batter practically the same way. And there never was any serious objection to this, for Cobb depended upon his mechanical ability and there was reasons for his faith in himself. There has never been a man in the history of the game who could break away as fast as Cobb. If Charlie Paddock had been gifted with Cobb's quick start, he would have established a new world mark for the 100-yard dash because Cobb was at the top of his stride with his second step. He moved at top speed almost at the instant he started.

It was because of this speed and developed judgment of fly balls that Cobb managed to be a good outfielder while playing a "stationary" position. But he would have been a better out-fielder had he moved according to the batter's position and the catcher's signals. He would have gotten more fly balls and stopped more ground-hit balls.

Still, this style of play would have taken from Cobb many spectacular chances. Cobb, a born showman, always tried to do everything in the most difficult manner possible. Innumerable times has he started late after a ball, or paused in his run, timing himself shrewdly so that he managed a shoestring or diving catch, or a stabbing of the ball with his gloved hand while leaping high — all on chances where easy and natural catches were possible. Cobb, skilled in theatricals, had trained himself to introduce every possible thrill into his play and where there was no natural opportunity for a spectacular piece of fielding. He created the opportunity. He was baseball's master show-man.

Opposite:* William H. "Germany" Schaefer (1876–1919) in 1918. As a veteran ten years Cobb's senior, Schaefer advised Cobb in 1909 to give up his dreams of ever becoming a pitcher. Schaefer had played for the Chicago Cubs in 1901 and 1902, and was out of baseball for two years before joining the Tigers in 1905. He played with Detroit until 1909, and with the Washington Senators until 1915 when he bolted to the Federal League. He finished his career in 1918 after appearing in only one game with Cleveland. Schaefer was known for his antics, the most famous of which was "stealing" first base, returning to it from second after a double-steal attempt drew no throw from the catcher. *Courtesy Library of Congress Bain Collection.

CHAPTER 3

Ty Cobb as a Boy

His fathers orders—
A shattered outlook—Ty Cobb goes to work

Ty Cobb as a boy learned what he regards as his most valuable lesson in life during a summer vacation. He had planned to spend the vacation—as his previous ones had been spent—in playing ball, fishing and swimming. One evening his father called him aside—he would have to go to work, the father said. Young Tyrus did not like the idea. His father was insistent. He told him the time had come when he must find out something about earning a livelihood, something about the demands of work and the rewards of work. He was old enough, said the father, to learn about the more serious things of life.

The plan still did not appeal to Cobb. He had been eagerly waiting for spring, and then for summer. He had counted the days until school closed, until he would be free to play from morning until night. He yearned for the companionship of the ball fields, the swimming hole. And now all that he planned for, all he hoped for, all that he visioned, was taken from him in a full sweep of parental command.

Ty's Ten Acres

"I have ten acres near here," said the father of Tyrus. "This ten acres I have been holding for several years until you grew old enough to work it. The soil will produce cotton and I want you to produce ten acres of cotton.

"We will go about the thing in a regular manner, the same as if you owned the land and were a cotton planter. You will keep books and supervise everything. It will be up to you entirely; I am putting the whole thing in your hands.

"Tomorrow morning we will go out, you and I. We will make all the necessary purchases, acquire all the necessary equipment. We will put down the cost of everything. Then you must keep in mind the cost and learn to make up all the cost and get the investment to earn money."

They started out the next morning, young Tyrus and his father. They went to a hardware store for a plow, to a harness shop for harness and to a seed store for seed,

Ty Is Given a Mule

The Cobbs had several horses. Tyrus suggested that he take one of those horses, and he asked his father which one he could have for use on the ten-acre farm.

"You can't have any of them," replied his father. "That would he borrowed equipment. I want you to be entirely on your own. A horse is too expensive. It would raise the investment; too high. We can not afford to buy a horse to pull the plow on the ten acres. A mule is less expensive and it will do the work required out there. We will buy a mule."

They bought a mule and the elder Cobb took the mule and the plow, the harness, the seed and other equipment to the ten acres and told Tyrus to get to work.

It was difficult work at first. It was also distasteful work. Tyrus went at it in a half-hearted, disinterested manner. He loafed on the job. All day long he saw visions of the baseball diamond, of the swimming hole. He heard the call of youth and he was figuratively shackled to a plow. How he hated plows! Hated mules! Hated cotton! Hated farming!

But his father made him stick. He was routed out early each morning and sent to the ten acres. He hitched up his mule and started on his job. It was hard work and he did not see the use of it, anyway.

A Hit in Cotton

Then, slowly, a change came over him. The cotton stalks began peeping above the surface of the ground. He became interested. He watched over his farm daily, walked the ten acres, noted how the stalks in one plot were outgrowing the stalks in another part, outgrowing them just a trifle, but still outgrowing them.

The idea came to him that he was producing something, that he was really contributing to the world. He was a person of importance.

He had a new interest in life, a mission to perform. He looked forward to each new day with eagerness. Always, when he quit at dusk, he mapped out his duties for the following day and went to bed at night, knowing that at dawn he would be eager to go out to his farm and carry on the work.

Rain clouds that had previously meant a spoiled day for him, now took on a new meaning. When the cotton fields needed rain he watched each fleeting cloud, eagerly hoping for a gathering of storm clouds. He speculated on what his ten acres would produce, on what he would get for his cotton in the market. He had his investment to overcome, the cost of the mules, the plow, the harness and the other utensils.

"That was the most valuable lesson I ever received," said Tyrus. "I learned to produce. I learned that money had to be earned. I learned the value of the dollar, the joy of earning it. I could not have learned it in any better way."

CHAPTER 4

Ty's Father

A Schoolmaster's Address—
Cobb Praises Gran'mother—The Boy Leaves Home.

Who discovered Ty Cobb? The question has been argued for more than 15 years and with apparently no definite answer. Many men have claimed the distinction and many arguments have resulted.

Also, it is generally believed that Cobb was born in Royston, Ga. He was not. Cobb's birthplace was in Banks county, Ga., and Banks county is close to the Carolina state line. His parents moved to Royston, a small town near Augusta, when Tyrus was a baby and Cobb spent his boyhood in Royston.

His father was a schoolmaster.* One day, 18 years after Cobb made his major league debut, he received a package. Enclosed was a faded manuscript, yellow with age. Written in long hand was an address. The handwriting was free, easy. To an expert in such matters the writer would appear as a man who knew his subject and who set down his ideas rapidly, and well. The address dealt with education in the state of Georgia, advocating more liberal education and setting forth citations from history to establish the point that education is the foundation of true democracy.

Written by Ty's Father

The writer of the address was Cobb's father. He delivered it before a state convention of educators, and, according to the man who sent Cobb the

*William Herschel Cobb (1863–1905) was a farmer and educator who served on the local school board and was elected to the Georgia State Senate. He was a graduate of North Georgia College in Dahlonega, Georgia. He also was owner and publisher of the *Royston* [Ga.] *Record.*

manuscript and who heard Cobb's father deliver the address 40 years previously, "the speech did a great deal for the development of educational facilities in the state and was the finest address ever delivered before a body of educators."

Cobb's father, as a result, became one of the leading educators in Georgia and until his untimely death, did splendid work in establishing a better system for the development of the school in his home state.

One of the greatest women in the world, in Cobb's opinion was his grandmother.* She has always had his keenest admiration.

"I never knew another woman like her," he says. "She had one of the most remarkable minds, if not the most remarkable, I ever came in contact with. Her memory is flawless. Her intuition is far more accurate than the logical conclusions of any man I know. I have never found a human being more frank and, at the same time, more diplomatic, than she is. Her insight into human nature is uncanny."

An Ordinary Boy

Cobb was an ordinary boy. He did the things that other boys did in much the same way. There was nothing about him that would indicate future greatness in any particular calling. He was the kind of a boy who, after he achieves high rank, finds the neighbors remarking: "You don't mean to tell me it's that same spindle-legged kid that used to run around here. I can't imagine it."

And he was a spindle-legged kid, extremely thin, a gangling youth. He rode a bicycle; he fished; he played ball. Finally he learned to swim.

A negro taught Cobb how to swim. The colored man, working for one of the families in Royston, used to go to the swimming hole. Cobb was timid about the water. The negro asked the boy to climb on his back and he would carry him out. Cobb did. The negro swam about with Cobb's arms around his neck, his legs pinned to his sides. He brought him back to shore. He repeated this the next day and the next. Then, one day, he carried Cobb to a mid-stream on his back. There he made him release his hold.

*Sarah Ann Elizabeth Waldroup Cobb (1837–1921). As a youngster Ty Cobb often spent summers at the farm of this grandfather and grandmother in Murphy, North Carolina.

Cobb, forced to swim or sink, discovered he could swim. He swam back to shore unassisted, and he swam ever after.

Not Best Boy Player

There have been many stories written about Cobb's accomplishments as a boy. There are stories tending to picture him as an infant prodigy. But Cobb had none of the outstanding qualities that set him apart from the other boys of Royston. He was one of a million or more boys within the boundary lines of his native land at that time, carrying the faults of the other boys and most of their virtues. He was "just boy."

He played ball much like the other boys. He was a shortstop for one of the sandlot teams. He improved in his play and soon was a member of the best sandlot team in his home town. He was one of the best players in town, but not recognized as the best.

Cobb was ambitious. He wanted to become a "regular" ball player. One day he left home and went to Augusta, nearby. He sought an interview with "Con" Strouthers, manager of the Augusta team that year, in 1904. Strouthers granted Cobb the interview.

"Well, young man, what can I do for you?" asked Strouthers.

"I'd like to play on your team," answered Cobb.

CHAPTER 5

He Takes the Plunge

A Skinny Lad of 17—
First Opening Day—The Boy's Chagrin.

Ty Cobb, a skinny boy of 17, had taken the plunge. He had made his bid for a place in the ranks of professional baseball. Con Strouthers, manager of the Augusta club, had agreed to give him a tryout.

A year before no thought of this had ever entered his head. He had other plans. He wanted to become a surgeon. He had intended entering the University of Georgia. His father approved of the plan. It delighted him to discover that his Tyrus had selected one of the leading professions.

Cobb also wanted to play college football and baseball. He says he had nursed this college ambition for years and because of it never accepted money for playing ball; he wanted to enter college as a simon-pure amateur.

The turning point in Cobb's life came when one of his friends, playing on the same Royston sandlot team, secured a trial with a club in the Southern league. It was then that Cobb first began reading baseball news. He wanted to follow his friend's professional career.

Writes for a Tryout

Cobb became interested in the professional leagues. Daily he looked through the box scores. At the end of the season his friend returned to Royston and gave him glowing accounts of the life he led as a professional ball player. It was easy to make good, his friend said. And, listening to the friend day after day, Cobb finally resolved to become a professional ball player.

The next spring, it was the spring of 1904, he wrote letters to two clubs in the old South Atlantic league, asking for a trial. The management of the

Augusta team said he could get a trial if he paid his own expenses. Cobb bought a ticket to Augusta, made his way to baseball headquarters and asked to see Con Strouthers, the manager. He lost no time launching his request.

Strouthers thought for a moment. There was no expense involved in giving the boy a trial and — well, you can never tell with these boys. Strouthers told Cobb to report at the park and get a uniform.

Cobb reported at the park and worked out with the Augusta squad. The season was close at hand but one of the Augusta outfielders, a regular of the previous year, was not eligible. He had played outlaw ball and was suspended. Strouthers told Cobb to play the outfield. If the player was not reinstated by opening day he would use Cobb in the regular's place.

Ty's First Opening Day

Opening day arrived — April 20, 1904. The regular outfielder had not been reinstated. And the name of Cobb that afternoon appeared in the lineup and batting order of a professional baseball team for the first time.

The scene of Cobb's professional debut still stands in Augusta as that city's baseball park. Across the street lies a cemetery and at three in the afternoon the yells of the Augusta fans, the cries of joy, the hoots and hisses, often mingle with the sobs of the mourners at an open grave across the street.

Here, on that April day, Augusta fans witnessed the entrance into the professional game of baseball's greatest performer. Augusta was playing Columbia, S. C. The new recruit, playing the outfield, did well. He made two hits, one a two-bagger and the other a home run. But his good hitting did not prevent Augusta from losing, for victory went to Columbia that day by a score of 8 to 7.

Cobb was back in the lineup the next afternoon. He did not do so well at bat but still he did not go hitless. He made a single. Augusta won the game.

Cobb Is Fired

Strouthers walked over to Cobb in the clubhouse that evening. He asked him to see him in his office the next morning.

Cobb, believing he was to be tendered a contract with a good salary, eagerly went to Strouthers' office the next morning. Strouthers arrived some time later and Cobb followed him into the office. Without waiting to ask Cobb to be seated Strouthers informed him:

"You're released."

Cobb was stunned. A moment later he blurted out:

"You mean I'm let out here? You're letting me go"

"Yes," replied Strouthers. "I'm letting you go. You're a free agent. I can't use you. My regular outfielder has been reinstated and I'm going to use him. You can join any club you like because you're a free agent now."

CHAPTER 6

Jobless

A Laconic Father—
Ty Gets His Contract—His Real Discoverer.

Ty Cobb had experienced his first great disappointment. He had thought he was making good, but the Augusta manager, Strouthers, had released him after his first two days as a professional baseball player. Now he was in a sore predicament. His father was opposed to professional baseball. He had asked his son Tyrus to forget his desire about playing professional ball. Cobb had come to Augusta against the wishes of his father and here he was—jobless.

He finally resolved to call his father, feeling sure that the elder Cobb would ask him to come home. He called him, said he had lost his job, but that he had a chance to go with a smaller club.

"All right, take the job. Don't come home a failure. You've decided on professional baseball and now show that you can be a success at it. Try and do your best, but don't come home until you succeed," Cobb's father told him.

Ty Gets a Contract

Cobb went to Anniston and got a contract with that club. At the time Anniston was in the Southeastern league, an organization that has long since passed out.

It was not long before Cobb became the star of the league. In 22 games with Anniston he batted for an average of .370. Augusta fans began reading about Cobb. They remembered he had been dropped from the Augusta team. They began criticizing the management.

Letting a ball player go who later makes good with another club is the dread of every owner and manager. Nothing brings so much criticism and nothing so hurts gate receipts as to show faulty judgment on the possibilities of a recruit. Augusta was in a slump and the patrons were saying, "If they hadn't let that kid Cobb go we might be somewhere in the standing. Look at what he's done for Anniston. He's hitting .370 and..."

Strouthers, tiring of the criticisms, tried to get Cobb back. He wired him an offer and Cobb's reply ran something like this:

"I won't play for you in Augusta and I'll never play for you anywhere else."

Several weeks later Strouthers lost his job. His release of Cobb was one reason and a losing team was another and the chief reason. In Strouthers place came George Leidy. The Augusta fans were still demanding the return of Cobb, and Leidy, acquainting himself with the facts attending Cobb's departure, wired him an offer, guaranteeing him fine treatment and assuring him that Strouthers was no longer connected with the club in any way. Cobb accepted Leidy's offer and returned to Augusta.

His Real Discoverer

When Cobb returned to the town of his debut he came under the management of the man who really discovered him — Leidy.

Leidy was never a big leaguer. He never had the mechanical ability to make the majors and as a manager he would never reach that high, for few men who have not played in the major leagues have ever managed clubs in either big circuit.

Leidy was one of an army of several hundred men whose managerial careers are confined to the minors. Only a small portion of the baseball public ever hears of these men. They shift often. Their jobs rarely last beyond a season unless they produce a pennant-winning team or one that finishes well up. They drift from team to team, from league to league, and few last longer than four or five seasons.

Never able to attain the baseball heights they try to do the next best thing — develop stars for the major circuits. They want to see others accomplish what they were never able to attain.

Such a manager was Leidy,* a medium-sized man, with a weather-beaten face and knotty fingers. A retiring man, unassuming, modest, plain, frank and honest. He had seen much of life and he had seen a great deal of baseball in the "bushes." He knew the ups and the downs, the breaks and the luck of the game.

Leidy had a "nose for baseball talent." He had imagination. After watching Cobb in a few games Leidy got a hunch that the boy held unlimited possibilities. He was quick, high-strung and nervous. He was timid, supersensitive and extremely temperamental. Leidy took all this into consideration. He weighed the qualities, the characteristics. He decided the boy could be developed into a great ball player, for Leidy imagined what Cobb's qualities could produce in the way of mechanical skill.

"Of course, he was the kind of youngster that a lot of managers would pass up," said Leidy one day years after. "But I figured him like a fine thoroughbred race horse. I said to myself, 'Now you wouldn't give a snap for a horse that acted like a plough horse at the barrier. This kid is high-strung and he can't be bullied. He's got to be nursed along. He's got the fire and the thing to do is break him to bridle. He's got to be handled like a prancing colt and that's how I'll handle him.'"

*George Leidy would spend only one year in Augusta, 1905. He played for the Mobile Sea Gulls in the Cotton States League in 1906, and then spent nine years as player-manager for three different teams in the Texas League.

CHAPTER 7

Genius Afire

Sowing the Seeds—
Instilling Confidence—Ty Cobb's Resolve.

The real development of Ty Cobb as a ball player did not take place on the playing field at Augusta, but in a summer amusement park. Here, where the working classes of Augusta sought relief and recreation in the summer evenings, the foundation was laid for Cobb's meteoric and dynamic career.

Leidy decided, after closely observing Cobb's play, that this boy could not be developed by ordinary coaching. He knew the boy had imagination and he concluded that the most effective methods with him would he to appeal to this imagination.

Cobb was a stranger in Augusta and one day Leidy asked him what he was doing that evening. Cobb replied that he had no engagement and Leidy invited him out to the summer park.

This park, at the end of the car line, maintained by the street car company because of the financial advantages to be gained, had the usual summer park equipment: merry-go-round, Ferris wheel, vaudeville show, cave-of-the-winds and so forth. To this place Leidy took his youthful recruit. They walked around and Leidy finally suggested that they sit down and rest awhile.

Sowing the Seeds

As they sat on a bench Leidy commented on the amusement offerings.

"You ought to see what they have in the big cities. This is nothing. Why in New York and Chicago, Boston and Detroit, Cleveland and Cincinnati and those cities they have parks that would swallow a dozen of these places and you'd never notice them. You've heard of Coney Island, of course. Well, now, Coney Island—"

And Leidy followed with a vivid word picture of Coney Island. He went into minute detail and as he saw the concentrated interest of his listener he called upon his imagination to supply added features.

They were back the next evening, Cobb and Leidy. Again they sat under the tree and the old iron bench, and while the barkers shrieked their wares, and the merry-go-round organ squealed out its old tunes and youth of Augusta laughed and yelled in amusement, Leidy gave Cobb further word pictures of the big cities, the hugeness of them, their vastness, the fascination of the metropolis. He opened the gates of Cobb's imagination to these paradises of the north.

Leidy's Narration

Finally, after Leidy had touched upon the other attractions, he began telling Cobb about the major league ball parks. "They're vast stadiums, built of stone and concrete, enormous places like palaces, just like the old Romans and the Greeks used to have for their games. Just like the places where the lions used to fight and where the gladiators battled hand to hand till one was dead.

"Why, you think we had a big crowd out today. Say, in them big cities, a crowd like this couldn't be seen in them parks. If they didn't have more people than that out to a game they wouldn't open the gates. They're more people out to a game in them big towns than there is people in all of Augusta."

Then he told him of the fame that came to major league stars. How all the metropolitan newspapers ran their pictures, how great writers devoted columns to them, how everybody honored them. A star ball player was, according to Leidy, much more important than the president.

The Picture Grows

He would tell the youngster of the stars the game had produced; the group of baseball immortals. He related their deeds of valor. He would give a detailed account of the base-stealing ability of some of the old stars and add, after a moment of reflection, "But to be frank with you, Ty, I think you got more speed than any of them fellows had." He told him of the great hitters the game had produced. Delahanty and Anson, Wagner and Lajoie, who were up then, and of others. He would pause and confide to Cobb, "But I think you could become a better hitter than any of them fellows."

And so, day after day, Leidy, the plain and unassuming Leidy, would call upon his imagination to build new pictures for his imaginative pupil. Day after day he added tinsel to the goal he was making brilliant; he was firing ambition in the boy. Leidy became more and more convinced that Cobb had all the dormant qualities and all that was needed to start the blaze was incentive. This Leidy was doing and he was pleased to note that the boy's interest became keener. He continually asked questions, sought information. The boy was constructing a picture of his own. It was his new goal. He had firmly resolved to become a part of the Leidy picture.

CHAPTER 8

Hard Work

Learning To Slide—
The Way He Learned To Field—His Worst Season at the Bat.

Ty Cobb had less actual instruction in baseball than any man that ever became a star in the major leagues. Cobb always preferred his own counsel. George Leidy decided this soon after he came to know Cobb. He felt certain that the best way to develop Cobb would be to fire his imagination and if that was fired sufficiently Cobb would develop himself. Trying to superintend that development would mean only retarding his progress as he would not take kindly to advice.

Leidy let Cobb figure things out for himself. He told him how various great batters of the past worked at the plate. He gave him various suggestions while narrating yarns, knowing that Cobb would perceive the baseball wisdom contained in his stories and adopt what was best suited to his needs.

Learning in Earnest

The manager soon noticed that Cobb was spending a great deal more time at the ball park than other players. Cobb would be at the park when the others arrived for morning practice, and he would linger after they departed.

Leidy had told Cobb a story about Christy Mathewson, then reaching his top form as a pitcher. "This Mathewson used to have poor control and so he'd come out to the park early and get a catcher to come along. He'd have the catcher to hold his glove in one certain position and keep on pitching, trying to hit the hollow of the glove. And in the winter he cut a hole twice as big as a baseball and about the height of the average man's waistline in the side of his barn and he'd pitch for hours trying to throw the ball through the hole. That's how he learned control. You got to keep pluggin' at one certain thing till you get it down pat."

Another time he spoke of Hans Wagner. The great Wagner at that time was becoming recognized as the best player of his time.

Wagner Held Up

"You know this Wagner used to be a poor fielder," Leidy would tell Cobb. "He was first an outfielder and he wanted to play the infield. They had him playing the outfield. They didn't think he could play the infield. Wagner used to get up early in the morning and go to the park. He'd get a couple of kids of the neighborhood to hit grounders to him. But he found he was slow getting started. He couldn't get the jump in going after a ball. So Wagner took off his shoes and would play in his stocking feet. He would dig little trenches around the short field and he would set himself in these trenches in his stocking feet. You see that gave him a chance to start quicker. He couldn't slip while he was standing in them little trenches. He kept this up for weeks and they couldn't figure out what made the infield so rough around short until one day one of the players happened to come to the park early and there he saw Wagner digging holes. But he learned to start quick.

"All of them fellows that made big reputations in baseball got their start that way. They practiced for hours and hours till they got the thing down pat."

Cobb decided to do likewise. He, too, practiced for hours and hours.

There was sliding. Cobb could not slide. He borrowed an old and torn base sack from the groundkeeper. In one corner of the field he spaded up the ground. At one end of this spaded plot he set the bag. Then he practiced sliding. He would slide for an hour at a time. He practiced early in the morning and late in the afternoon, after the game. Sometimes his hips were raw. Often he came into the clubhouse with his uniform soaked with blood. He learned to slide. He did not stop at the conventional slide. As soon as he mastered that he developed other slides. After a few years in the majors Cobb was sliding in eight different ways.

Learning to Field

He had started as a shortstop. He was now playing the outfield. Judging fly balls was difficult for him. He missed many. He started to learn. He had players bat fly balls to him by the hour. Leidy did it often, gladly. Cobb asked for short flies and long flies, flies to the right of him and to the left of him. He learned to go to the left and the right much sooner than he got the knack of coming in and going out on a direct center line. This is the most difficult chance an outfielder encounters. A ball hit in the air directly at him is extremely hard to judge. Those to the left and right are easy in comparison. They look by far the hardest. Most outfielders miss the chances that to a spectator seems the easiest. Ball players understand why, the spectator never seems to realize it.

Cobb played for Leidy during the remainder of the season of 1904. He participated in 37 games and batted for an average of .237, the lowest he ever hit during his professional baseball career. "You've made a fine start." he told Cobb. "You'll set the league on fire next year." Leidy was still working on the boy's imagination.

CHAPTER 9

The Nut

"Germany" Schaefer's Joke—
Navin Watches The Nut— Cobb's Batting Average Jumps.

In the spring of 1905, Frank J. Navin, who had for several years served as bookkeeper for the owners of the Detroit Baseball club and who recently had succeeded in buying an interest in the franchise, decided to go south and see what ball players did during the spring training season.

The Detroit team was training at Augusta that spring and in the hub of Augusta's downtown section stood the old Albion hotel, since burned down. As Mr. Navin entered the lobby he was met by "Germany" Schaefer, captain and second baseman of the Detroit team, and "Wild Bill" Donovan, star pitcher, both of whom have since passed on.

The two players called Navin to one side and Schaefer told him:

"We've got the richest joke in the world for you out here. There's a kid playing on the local nine who thinks he's a ball player. He's just a nut but a scream. Wait till you see this baby run bases! You'll laugh yourself sick. But don't let him know he's a joke. We've been having a swell time just kiddin' him along. If you talk to him tell him you think he's a great ball player. Whatever you do don't let him get wise to what we think about him or you'll spoil the best laugh we ever had."

His Speed Noticed

Navin went out the next day to see the "nut." He was not like other players. Navin noticed that he was extremely fast, that he got a quick start from the plate, but that he still needed a lot of polish. He had certain ability but he ran loose, like a wild colt.

The new owner met George Leidy that afternoon. He happened to mention the "queer" youngster.

"I'll admit he needs a little polishing," said Leidy. "but as soon as that boy gets used to a bridle you're going to see the world's greatest ball player and nothing less."

Soon after the Detroit squad started back north, playing exhibition games along the way. The players laughed and joked about the "queer one" in Augusta for awhile and then forgot about him. The pennant race was about to start.

Before the Tigers left Augusta, Detroit was expected to pay ground rent for use of the Augusta field, but instead of paying in money the club offered Augusta the use of a player. Detroit had on the payroll a pitcher named Eddie Cicotte. Augusta needed a pitcher and so Cicotte was turned over to Augusta. This saved railroad fare on Cicotte and also saved the money that would have been paid for ground rent. There was also a clause in the agreement stipulating that if Detroit wanted a player at the end of the season it could have any man on the Augusta roster for $750.

Jumps His Average

Detroit plunged ahead into the pennant race, the Augusta deal put aside for several months and down in Georgia old George Leidy continued working on Cobb, nursing the player along.

He batted .237 in 37 games in 1904, but Leidy had convinced Cobb that this was highly satisfactory since Cobb was changing his style at bat and that he would improve constantly. Leidy created self-confidence in Cobb and as a prophet he proved correct. He played in 103 games that season and his batting average was .326, just 99 points above his average for the preceding year.

Leidy also noticed that Cobb's base-running was taking on form: Cobb now had a definite purpose when he did things. It was the same with his fielding and batting. He was learning quickly and developing fast.

Cicotte was pitching for the same team. He won 15 out of 21 games for Augusta and when the season was drawing near the close the Augusta club asked Detroit to select a man, according to the clause in the agreement.

Augusta had another player that looked like sure major league material. He was Clyde Engle, who later came to the American league.

Cicotte Discarded

Detroit finally discarded Cicotte. He weighed 135 pounds and Detroit considered that much too light for a pitcher. Few major league clubs ever cared for little fellows as pitchers. This is a matter of psychology. They believe that a batter has no respect for a little fellow. The batter concludes: "A little guy like that can't have nothing," and he has full confidence at bat. When the batter faces a giant, who looms big before him, he believes that the giant has a great deal of stuff because "a guy that big can't help but have a lot." There is a great deal in that. A little fellow is under a handicap because of his size, a big pitcher holds a psychological advantage. Confidence is the thing at bat.

Detroit decided it did not want Cicotte. He was too small. He would be of no help. Batters would not respect. History proved Detroit wrong.

CHAPTER 10

Cobb's Debut

Ty's Debut—1,200 Fans See It—
A Nervous Substitute—Two Strikes and a Hit.

Near the end of the 1905 season Augusta was still asking Detroit to select a player. The Detroit club still was considering the matter. The club did not want Cicotte. He was too small. Engle looked fairly good. But he was not speedy enough. And then someone suggested Cobb.

They had quite forgotten about Cobb. Finally, they recalled the "nut" on the Augusta team. Yes, he had a good season, and he seemed to show promise. George Leidy was recommending him strongly. Several other clubs were going to put in a draft for him. Someone was sure to get him.

After several days of discussion it was decided to take Cobb. He became the property of the Detroit club for $750. A week later the draft was held. Four clubs were after Cobb. Each club was willing to pay $500 for him, the draft price. But Cobb was in Detroit by that time.

1,200 Saw His Debut

Cobb's major league debut was at old Bennett Park, in Detroit, on August 30, 1905. A crowd of about 1,200 saw that game, Detroit opposing New York. Dick Cooley, one of the Detroit regulars, was ill and Bill Armour, managing the Tigers at that time, used Cobb in center field. He was fifth in the batting order, just behind "Wahoo Sam" Crawford, one of the greatest natural hitters and sluggers of all time.

Big Jack Chesbro, at the top of his splendid career, was pitching against Detroit that August day. In the first inning of that game Matty McIntyre, leading off for Detroit, drove out a two-bagger. Lindsay, next up, singled, scoring McIntyre. Schaefer sacrificed Lindsay to second. Crawford tapped weakly to the box and Chesbro threw him out. Lindsay going to third. And then walked to the plate a tall, gaunt, almost, gawky-looking boy, who appeared extremely nervous.

A murmur ran through the crowd. Score cards were scanned. A newcomer. Who is he? Oh, just filling in for Dick Cooley.

Jack Chesbro wound up and shot a high, fast ball past Cobb. Minor league players in those days were all regarded as high ball hitters. They would bite on the high ones. Here was a minor leaguer and Chesbro used the orthodox method of major league pitchers. Cobb lunged at the ball. He missed. He had never seen a high one pitched quite so fast.

"Strike Two!" Cried Silk

Chesbro wound up again and pitched. This time it was a curve that broke over the plate, waist high. Cobb did not offer at the ball. "Silk" O'Loughlin, umpiring, called it "Strike two," as only the picturesque O'Loughlin could call a second strike.

Once more Chesbro wound up. He figured he had the batter's number. Another high fast one is what he would expect. Chesbro would cross him up. He would pitch a fast one but waist high.

The ball did not pass the plate,

Jack Chesbro (1874–1931) in 1904. In his first major league at-bat in 1905, Ty Cobb faced New York Highlanders pitcher Jack Chesbro. On an 0–2 count, Cobb connected with a waist-high fastball, driving it deep into center field. Cobb sped past first base and slid safely into second for the first of his 4,191 career hits. Jack Chesbro won an amazing 41 games for New York in 1904, and won 19 games in 1905. He finished his career in 1909 with a record of 198–132 and an ERA of 2.68. Chesbro was elected to the Hall of Fame in 1946. *Courtesy Library of Congress Bain Collection.*

Cobb met it. He "got a hold of it." Out in center field, Hahn took one look at the ball, then turned and ran fenceward. Cobb, streaking to first, turned sharply and without apparently lessening his stride in making the turn, headed for second. He slid into the bag safely. Cobb had successfully launched his major-league career.

That was the only hit he made in his opening game, but it impressed the patrons. The following day this paragraph appeared in one of the Detroit newspapers:

"He hit .326 in the south, leading his league. Of course, he does not expect to hit anything like that up here. If he hits .275 he will be satisfied. So will the fans."

Before the season ended Cobb was regarded as a regular. He played in 41 games. He went to bat 150 times, scored 19 runs, made 36 hits, stole two bases and batted for an average of .240. It was the only season in his major-league career that he failed to hit above .300.

Bill Byron (1872–1955) in 1915. It was South Atlantic League umpire Bill Byron, along with Augusta manager George Leidy, who convinced Detroit manager Bill Armour to bring Ty Cobb (rather than Cobb's Augusta teammates Eddie Cicotte or Clyde Engle) up to the majors in 1905. Byron umpired in the South Atlantic League from 1905 to 1907, the Eastern League in 1910, the Southern Association in 1911 and the International League in 1912. He moved up to the National League from 1913 to 1919, then went to the Pacific Coast League from 1920 to 1924. Byron umpired the 1914 World Series. *Courtesy Library of Congress Bain Collection.*

Cobb's Advantage

Cobb was fortunate enough to have an advantage when he joined the Detroit team. Bill Armour, the manager, had selected Cobb over Cicotte and Engle. It was Armour, holding out for Cobb, that had finally swung the vote to the boy. The owners favored Engle. Bill Byron, the "singing" umpire, who worked in the south that season, had watched Cobb and came to the conclusion that he would make a great player. Byron and Leidy convinced Armour. Since the manager had insisted on Cobb, it was up to him to show that his judgment was correct.

If Cobb had been wished upon Armour, chances are that he could not have held his place in the lineup. The manager would have been prejudiced. The situation in Cobb's case was the reverse.

But managerial favor did not entirely make Cobb's path a smooth one. No player ever found the road rougher than did Cobb; for which his temperament chiefly was to blame. It was difficult to get along with him, and he was thrust into a situation where a disposition such as his causes strife.

CHAPTER 11

The Griddle

The Recruit Bullied—
A Youth in Despair—His Only Pinch-Hitter.

Ball players, at the time of Ty Cobb's major league debut, were a different type than the players of today. They were a hard, rough and ready lot, as a whole. They battled on and off the playing field. A man had to win his position in those days by showing that he could take it.

The veterans were clannish. They held as common enemy any recruit who tried to break in. They did everything to handicap him. They made the youngsters the butt of coarse jokes, bullied them, "ragged" them.

Such was the feeling, the attitude and the situation Cobb faced when he broke in. They resented Cobb's appearance. They were more resentful than usual, because he had broken into the regular lineup as soon as he arrived, instead of warming the bench for a season or two as recruits were expected to do.

When the season of 1906 opened Cobb was in center field. He had a certain amount of success and this reacted on him in the clubhouse. Few of his teammates spoke to him, except to fling some new insult in his direction.

They Broke His Bats

Cobb showed ability to bat. The day after he made three hits in four times up he arrived at the park and discovered his favorite bats were missing. He had brought them with him from Augusta—two black bats that he had used ever since he started with Detroit. Cobb hunted for the bats. He was told he could find them outside the fence. Cobb found them—in splinters.

Some of his teammates had taken a hatchet and destroyed the bats. They believed that by destroying the bats they could lessen his hitting ability, for it is the belief of most ball players that certain bats "hold more hits" than other bats. If they are lucky with a certain bat they treasure it more than anything else, crediting most of the hits to that particular bat. Cobb had such a faith in his bats, and when he returned to the clubhouse he slouched to one corner of the locker room — in despair.

Charlie Schmidt, then the regular catcher of the Detroit team, had witnessed the destruction of the bats. Schmidt walked over to Cobb and extended one of his own pet bats.

"There's just as many hits in this one as the bats they broke up for you. Use it." Schmidt told Cobb, "If anybody tries to break up that bat they'll reckon with me."

Charlie "Boss" Schmidt (1880–1932) in 1901. Schmidt was Detroit's catcher and befriended Cobb in 1906 after watching their teammates saw Cobb's bats in half. He lent two of his own bats for use until new bats that Cobb ordered arrived. Salsinger writes that his continued good hitting while using Schmidt's bats ultimately led to Cobb's acceptance as a legitimate major leaguer by his Tiger teammate detractors. Later, in 1907, Schmidt and Cobb would fight on two different occasions, with Schmidt besting Cobb the second time by giving him a broken nose and two black eyes. By the beginning of the 1908 season, the feud had subsided and Schmidt told Malcolm Bingay that "Cobb last year was a player so great that his work can't be described: it's kind o' beyond belief.... [His base-running] is baseball science reduced to such a remarkable state that it's hard to grasp it." The London-born Schmidt played for the Tigers from 1906 until 1911, appearing in 477 regular season games and catching 14 of the 16 World Series games that the Tigers played in 1907, 1908 and 1909. *Courtesy Library of Congress Bain Collection.*

George Mullin (1880–1944) in 1913. On September 18, 1906, Tigers pitching ace George Mullin pinch-hit for Ty Cobb, something that would occur only twice in Cobb's 24-year career. When a slumping Cobb left the game early that day, Mullin came to bat in his place in the bottom of the ninth inning and blasted a triple to center field. Mullin pitched 11 seasons for Detroit beginning in 1902, and won 20 or more games five times. For the championship 1909 Tigers he won 29 games and lost 8. A better-than-league-average hurler for much of his career, Mullin was also a standout hitter among pitchers, compiling lifetime batting average of .262 and striking out only once in 1,555 plate appearances for Detroit between 1902 and 1913. *Courtesy Library of Congress Bain Collection.*

Cobb used Schmidt's bat. He made two hits in that game. The next day he made two more. He continued using it for a week. Then there arrived two new bats that he had ordered. But he had demonstrated with Schmidt's bat that he could get hits out of a strange bat, so they did not bother to chop up the new ones.

Outside the Circle

That season, as well as the succeeding year and even a few after that, witnessed a succession of feuds. Cobb, the tempestuous, found it difficult to get into the ways and habits of his team-mates. He did not like them and they detested him. He was pretty much alone.

In 1906 Cobb was beginning to find himself. The spark of ambition that Leidy had lighted flamed secretly. Cobb had faith in himself, but this faith was not shared by his teammates. And Manager Armour, who had selected him, also had little confidence in Cobb's possibilities. He was regarded as a "morning glory," a "flash in the pan," a "gold brick." "He'll be back in the minors inside of another year," they said.

Cobb played in 97 games in 1906. He scored 44 runs and made 112 hits in 350 times at bat and he stole 23 bases. His batting average was .320 and players that can bat .320 in their first full season in the majors are not sent back to the minors. They are kept at least until they furnish proof that they are morning glories.

"Payne Batting for Cobb!"

During this season Cobb, although batting above .300, had not convinced his manager that he was a sure hitter. In that season Cobb saw a pinch batter go to the plate for him; the only time in his career that this has happened because the manager wanted a better man at bat.

Detroit was playing Chicago, "Hitless Wonders" of that period and world champions that year. "Doc" White, a smart left-hander, was pitching. White was the hardest man in the league for Cobb to bat against and he was particularly hard on this particular afternoon. Cobb had faced White three times and struck out each time. When it came Cobb's turn to bat again Manager Armour called him back and sent up instead Freddy Payne, second-string catcher. And Payne, who went out of the majors a few years later, won a distinction that never fell to the lot of another player.

In later years George Mullin, a pitcher, batted for Cobb one day, but that was because Cobb had left before the game was over. Somebody had to bat for him.

CHAPTER 12

A Star Evolves

Hughie Jennings' Tact—
Turning Point in Cobb's Career—Envy and Jealousy.

The turning point in Ty Cobb's career came in 1907, the year that Hughie Jennings took charge of the Detroit team as manager. The Detroit team had enough power, but there had been lacking a leader to harness this power. Jennings proved to be that man.

There never lived a keener judge of baseball talent than the redheaded Jennings. Few men have been his equal. He had heard about Cobb and he was eager to see him. After getting his first look at the youngster Jennings formed his judgment. He watched him closely a week and then ignored him entirely.

Cobb noticed the slight and spoke about the matter to a friendly newspaper writer. The newspaper man told Jennings that Cobb was hurt because he was ignoring him. Incidentally he asked Jennings why he did not pay some attention to Cobb, since the boy showed a certain amount of promise. Jennings said he would take the matter up with Cobb. In the meantime he would assure the writer that he had in no way neglected Cobb. He had fully observed that young man and his mind was made up as far as he was concerned.

Advice of Jennings

Jennings took Cobb aside the same evening.

"My boy," began Jennings, "you may think I've been overlooking you. I haven't anything of the kind. I've been watching you closely and I want to tell you this: There isn't a thing about baseball that I can teach you. Anything

I might say to you would simply hinder you in your development. The only thing for you to do is to go ahead and do as you please. You just use your own judgment. You can teach yourself better and get along faster than by the aid of any man I know. Now just go head and work things out in your own way and do what you think is best, and I'll back you."

The next morning Jennings met the newspaperman on his way to the training grounds.

"I think you'll see Cobb do a lot better work from now on," observed the new manager.

"Do you think he has the making of a good ball player?" asked the newspaper man.

Jennings took him by the arm and answered slowly:

"Listen to me! He has the making of the greatest ball player that ever lived and that's exactly what he will be within the next three years. Mark my word and play that as strong as you like. You can't go wrong."

An Exclusive Story

The newspaper man took Jennings' word. He played his opinion in eight-column lines. He did not go wrong.

Jennings adhered to his decision. He let Cobb attend to his own development. He never gave him orders. He permitted him to "run wild."

There has never been another player who was such a law unto himself as Cobb. No other manager would have handled him as Jennings did and it would have been impossible for Cobb to develop under another man the way he did under Jennings. Another man would have tried to make Cobb part of a machine and Cobb could never have developed as one of a whole; to develop he had to be one, all alone and apart from the whole. Jennings, great judge of playing talent, realized this. Also he realized that, permitted to be a law unto himself, Cobb would be far more valuable than Cobb as a spoke in a wheel, figuratively speaking. He could let Cobb play his own game and create opportunities from which the team would benefit.

Jennings studied Cobb from the standpoint of psychology, as well as from mechanical playing standards. He knew that Cobb, being what he was, could not work with other men. Cobb, as he was, could not shape his play to conform with that of others, for there was no one else near his style nor was there any other man that could fit into the system that Cobb used. He was adapted to his own system; other men were not, either mechanically or mentally.

Center of the Stage

The perfect freedom that Jennings gave Cobb enabled him to cut loose. Having only himself to consider, Cobb was in no way hampered by signals and team play. He did engage in a certain amount of team play, but never when it interfered with his individual game. He was never subjected to any of the rules that applied to other men. He rarely ever showed up for morning practice and rarely ever did he report before the opening of the season. Cobb never went to bat with instructions. He could bunt or hit, as he saw fit. He was not subject to the signals of the men coaching at first or third. He ran as he pleased.

While this method enabled Cobb to develop to the fullest possible extent, it made Jennings' position extremely delicate. Other players could not see why they had to report for spring training when Cobb did not. Other players could never see why they had to get up in the morning and go to ball park and practice when Cobb did not. Other players could not understand why they had to be back in uniform at 1:50 o'clock when Cobb rarely got to the park until an hour later and sometimes was not on the field when play started, a substitute going to his position. These protests often reached Jennings' ears and he had but one reply:

"What's your batting average?"

CHAPTER 13

Revolution

Studying the Leading Hitters—
Cobb's New Batting Stance—Knocking Them for Position.

Ty Cobb's meteoric career got its real start under Hughie Jennings in 1907. In that season he gained the batting championship of the American league with an average of .350. He held the title for nine consecutive seasons.

But, what is more important to the history of baseball, is that Cobb began the revolution of baseball in 1907. He introduced a new style of batting and base-running. Others copied him and the result was that the attack of the game was gradually changed. To meet this attack the fielders had to change the defense, a natural result. So, because of the innovations that Cobb brought into play, batting, fielding and base-running underwent a change.

At that time most of the players still considered Cobb a "morning glory" and a "flash in the pan." Cobb was introducing new ideas and baseball loves the conventional. Ball players are the most orthodox of athletes and the most suspicious of new ideas. They explained Cobb's success by calling it luck and added "the luck of a crazy man." The veterans of the game disliked his style of play and could not see why people took a fancy to it. As Cobb's star rose they became insanely jealous of his success. They belittled him wherever possible and sought to discount his efforts. But they failed to stop him on the field.

In the Anvil Chorus

Even as wise a baseball man as old Bill Donovan said Cobb would not repeat, at the close of the 1907 season when Cobb had electrified the nation.

"He won't finish in the league next year." said Bill who had befriended the boy on many occasions. "He plays contrary to all baseball law and he won't last. He can't. He's a wild man. Next year they will just throw the ball to the home plate and wait for him to dash around to it. These freak player never last because they go contrary to the law."

But Bill did not understand; very few did. Cobb was not going contrary to the laws of the game — he was creating new laws. He was making over a nation's sport.

To batter his way to the top of the batting averages was a heavy task. Cobb had two men in his own league who stood eminent as batsmen. One of these was his teammate. Samuel Crawford, the former barber of Wahoo, Neb., known in baseball circles as "Wahoo Sam." Another batting leader was Napoleon Lajoie, the

"Wild Bill" Donovan (1876–1923) in 1915. A veteran of ten years in the majors in 1907, Donovan predicted that his youthful teammate Cobb would not finish the next season in the major leagues. He thought Cobb was a "wild man," playing contrary to all the existing laws of the game of baseball, and that he would surely burn out. Donovan pitched 18 seasons in both leagues, staying with the Tigers for 14 of those years. He had a career won-lost record of 185–139 with an ERA of 2.69. *Courtesy Library of Congress Bain Collection.*

Opposite: **"Wahoo" Sam Crawford (1880–1968) in 1909. As Detroit's leading hitter, outfielder Crawford was threatened by the young upstart Ty Cobb, who began to overshadow him in 1907. That year, Cobb blamed Crawford for instigating the second of two incidents in which his bats were sawn in two. In 1907, Manager Jennings moved Crawford to center field to separate Cobb from his most determined detractor, Matty McIntyre. Despite Crawford's contentious relationship with Cobb, they developed a powerful hit-and-run threat with Crawford following Cobb in the batting order. Crawford played 15 of his 19 major league seasons with Detroit, retiring in 1917 with a lifetime batting average of .309. As a power hitter, he twice led the league in home runs, and six times led in triples. He was elected to the Hall of Fame in 1957. *Courtesy Library of Congress Bain Collection.***

former cab driver of Woonsocket, R. I., known as "Larry" and "The Frenchman." The third member of the leading trio was not in Cobb's league but in the National. He was John P. Wagner, known as "Hans," "Honus" and "The Flying Dutchman." While Wagner was not an actual competitor, he was the king pin of baseball in that day, a player with a long record of brilliant performances at bat and with whom Cobb would be constantly compared if Cobb continued on his road to baseball's top place.

Like None of Them

Physically there was no comparison between Cobb and the three men mentioned. They were not alone all natural hitters but they were sluggers besides. Lajoie, big and thick, remarkably well built, king as second basemen and a great batter. Crawford, another giant, slow, methodical, powerful. Wagner, broad-shouldered, thick-chested, bow-legged, long-armed, etc., described once by a cartoonist as a "splendid piece of Mission furniture."

As batters they were nearly all of one type and this type was directly opposite to Cobb's type. They were heavy, solid and they batted in that style. Each outweighed Cobb by at least 20 pounds and each could drive a ball a great deal farther than Cobb ever did. They were powerful hitters; Cobb lacked their power.

Because Lajoie, Crawford and Wagner were the leading batters, they were the accepted type. No one expected Cobb to compete successfully against them because he was so entirely different. And, naturally, when Cobb introduced a style contrary to the style used by the leading batters of the day, he was rebuked.

Lajoie, Crawford and Wagner had a set style at bat. They would step to the plate, plant their feet firmly on the ground, set themselves and await the pitch. When they elected to hit they would throw their shoulders behind the swing and follow through. They stood flat-footed and firm so they could set their entire weight behind the swing.

He Studied Crawford

Cobb studied all the leading batters. He paid particular attention to Crawford. He quickly noted that Crawford was a "groove ball" hitter; in other words, the pitcher had to get the ball over the plate before Crawford would swing. Also, he noticed that whenever Crawford came to bat, the entire infield and outfield shifted to the right; for Crawford, using the style at bat that he used, could hit only in a certain direction. He was a lane hitter, or, as ball players say, a "dead" rightfield hitter.

So Cobb set about to improve on this batting style. He realized that he lacked the power of a Crawford, a Lajoie or a Wagner, so he had to invent a style that would offset their physical advantages. And, further more, he had to invent a style which would enable him to hit to all fields. There would he extreme advantages in that.

From Crawford's style at bat, Cobb learned that a man standing in a position like Crawford, was certain to hit almost always to a certain part of the field. To overcome this result Cobb adopted a system by which he could change his position to suit the pitch, something Crawford and nearly all the others could not do. Instead of spreading his legs and planting his feet firmly on the ground and standing flat-footed, Cobb stood at the plate with feet close together and balanced on the balls of his feet. In this position he was able to switch instantly, jump into any desired position after the ball left the pitcher's hand. By this stand at the plate Cobb struck his first revolutionary note in baseball.

CHAPTER 14

New Phases

Swinging Three Bats—
Crossing the Infield—A Bit About Hitting Left-Handers.

Ty Cobb began revolutionizing baseball in 1907. Having discovered a way to cross up the fielders in batting Cobb set about to discount the advantages other batting leaders had in weight and power. He realized that a bat in the hands of a giant like Lajoie, Crawford or Wagner was much lighter and easier to handle than a bat in his hands.

Cobb decided that this handicap could be offset by using three bats. Just before his turn at bat he would pick up three bats and swing them until he took his position at the plate. Then he would throw away two of them and the weight would be reduced two-thirds. That is what he practiced and he discovered the idea correct. He was the first player to carry three bats to the plate and nearly all players do that today.

By using what was regarded as a freak position at the plate, and by swinging three bats until the pitcher was ready to deliver the ball, Cobb overcame the physical handicaps. Instead of planting his feet flat and firm and getting set for the delivery, Cobb was on his toes. He used a snap swing, a quick chop, and therefore he did not have to set himself.

Could Meet Any Ball

Being on his toes he could quickly shift his body and using the chop he could meet any kind of ball the pitcher delivered and place it. Where the orthodox system demanded that the batter wait until the pitcher put the ball over the plate, or gave him one that he liked, Cobb could shift into position quick enough to meet a ball on the inside or outside, low or high, and still have time to hit the ball because he saved a fraction of a second in chopping, instead of swinging. His eye, wonderfully quick and accurate, helped.

Cobb's style revolutionized batting. He perfected the chop stroke and with his stand at the plate the quick, changing shift, he perfected the scientific style of hitting. There are not six players in the major leagues today who are on the Lajoie-Wagner-Crawford style. All followed this style when Cobb broke into the big leagues. Now, nearly every batter shifts. Only about half a dozen men can be described as natural hitters, men that stand firmly at the plate and swing, always in the same fashion. The others shift and mix their style.

Cobb proved that his style enabled him to hit in any direction. Fielders found it impossible to play Cobb accurately. He had no specified lane. He has hit to center, left and right fields on three successive times at bat. Fielders found it impossible to play him accurately. He could place a ball as well as any man that ever lived and he always tried to pull the ball through the opening. If the team Detroit opposed had a good first baseman, Cobb never hit in his direction. We do not remember Hal Chase ever fielding a ball batted by Cobb. If the opposing team had a good third baseman Cobb never hit the ball in his direction. If the opposing team was weak at either corner Cobb would invariably try to pull the ball outside the fielder.

Mastered Them All

Cobb could hit any kind of ball that he could reach. Some pitchers stopped him for a while but sooner or later he mastered them. Fielders became nervous whenever he came to bat. He almost always had them crossed up. No man ever took quicker cognizance of an opening in the defense; no man ever took quicker advantage of it. He would bunt when he was expected to hit and he would hit when the infield was sure he intended to bunt. He nearly always did the unexpected.

It was Cobb who first used the system of swinging hard on a ball, fouling it off or missing it altogether, with the purpose of driving back the infield, sure that, he intended to hit. And then, with the infield back, Cobb would bunt. Or, he would reverse this order. He would miss a bunt or bunt foul for a first strike, pull the infield in, and drive through on the next ball that he liked. If he bunted a foul or missed a bunt for the first strike and the infield refused to be pulled in, then he would bunt on the next one. He managed to cross the infield either way it played him.

Drove Between Fielders

With the style he developed Cobb never became a slugger. He tried to drive the ball between fielders and not over them. With his unorthodox stance he could not get the power behind the ball. He never tried for distance; his object was always to get on base.

Cobb, a left-handed batter, was weaker against left-handed pitchers than against the right-handers. He set about to overcome this weakness by practicing against left-handers. He would induce the left-handers on his own club to pitch to him. If they were not available he would engage the services of any left-handed thrower to pitch to him. In this way he accustomed himself to meeting balls thrown from the left side of the body. He practiced so long that he became as proficient in hitting left-handers as he was in meeting the deliveries of right handed pitchers.

CHAPTER 15

The Observer

Studying Pitchers—
Solving "Doc" White—His Greatest Nemesis.

Before Tyrus Cobb became a national figure in baseball it had always been taken for granted that it was up to a pitcher to study the batsman, discover in him the strong and weak points and pitch accordingly. But ball players had never considered that it was just as important for the batter to study the pitcher. Cobb decided it was. He believed that a batter could get just as much advantage in studying the strong and weak points of a pitcher as the pitcher got by studying the batter, so he set about to study every pitcher that came into his line of vision.

No man ever studied pitchers more closely than Cobb. No man ever found out more about them. Cobb knew faults about pitchers of which the pitchers themselves were never aware. Certain twirlers who could never figure out why Cobb was able to hit their curve ball do not know to this day that in pitching the curve they had a peculiar little move that they did not have in pitching a fast or slow ball. Cobb discovered these individual physical characteristics. Often, when he was given credit for outguessing a pitcher he did not outguess the pitcher at all: he knew every minute movement the man made in pitching; there was no guess work; Cobb knew what was coming.

He Solved White

Cobb sooner or later mastered every pitcher that he faced. It look him some time to solve the delivery of certain men.

The pitcher who gave Cobb the most trouble for a while was "Doc"

White, a star of the world champion Chicago While Sox in 1906. White was a tall, slender lefthander, a hard pitcher for any team to beat. Many batters had difficulty in batting against White, but of all the men he pitched to he found Cobb the easiest. In one game he struck Cobb out four times and in another, as has been told, he struck him but three times in succession and when it came Cobb's turn at bat again Freddy Payne, second-string catcher, pinch-batted for Cobb.

White pitched a ball that dropped and it was this delivery that fooled Cobb. The star batter of the league was lucky if he ever touched White's drop ball. Cobb would "break his back" swinging at it. Cobb continued studying White. He noticed that the ball which he could not hit always broke right over the plate. He decided that if he stood far back he could "get hold" of the ball after it broke.

The next time that Cobb faced White he stood as far back as possible in the batter's box. In that position he was two feet behind the home plate. White broke his drop over the plate as usual. But the ball traveled two feet after the break before it reached Cobb and the batter was able to connect. White never again struck out Cobb and the batter who had been the easiest in the league for While, the man who could not hit a foul off his delivery, became his Nemesis. Cobb batted against White in 46 American league games and his life-time average against White is .335, so Cobb made up for lost opportunities when he finally solved White's delivery.

Joss Bothered Him

The pitcher who had the most success against Cobb was Addie Joss of Cleveland. Addie died several years ago but he is still remembered as one of

Opposite:* Guy Harris "Doc" White (1879–1979) in 1910. Chicago's left-hander Doc White was the most difficult pitcher for Ty Cobb to hit early in his career. White fanned Cobb four times in one game and three times in another, leading to the second time in Cobb's career that a pinch-hitter replaced him at the plate. After a long study, Cobb discovered that by standing at the back of the batter's box, he could hit White's breaking pitch after it had curved, and he never again struck out against White. Doc White played 13 seasons in the majors, 11 of those with Chicago. He had a career won-lost record of 189–156 and a career ERA of 2.39. He led the American League in 1906 with an ERA of 1.52, and in 1907 he had a career high of 27 wins. *Courtesy Library of Congress Bain Collection.

the great pitchers of baseball. Among his achievements was a no-run, no-hit, no-man-reaching-first game. Cobb batted against Joss in 23 games and his average for those games was .253.

Carl Weilman of St. Louis, who was just as tall and just as thin as Joss, was almost as difficult for Cobb. This pitcher, who also has passed on, was the most difficult man a Detroit team ever faced. In one season he beat Detroit eight times. His success against other teams was not pronounced but he could beat the Tigers by "tossing his glove into the box." Before the tall and skinny Weilman they were helpless. He had little on the ball. Many clubs would find him an easy man to hit. But Detroit could not get hold of the ball. Cobb had little more success than his teammates. His average against Weilman was .276 in 23 games.

"Dusty" Rhodes of Cleveland, a teammate of Joss, was just about as hard as Weilman for Cobb. He batted against Rhodes in 20 games and batted .275.

After considering all pitchers that Cobb has faced, Weilman must be regarded as the man who gave him the most trouble. Joss and Rhodes were pitching when Cobb broke in and most of their pitching against him was done before Cobb fully developed as a batter. After he blossomed out at bat he was able to hit Rhodes and Joss. But Weilman made his debut after Cobb was well on the high road to success. Cobb had fully established himself as a leading batsman before he saw Weilman and therefore the success that Weilman had against Cobb in the 23 games he pitched against him must be regarded as the most successful showing of any pitcher in relation to Cobb.

CHAPTER 16

Ty's Opinions

His Pitching Choice—
What Ed Walsh Thinks—What Records Show.

Ed Walsh was, in the opinion of Tyrus Raymond Cobb, the greatest pitcher the American league ever produced.

This opinion conflicts with a belief that is almost unanimous and which places Walter Johnson as the kingpin of American league twirlers.

Cobb, in explaining his preference, says: "Take the best five years of Walsh's pitching career and the best five of Johnson's and you will find the edge with Walsh.

"What pitcher ever did as much work as Walsh in modern baseball? He pitched his arm away, working in about one-half the games his team played.

"Johnson's record looks the more impressive. Of course, it does. Look at the number of years he has pitched.

"Here's one thing you've got to remember about Walsh: He had to win his own games, He had to win them almost alone. Johnson always had some help, but Walsh had next to nothing."

Worse Than Washington

"Walsh pitched for a team that had such little batting strength that it was called 'Hitless Wonders.' You will say that Johnson pitched for one that had little more. That is true but still they had more batting strength that Walsh's Chicago team."

"But, there is one thing that you overlook. Johnson did always have a good fielding team behind him and Walsh never did. Walsh pitched before one of the poorest fielding teams I ever saw in the major leagues. His infield was a sieve and his outfield — well, it was the poorest in the American league; the poorest I ever saw."

"There never lived a pitcher that could work the way Walsh did. Look at Walsh going in as relief pitcher, which he often did three and four days in succession. I have seen Walsh strut from the bull pen with bases filled and none out and three batters coming up and not one of three reaching first base. Walsh struck them out in a row. I never saw a pitcher who could so completely, thoroughly and quickly subdue a team as Walsh. He ended batting rallies quicker than any man that ever pitched."

One day we asked Walsh whom he regarded as the greatest batter that ever faced him and Walsh replied without hesitating the fraction of a second:

"Larry Lajoie. That Frenchman is the greatest hitter that ever lived. He was one batter that put fear into my heart. Boy, how he could hit that ball! Get it anywhere near to where he liked it and you were gone. That baby had the old power behind his swing. When the Frenchman hit 'em they shot through or over. He was a tough bird to pitch past. He had a great eye. He could hit."

Walsh was asked whether he did not consider Cobb a better batter than Lajoie. And Walsh replied:

"I do not. I think Lajoie the greatest hitter that ever

Ed Walsh (1881–1959) in 1912. In Ty Cobb's opinion, Chicago White Sox pitcher Ed Walsh was the greatest that the American League had produced, even surpassing Walter Johnson. Walsh led the league in games, starts, and completions in 1907 and 1908, achieving a league high of 40 wins against 15 losses in 1908. He played 13 of his 14 years in the majors with Chicago but appeared in only 33 games during his last five years after 1912. His career record was 195–126 with an ERA of 1.82. He was elected to the Hall of Fame in 1946. *Courtesy Library of Congress Bain Collection.*

lived. He was an honest-to-goodness natural hitter. He earned everything he got. Cobb was more of a trick hitter. He never impressed me the way Lajoie did.

"In one game I struck out Cobb three times. He did not get a foul off me. And I struck him out on nothing but fast balls. You see Cobb was up there looking for the spit ball, I figured he was doing that. I shot a fast one by him. Cobb let it go, thinking it was the spitter. Then I figured he'd keep looking for the spitter and throwing by the fast one. Yes, sir, he fanned three times, on nothing but fast balls."

But—Ah!—The Records

Still, the baseball record books do not show that Cobb proved an easy mark for Walsh as a rule. He opposed him in 30 games. Cobb batted 110 times against Walsh, a fair test. His average was .337. He made 40 hits off Walsh in the 110 times at bat.

Another pitcher whom Cobb much admired was Ed Plank. Of him Cobb says:

"Plank had just about everything a pitcher needs, fast ball, drop and curves. He had a deceptive delivery, shooting his stuff from three and four different angles. His cross-fire was one of the most deceptive deliveries of all time and it's a wonder that more pitchers don't develop the cross-fire.* And above all, Plank had brains. He was one of the smartest pitchers of all time. He had the batter in the hole from the time he stepped into the box. Even after he lost his fast ball he remained in the big leagues and most players say a left-hander without a fast ball can't pitch in the big leagues. Plank did. He was smart."

But good as Plank was, and intelligent as he was, Cobb managed to hit him for an average of .310 in 52 games.

*The cross-fire pitch was a side-arm curveball that came across the plate at an angle, making it difficult for batters to hit. The left-handed Plank threw with a natural cross-fire motion, landing on his right leg on the first base side of the pitchers mound and then throwing across his body to the plate. This off-balance delivery usually resulted in wildness, but in time Plank learned to control the ball and became the greatest cross-fire pitcher in the league.

CHAPTER 17

A Wrong Pitch

Wrong Pitch—Rube Waddell Threw It—
Ty Cobb Hit It—It Won a Pennant.

Baseball historians, setting down how a pennant was won, often point to one series that was the break in a season's race. One can go deeper in this analysis. One can point to a certain game as the deciding one of that particular series, and that game probably had one play that was the break of the game and that one play came on a certain pitched ball.

Ask any major league pitcher and he will tell you that one ball pitched wrong can decide a ball game: it not alone can, but often does.

It is a long time since Detroit under Hughie Jennings won the American league pennant in 1907. All who studied the matter were agreed that one series decided the pennant, a series between Detroit and Connie Mack's crack Philadelphia machine, played late in the season. And one game decided that series, a 17-inning tie that broke the Athletics, one of the most famous games in history.

The Hit of 1907

Going further into the matter that game was snatched from Philadelphia in the ninth inning on a home run by Ty Cobb and that home run stood out as the most important hit of the season of 1907. But that home run was made possible because Cobb outguessed the late "Rube" Waddell, a remarkable left-handed pitcher, illiterate but cunning, with vast physical power and with all the stuff a pitcher wants. He had just about everything and Connie Mack had sent him to the box that afternoon to stave off the Detroit attack and give Philadelphia the break that she needed to win the championship.

How this game was snatched from Philadelphia, was later told by Waddell himself. We have a vivid recollection of his recital and the story follows:

"Up comes this Cobb, and I feeds him a fast one on the inside where he wasn't supposed to particularly like to see 'em pitched. I always figured that if this fellow had any weakness it was on a ball pitched close in. The way he stood at bat made him shift too quick to get a good hold of the ball.

"Well, I shoved the first one in over the inside corner of the plate an' he never looks at it. The umpire calls it a strike but he pays no attention to it. I immediately figures this bird is looking for a certain ball, thinking I'd give him just what he wanted on the next one or the one after that. He figures I'm going to be working on him. So I see my chance to cross him up. I says to myself: 'I'll feed this cuckoo one in the same spot an' get him in a hole, then let him guess on what's comin'.

"Once more I shoots a fast one for the inside corner an' the second the ball leaves my hand I knows I made a bum play. This Cobb, who didn't seem to have noticed the first one, steps back like he had the catcher's sign, takes a toe hold and swings on her. I guess that ball is going yet.

"Later on I meets this Cobb on the street, an' I says to him. Listen here, Cobb, it's all over an' everything, an' there ain't no hard feelin' or nothin', so tell me, why don't you swing at that first one, the fast one I send over. You don't give it a look an' you're all set for the same thing when I repeats. Did you have the catcher's signal or somethin'?

"An' this Cobb says to me: 'Why I figures if I lets the first one pass and makes out I don't notice it and is lookin' for somethin' else, you'll try to cross me up and shoot the next one over the same spot, feeling sure you double crosses me. I feel so sure that so soon as the ball leaves your hand I jump back, take a toe hold an' swing. Sure enough I was right. You hand me the same thing back.'

"An' I says to this Cobb, 'Kid, you had me doped 100 per cent right!' An' sure enough the lucky stiff did."

One Wrong Pitch

The eccentric Waddell pitched one ball wrong in that game. He did not know it was wrong until he talked to Cobb. Then he knew that one pitched ball robbed the Athletics of a victory, and that one pitched ball enabled Detroit to win the pennant in 1907.

After having batted against all kinds of pitching over a stretch of many seasons Cobb made this observation:

"Most pitchers follow a set system of pitching to you. You can get this system after batting against them once or twice. If they throw you a fast ball, screw ball, curve, fast one, in that order the first time you come to bat it is almost certain that they will throw you the same thing in the same order the next time you come up. Few pitchers vary from this system, and the few that do are the leading pitchers.

"Knowing what is coming is one thing but hitting the ball is another. You often know just where the ball will be pitched, but often it carries so much stuff that you can not get the proper hold on the ball and you fail to hit safely even when you have the advantage of knowing what it is."

CHAPTER 18

Three Failures

3 Failures — 3 World Series —
3 Chances To Star — Ordinary Efforts.

Among the world series heroes of baseball you will not find the name of Ty Cobb, although he played in three, against the Chicago Nationals in 1907 and 1908, and against Pittsburg Nationals in 1909.

He had just finished his first full and successful season in 1907 when Detroit, under Hughie Jennings, met Chicago for the world title. He had won the batting championship of his league, had made 212 hits and stolen 19 bases. He established himself that season as the most important baseball figure of the year.

Cobb was expected to do some remarkable work against Chicago. He was picked everywhere to be the star of the series. Most of the pre-series discussion concerned Cobb. And that was the trouble. Cobb, sensitive, reading much of what was written, hearing more, went into the series to outdo himself, to do all he was expected to do — and more. The result was that Cobb over tried. He over-pressed. He failed absolutely. There has probably never been a bigger failure in a world series than Cobb. His work was most ordinary. His team lost the series and much of the glory that he had accumulated during the playing season was lost by his poor showing in the world series.

Alibis Were Out

Various excuses were made by those who had faith in Cobb. They were sure he would get another chance and then vindicate their predictions.

He got another chance. Cobb enjoyed another brilliant season in 1908, although not as good as in 1907. He managed to retain the batting championship of the American league although he batted for an average of only .324. But in 1908 the American league saw the best pitching in its history, a fact that may be surmised from the top batting average. Cobb stole 10 bases less than the year previous and made 24 less hits. But, when the Tygers met the Cubs again in the fall of that year, Cobb was expected to vindicate himself. He was once more the most discussed player in the world series.

His second attempt to establish himself as a big series player did not meet with much more success than the preceding effort. He once more was a disappointment. Cobb deeply felt the humiliation of his failure in 1907 and tried to make amends. He tried too hard. He pressed himself too much. He felt too keenly how much depended on his showing. And he was just an ordinary player. The demand had been too great.*

Flashes a Spark

He got his third chance in 1909 when Detroit won the pennant for the third successive time. The Tygers met the Pirates under Fred Clarke. Cobb had finished one of the best seasons of his career. He batted 53 points higher than in the previous season. He won the batting championship of his league again, with an average of .377. He made 216 hits that season and stole 76

Babe Adams (1882–1968) in 1910. In the 1909 World Series between Detroit and Pittsburgh, Babe Adams won the three complete games he pitched, becoming the star of the series for Pittsburgh. He held Ty Cobb to only one hit in the eleven times he faced him. For the series, Adams pitched 27 innings, striking out eleven Tigers and walking only six. In his 18 years with Pittsburgh, he won 194 games and lost 140, with an ERA of 2.74. He led the National League with eight shut-outs in 1920. *Courtesy Library of Congress Bain Collection.*

*Cobb actually batted .368 in the 1908 World Series. This was far below his 0.681 five-game average at the end of the 1907 season, but it was still higher than "ordinary."

bases. He scored 116 runs. It was a record that made him the biggest sensation in baseball, that established him as the kingpin player of the season.

Due to his improved play in 1909 he was expected to turn the trick in the world series. Cobb alone made the Tygers favorites. His two successive failures against the Chicago Cubs were forgotten.

And, in the first Detroit-Pittsburg game Cobb was the sensation that he was expected to be. In that game he made a clean steal of home with "Babe" Adams pitching and Gibson catching. It was a perfect play and his work that day made the baseball sharps predict that he would carry away the individual honors of the series.

But Cobb ceased to shine after the first game. He was trying harder than ever but his best efforts were wasted. This was due chiefly to "Babe" Adams. This pitcher had rarely been mentioned in the pre-season stories. He was not one of the dependable regulars and when Fred Clarke started him against Detroit he was severely criticized for picking an untried youngster. Adams, they said, lacked the needed major league experience to pitch in a series as important as the one with Detroit.

Adams the Hero

Clarke made a fortunate choice. Adams was the hero of the world series of 1909. The series was won by Pittsburg and Adams pitched the Pirates to victory in three of the games they won. He had a curve ball and a slow one that Detroit could not hit and Cobb, star player of the majors, made one hit off Adams in the three games. He faced him 11 times.

In the two preceding world series, against Chicago, Cobb found a Nemesis in big Jeff Overall. He pitched four of the games these two teams played in two years. Cobb faced Overall in all four games. He batted 16 times against him and made two hits, one of these a three-bagger.

Cobb played 17 games against Chicago and Pittsburg in the three world series. He was at bat 65 times, scored seven runs, made 17 hits, stole four bases and batted for an average of .202. His average against Adams was .091 and against Overall it was .125.

He always keenly felt his failure in those series. He always wanted to get into another world series to redeem himself. But the opportunity never came again.

CHAPTER 19

Confidence

Confidence Begets Base Hits—
Lost, Slumps Follow—Curse of a Slump.

Probably the most valuable asset in batting is confidence. The man who has faith in himself will be able to hit, provided he has mechanical ability. But a great many men with mechanical ability have been forced out of the major leagues because of falling off in batting. They got into a slump and never got out, so they passed from the charmed circle of the majors.

One of the reasons Ty Cobb was a super-player was because he believed himself to be one. He was convinced that he could play ball better than any man that ever lived. His faith in himself was unlimited.

"When you step up to the plate, look the pitcher in the eye, straight into the eye. Let him know that you have confidence in yourself, that you know you're going to hit the ball. Convince him of it and you'll have an advantage over him; you'll put him in a hole."

Hits Follow Confidence

Any player that fully believes he can hit a pitcher is quite likely to hit him. The reason certain pitchers are able to beat certain clubs is because the belief has spread on those clubs that the pitcher has something on them and they can not beat him. They rarely do.

Carl Weilman, as previously narrated, beat Detroit eight times in one season, and that is nearly a record. Detroit was beating far better pitchers than Weilman consistently and weaker clubs were beating Weilman. But the Tygers believed that they could not beat Weilman and they did not. Cobb evidently shared the belief that Weilman was his master, for he never had any success to speak of in batting against him. But Weilman was the exception in Cobb's case.

"When I go to the plate I say to myself, 'I am going to hit the ball: I'm going to hit it; I can hit it.' I keep telling myself I can and I become convinced I can and often I do." said Cobb.

He has had his slumps. He never had long slumps, but he did have slumps where making hits was a hard job. But he was successful in batting himself out of the slumps.

He has been asked several times to analyze a slump, to explain its cause.

"That's difficult." answered Cobb. "I guess nobody knows. They just happen. If you knew what caused batting slumps you could prevent them. The trouble is you don't know. This thing of getting into a batting slump is unconscious. Often it is a matter of psychology; other times it is just plain mechanical. A man may change his style at bat without realizing it. He doesn't know that he is doing it."

To get out of a batting slump Cobb has frequently asked other players who played with him to watch him at bat and tell him what he was doing wrong, or what he was doing that he did not generally do. They would try to tell him. But he would also help himself by changing his style at bat. He would continue changing until he got out of the slump.

Cobb believes that many batting slumps are caused by the desire to hit home runs. Ball players, like golfers, love to hit the ball a long way. If a player makes a home run, the thrill of making it will cause him to keep on trying for home runs. He will change his batting style entirely to drive the ball out of the park. He will get into a slump as a result. He will be unable to get out of the slump. That is how some players passed from the major leagues.

Curse of a Slump

The curse of a slump is that it destroys confidence. If a player goes to bat a week or so without making more than two or three hits he becomes disheartened. He loses faith in himself. He believes all luck has left him and this mental state, more than mechanical, will cause the slump to continue. It may mean the end of his major league career. It takes a great deal of courage and extreme self-confidence to work out of a batting slump. There is nothing in baseball that will destroy a player's poise more quickly, and the trouble is that he begins to worry and falls off in fielding when he quits getting hits. He begins making the wrong play and he plays wrong position for batsmen. He goes into a panic and sooner or later destroys his usefulness.

Batting slumps come to all players. Cobb, in a slump, sits down and tries to figure the thing out. He is doing something he should not do, but just exactly what! He tries to find out himself and he tries to find out from others. He continues changing his style and he gets out of the slump. But all the while he never loses faith in himself.

"I've been able to hit before and I can still hit," says Cobb. He believes it. Most players do not say that and this is one reason that there has been but one Cobb.

CHAPTER 20

Features

An Original Idea—
Why Ty Was Fast—Lazy Ball Players

Several new features were introduced into baseball by Ty Cobb. One of them helped his batting and this has been copied by nearly every player. Another helped his base running, but as far as is known, no man ever employed the same means to increase his speed.

In the early spring Cobb had a shoemaker fix weights in the soles of his shoes. Both shoes were equally well leaded. Cobb ran with the added weight on the bottom of his feet. This put him under a handicap, but it developed his leg muscles, made them fit, and the running developed wind and stamina.

When Cobb got ready to launch his campaign the weights were removed and he felt as if he were running on air. It helped his speed. The training with weights was difficult, but when actual play started his work was much lighter.

For Same Purpose

The other stunt that Cobb worked was for the same purpose, making lighter the burden imposed. This was his mentioned habit of carrying three bats out of the dugout and swinging the three until the pitcher was ready to deliver the ball. Tossing two away, the one he held felt as light as a lead pencil. Nearly all players carry three bats to the plate now, but probably no other player ever wore lead in his shoes during spring training,

The plan of using the lead was original with Cobb. We do not believe that he got the idea from anyone else, but he was not the only one who used it. Alfred Shrubb, England's famous distance runner, who at one time held every record from one to 10 miles, used the same system. Shrubb also wore leaded shoes while in training and credited much of his success to this system.

Other successful champions have done similar things to carry them to the heights. Their rule, like Cobb's, was thorough preparation.

Jack Dempsey had a weak left hand. He did all his punching with the right at the time he started his climb to a championship goal. When Dempsey became champion it was noticed that his left hand was as good as the right and probably better. Most of his success in the ring had been due to the powerful left. He developed the left by tying his right hand to his side and punching the bag for hours, or boxing, using only the left. He did this until the left was as useful as the right.

What Travis Did

Walter J. Travis* is one of the best golfers this or any other country has produced. Travis' strongest point is his putting. And yet, Travis used to be a weak putter. The size of the normal golf cup is 4¼ inches. Travis got some cups made that were about one-half that size, or just a bit larger than a golf ball. He practiced putting for hours, trying to roll the ball into these half-size cups. After practicing with the smaller cups over long stretches, Travis returned to putting greens that had the normal size cups and these looked about a foot in diameter to him then.

Paavo Nurmi,† sensation of the 1924 Olympic games at Paris and regarded as the greatest distance runner of all time, did not do his training by running the exact distance he was to run in the Olympic events; he would run two, three, four and five times that far. Some days he ran from 20 to 30 miles and at times he run as far as 40 miles. He was developing muscular power and lung power. After running these long stretches daily it was little

*Walter J. Travis (1862–1927) was the most successful amateur golfer in the U.S. during the early 1900s. He was also a noted golf journalist and publisher, an innovator in all aspects of golf, a teacher, and a respected golf course architect.

†Paavo Nurmi (1897–1973) was the best middle and long distance runner in the world in the 1920s, setting world records at distances between 1500 m and 20 km. He won three gold medals in his debut at the 1920 Summer Olympics, and won five gold medals at the 1924 Summer Olympics in Paris.

more than a jog covering the distance he was asked to run in the Olympic games. That is why he ran so easily and that is why he finished so fresh when other runners dropped exhausted. The other runners had trained for the exact distance and no further.

Just as Others Did

These instances are cited here to show that Cobb, while a super ball player, gained his eminence by working in the same way that other leaders in sport worked. He was an exception among ball players, but it was not a natural gift. Cobb attained results by long and hard effort and by using his brain.

He was asked one time why there were not more good ball players and why he stood out so far over the field. His reply:

"The trouble with nearly all ball players is that they try to cover their faults instead of correcting them. There is hardly a ball player who doesn't know his weaknesses. But there hardly ever is a ball player who tries to correct them. Nearly all try to gloss over them: to hide them; they think they are fooling people, but the only person that is fooled is the ball player himself.

"It isn't fun to go out and practice for hours and for days trying to overcome some weakness. There is no joy in concentrating on one thing. That is monotonous and most men don't care for that kind of monotony. Hiding the fault is so much easier and that is what they try to do. But they don't. And that's the reason you don't see more good ball player. There are too many lazy ball players."

CHAPTER 21

Tricks

Cobb Used Them All—
Baseball Byplay—Secrets of the Clubhouse.

There is no player in baseball who ever knew as many tricks as Cobb. He was "slick." He had studied all the by-play of the game. He knew the turns and twists. He could fool them.

On the field Cobb has limped for days with nothing the matter with either leg to fool some opposing team into the belief that there was something wrong and that he was handicapped in his speed and then, when he had the opposing team fully convinced that he was crippled he put on one of his dazzling bursts of speed at the right time to win a ball game

He often pulled stupid plays on opposing teams with full knowledge that they were stupid and full intentions to make them look stupid. He wanted to make them look stupid. He wanted to create the impression that he did not know any better on a certain play, and then, when he had the opposing players thoroughly believing that he really did not know any better, he calmly took advantage of that belief at the first opportunity where he could gain heavily through a move that was based on the wrong impression.

Faked Lame Arm

He used to pretend that his throwing arm was lame. He would warm up throwing with a decided effort and making short throws. Ball teams, always looking for a pronounced weakness, would notice this. Soon a base runner tried to take advantage of the observation and Cobb's "sore arm" suddenly became well. He would have the runner flat-footed.

Sooner or later he passed up these tricks. He had to. They got wise to the fact that Cobb had been acting and that they had fallen victim to his ruse.

At the time when Cobb was at the height of his playing career he made it his business to get on friendly terms with certain players on each team. From them he would get whatever information he could. Every club has its clubhouse secrets. It is the aim of every team to cover its weaknesses and prevent the opposing teams from discovering them.

Cobb became extremely friendly with a player on the Washington team. He would meet him whenever Detroit played Washington, and the two would get into a conversation on the merits of their teams.

Free Information

The player would seek information from Cobb, and Cobb would give it freely. He would tell his Washington friend that a certain pitcher on the Detroit team had trouble with his fast ball. Yes, sir; the fast ball had lost its hop and every bit made off this pitcher was off his fast one. And Bobby Veach had a sore arm. He had trouble throwing a ball to the infield. And the Detroit catcher had strained his arm in a wrestling match. He was the only good catcher Detroit had, so Jennings had kept him in the game, but he really should be out, nursing his arm. Some teams would get wise to the fact that this catcher had the bad arm and run bases wild on him.

The player would confide in Cobb. One of the Washington outfielders had a bad arm. Griffith had succeeded in keeping the fact secret, but it was bound to leak out. The arm was very, very bad. And one of the Washington catchers was also going badly. He had some intestinal trouble and he was slow in getting the ball away on a runner going down.

That afternoon the Washington team would be all set for the Detroit pitcher. Batters would be going up waiting for the fast ball "that didn't have a hop any more," They were to slug the fast one. And about all they saw was curve balls and slow balls. They saw them too late to hit them safely. Once in a while the fast one came along, but it seemed to be hopping better than ever, from all they saw of it.

What Happened

And every time a Washington base-runner tried to run on the Detroit catcher's bad arm he found the ball in the infielder's hands ahead of him.

Whenever a Washington player tried to run wild on a hit to left because Veach "couldn't throw the ball to the infield because of a sore arm," he would find the ball traveling ahead of him as if shot from a rifle.

In the meantime the Washington team could not figure out why Detroit ran wild whenever a certain outfielder got the gall. They could not guess why Detroit should run wild on the only Washington outfielder that had a sore arm. Why did they single out the particular one that did not have the power to throw to the infield with any speed?

They could not understand why Detroit baserunners who never took a chance on any catcher, suddenly ran wild on the Washington catcher who had intestinal trouble and was slow in getting the ball away. No one knew about it except the members of the Washington team.

Griffith finally suspected what was happening. Walking into the clubhouse after another defeat at the bands of Detroit, he shouted:

"The first man on this team that's caught talking to this Cobb, even to say 'Hello' to him, is going to get fined $300 and the fine is goin' to stand. Get me and get me right. What I say goes."

CHAPTER 22

Tact

Courting Umpires—
How He Won Them—One Boomerang.

Tempestuous, a fighting player, Ty Cobb was never a source of trouble to the umpires before he became manager. He was, as any umpire who worked in Detroit games previous to 1920 will tell you, the easiest man in the league to work with. He never questioned decisions; never criticized; never argued.*

"A great player an' a fine man," the battle-scarred Timothy Hurst† used to remark. "Never gives you a bit of trouble. Always kind an' considerate, overlooking your bad days. A gran' boy indeed is this Cobb."

And he was. Because it was good policy to be. Cobb decided that early in his career. A friendly umpire was helpful; an unfriendly one not so good. Umpires are honest—the breath of scandal has never reached them. But they are also human; most players overlook this fact. Cobb did not, but then Cobb was not an ordinary player. Cobb has always worked on the policy that honey catches more flies than vinegar. He made it a point to treat umpires with respect, kindness and consideration; they were honest, of course, but being human they could not help being prejudiced in his favor; they were bound to be, no matter how hard they tried not to be—Cobb won them.

*After contesting a call at the plate by umpire Billy Evans in September 1921, Cobb and Evans fought under the grandstand after the game, with Evans besting Cobb but appearing bandaged in the next few games.

†Timothy Hurst (1865–1915) umpired for 16 seasons from 1891 to 1909, in both the National and American Leagues. For one season, 1898, he managed the St. Louis Browns.

Got the Close Ones

He never suffered because of his attitude toward the judges of play. If a decision was a toss-up between out and safe, Cobb was certain to get the break. He never lost anything by his treatment of umpires, and one could never say that he gained nothing. There is no denying the fact that Cobb got the close ones, at least the vast majority: and Cobb figured in more plays that were close, and extremely close, than any other man — it was nip and tuck most of the time when he was at bat or on the bases.

In those days you never heard an umpire say an unkind thing about Cobb. They were all exuberant in their praise of him. They went out of their way to give glowing accounts of his greatness and much of his fame was spread by these judges of play. Why shouldn't they? He was the best friend they had among the players. He understood them.

Cobb in turn praised the umpires. We vividly recall the time he gave an interview, extolling the professional virtues of Tommy Connolly. This clever Irishman deserved the praise, but the boomerang came when he read in the public prints what Cobb said about him. A day or so later Cobb was at bat with the winning run on second. The pitcher was trying to pass Cobb purposely, for two were out and the pitcher would rather take a chance on the next man.

Steps Across Plate

Connolly was umpiring behind the plate that day, calling balls and strikes. Cobb was eager to hit — he had already made three hits off the pitcher and felt sure that he could hit him safely a fourth time. The pitcher had made three pitchouts and on the next ball pitched wide of the outside corner. Cobb stepped across the plate and chopped. He lifted the ball into left field for a single, streaked to first and cut the inside corner of the bag, ready to take second on the throw home to nail the runner going from second. The left fielder had to go quite a way for the ball and he made the throw to second, Cobb not trying to advance. Cobb slid back into first, arose, dusted his clothes and then his attention was attracted to Connolly, standing at the plate, yelling: "you're out."

"I'm what?"

"You're out, I say. O-U-T!"

Cobb ran to the plate.

"Why am I out? How can I be out? I hit safely, didn't I?"

"That you did, but you hit outside the rules. You stepped across the plate to hit and the rules don't allow that. When you step across the plate you're out."

"But I didn't step across the plate."

"Well, you stepped on the plate and you're out."

Why It Happened

And Cobb was out. The decision was final. He lost a base hit, and losing a base hit is something a ball player cannot endure.

It probably never would have happened had not Cobb given out that interview. If Cobb had not called Connolly a great umpire Connolly would not have been so technical in all probability; he would have been prone to overlook the overstepping. But Cobb had called Connolly a great umpire and Connolly stepped out and proved it, or tried to. Connolly at least showed that public flattery cannot sway his judgment. He wanted to show the multitude what kind of a man Tommy Connolly really was.

It was a long time before Cobb forgave Connolly. He never forgot the base hit that he lost, but in time he admitted again that Tommy Connolly was about the best umpire in the league. Maybe not the best, but anyway about the best.

CHAPTER 23

A New Role

Baiting Umpires—
Public Condemnation—Constructive Criticism

Later in his career Ty Cobb changed his mind about the umpires, rather his attitude toward them. He became critical and soon was recognized by them as one of the worst kickers in the league. Also he criticized them publicly; something he had never permitted himself to do when at the height of his career.

In one of his publicly-expressed opinions on umpires he said:

"My opinion of an ideal umpire is one who has the official attitude. The trouble with the vast majority of umpires is that they lack this attitude. Some of our well-known umpires act as if they were on the wrong side of the bench. Instead of making decisions on the facts in the case many of them make up their minds regarding a play before it is completed. I ask you, is that a judicial attitude?

"Imagine, if you can, a judge antagonizing the person that appears before him, or the persons! Some umpires are worse to get along with than a mother-in-law."

Condemns Attitude

"Perhaps you have a legitimate kick on a decision that is close. Perhaps the umpire even missed the play. But, what do you get? The first thing the umpire says is:

"'G'wan, now, or I'll chase you to the showers if you open that trap of yours once more.'

"Men under the strain of competition should not and can not be handled in that manner by umpires or anyone else.

"The umpires have taken the fight out of baseball. It is believed by many that the clubs pay the fines of players, but even if that is true the man on the field does not want to be regarded as a rowdy.

"Make the umpires adopt a different attitude. They need to be called on the carpet just the same as anyone else.

"Any man, whether he is laying bricks, working on a newspaper or on the stage or on the diamond, is inclined to get into a rut, to drift into inefficiency. He needs to be pulled out of the rut ever so often. It is a mighty hard thing to keep out of the rut by yourself.

"Have the man who is in charge of the umpires call on the carpet the umpire who is having trouble with the players. Then he can ask him how it comes that he is having trouble so often with players Smith, Jones, Brown when the other umpires are getting along with them. If the umpire can not explain satisfactorily then get someone else."

"Undue Authority"

"The umpire should be able to get along as well as the players. He should be able to get along without taking undue authority. The minute some of these umpires get on a blue serge uniform they set out to make themselves felt. They try to show their power.

"I don't think that anyone pays money at the gate to see any of the umpires perform. If I am not mistaken the reason people come to the ball parks is to see the ball players but when you notice some of these umpires you imagine that all anybody is out at the park for is to see them. They try to make themselves the most important persons on the field.

"Above all things in baseball I hate a 'homer.' By the word 'homer' is meant an umpire who always gives the home team the better of the close decisions because the fans in the stands are with the home club. The umpire is following the course of least resistance, knowing full well that he will be thoroughly razzed it makes a close decision against the home team.

"How a man can lower his self-respect enough to adopt this attitude is beyond me. But unfortunately you can find a few 'homers' in every league.

Praises for Two

"Jack Sheridan was no homer. Tommy Connolly never was a homer. In fact there are a number of umpires past and present who stood up and called plays just as they saw them. All umpires tell you they call them as they see them but a lot of them do nothing of the kind; they call them the way the crowd wants to see them called. The men that do call plays as they see them will be wrong at times in their decisions. It is only natural that they should be wrong at times. But you are always going to have deep respect for them whether or not they happen to be right.

"If real baseball is to return the major league owners must shake up the umpire situation first of all. If you set down the faults of baseball you can use the umpires to head your list and you will not be wrong."

Cobb has ever been a critic. He criticized freely but he rarely gave anything but a constructive criticism. He would pick faults and point them out but he would suggest a remedy at the same time. Anybody can criticize but few can criticize constructively. Some of Cobb's suggestions may not have been good but they were still the best he had and considered by him an improvement over the condition with which he found fault.

CHAPTER 24

On the Bases

The Greatest in the Game—
Why Cobb Succeeded—Cy Young's Secret.

In Ty Cobb baseball has the greatest base runner of all times. There have been other players who stole more bases than Cobb and others who were considered great base runners,* but they performed in what is regarded in sport as "the long ago." When they played, the rules of the game were different and the style of play also was entirely different; a combination making base stealing an easy matter compared to the rules and system of play in vogue the last 25 years.

When Cobb first began making records as a base runner (and his mark continues to stand and promises to continue for many seasons) he was regarded as a child of fortune. "Just blind luck," players would say in explaining his success. A certain percentage of success in baseball is due to luck, but a player can not continue season after season on luck alone to accomplish what Cobb did; he has to have something besides luck. Cobb had it.

What puzzled unbiased students of baseball was how Cobb could run bases so successfully. Analyzed, Cobb lacked qualities that other men had. In no department of play was he the best equipped player from a mechanical standpoint. To run bases successfully a man must be fast. Cobb was fast but there were other players who were just as fast and a few that were regarded as faster. Still, they never compared with Cobb as base runners.

*Billy Hamilton (1866–1940) stole 914 bases between 1888 and 1901, with Kansas City, Philadelphia and Boston. Hamilton safely stole over 100 bases in four seasons, with a high of 111 in two of those years, and averaged 93 steals per season over his 14-season career.

BOSTON

What Cobb Possessed

In base running Cobb had speed but he also had brains and it was this combination that made him a great runner. He was not a faster man but he was a keener observer. Cobb had knowledge, nerve, courage and speed. The most valuable of these qualities was knowledge.

Cobb, figuratively, always had an ace in the hole in running bases. He did not run haphazardly, depending upon his speed to get him by. He had made a study of pitchers as a batter and he also made a study of pitchers as a base runner. He realized that two things were necessary to run bases successfully. One was a long lead and the other a quick start.

He had the quick start. No player ever broke away as fast as Cobb. He was going at top speed with his second stride. He had developed that better than anyone else. But to get a long lead was a different matter.

In his study of pitchers Cobb had observed that certain of them had an individual move just before making a throw to first. A pitcher has to make some kind of a move to turn to first and Cobb decided that most pitchers had certain little tell-tale movements. He studied them closely and discovered that all of them had.

Stole on Cy Young

Cobb had little difficulty in stealing bases on Denton T. (Cy) Young, one of the greatest pitchers the league ever saw. This was always puzzling to other players. Young had a good move to first. He caught many players napping. It was unwise to take a long lead with Young in the box and the wisest thing a runner could do was to keep close to the bag. But good as Young was, Cobb found it easy to steal on him. It was always a mystery and still, this explanation of Cobb's success shows that it was really no trick at all.

Opposite: Cy Young (1867–1955) in 1908. Cy Young was notoriously difficult to steal on, having a unique ability to hold runners near the base. Ty Cobb, however, discovered that Young never threw to the base after putting his hands to his chest in the windup. Young pitched for five different teams in his 22-year major league career, setting the record for most career wins, with 511, and most innings pitched, with 7,255. He won thirty games five times, and twenty or more another five. He was elected to the Hall of Fame in 1937. _Courtesy Library of Congress Bain Collection._

In observing Young, Cobb discovered one day that Young, who always held the ball with both hands near his chin when in pitching position with men on bases, drew the hands against his chest as he started to wind up. Cobb watched him for several innings and saw that Young never threw the ball to a base after pulling the hands to his chest. As long as the hands were extended from the body he was likely to throw to a base, but as soon as the hands hugged the chest Young threw the ball only in one direction and that was toward the plate.

While He Had Ball

After that Cobb always watched Young's hands. While they were out in front of him, clasping the ball, Cobb stayed close to the base, but as soon as the hands were drawn in against the chest Cobb broke for the next base. Because he was sprinting while Young still had the ball he got such a start that it was impossible for the catcher to throw him out.

Young could never understand why Cobb was able to steal on him. His catcher could never understand why. Young probably never found out. Cobb kept his secret.

Every pitcher in some manner tipped off his intentions of throwing to a base. It may have been a movement of the head or neck, a slight twist of the shoulder or the elbow. There was always one part of the body that never failed, even if the pitcher succeeded in covering up elsewhere, and that was the feet. If Cobb could not get the signal from the head, neck, shoulders or elbow, he was always sure to get it from the feet. No pitcher can throw without turning the feet and Cobb, in taking his lead, would watch the feet. He got the signal for a coming throw a fraction of a second sooner than he could get it by watching the upper part of the body.

CHAPTER 25

Sliding

Sliding—Going at Full Speed—
Eluding the Ball—Wallace's Knack.

One of the reasons Ty Cobb was the greatest base runner of his professional sport was his lack of "take-off" sliding.

Other players, in running bases, always had to hesitate a moment before starting their slides. They slowed down a trifle and threw their bodies into the slide. Cobb did not. Cobb never hesitated but hurled his body at the bag while going at full speed. He had studied the advantage of this. It insured him of reaching the base in less time, of making him a more difficult target for an infielder to tag. He learned to do this through hours of grueling practice, hours when he threw a tired and sore body into action until he was so bruised that it was only with difficulty that he could walk. He never went into a base in upright position. He took advantage of every opportunity to slide. He was perfecting himself in the art, training his body so that he would hurl himself in the direction of the bag while going at top speed without wasting the fraction of a second that others needed to poise themselves.

What He Gained

The momentum that Cobb gained by hitting the dirt while going at full speed gave him a better opportunity to twist his body away from the fielder. He could do so much more and do it so much faster while going at top speed. As he added different styles of sliding, he needed speed and momentum that carried his body not alone to the bag, but beyond the bag. At least half the Cobb slides depended upon his ability to slide farther than the bag. It was so with the hook slide, where Cobb hooked his toe inside or outside.

Umpire Billy Evans, who broke into the league about the same time that Cobb did and who closely studied his methods throughout Cobb's career, said of his sliding:

"He has nine different slides and a thousand variations of each slide."

Infielders went frantic in their efforts to tag Cobb. That is exactly what he tried to make infielders — frantic. But there was one who did not get frantic over Cobb's methods. There was just one who sat down and coolly figured out a way to tag Cobb. This exception was Rhoderick Wallace. Few men have served as long in the major leagues as this infielder did. He later became an umpire but did not last long. He did not like umpiring and so retired from the major league lots. But while he was in active service, Bobby Wallace was one of the smartest infielders in the game and there have been few men in all baseball history who could be regarded as his equal in touching a base runner. He was the best of his day, by far.

How Wallace Tagged

Wallace decided that it was sheer folly to try to put the ball on Cobb's body. Base runners ordinarily could be retired that way but Cobb could not, for Cobb was the exception among base runners. Most infielders failed because they tried to tag Cobb's body and they always discovered the body going away.

Whenever Wallace was playing against Detroit he informed his teammates that he would take the throw at second when Cobb was making for that sack. When Cobb thundered down the base paths, towards second, Wallace ran over and took the throw. He straddled the bag, legs far apart. Talking the ball from the catcher Wallace would look for Cobb's outstretched feet. Cobb always slid with one foot on the ground to touch the bag, the other foot free, about a foot above the ground. Wallace would reach out with his right hand, holding the ball, and give the free foot a twist. This quick twist caused Cobb's body to swerve to one side, out of a line with the bag. The position of Cobb's body left no doubt in the minds of the umpires whether Cobb was safe or out.

The Wallace system of tagging Cobb was a trick peculiar to Wallace. Others tried it but could not do it with his success. There was only one other man who could use the method and that was Charley O'Leary who has been assistant to Miller Huggins, manager of the New York Yankees during the years when they won the league championship. But O'Leary did not trouble Cobb because O'Leary was a teammate of Cobb's. O'Leary had the same knack of touching the ankles of base runners as they slid in and giving that sharp twist which changed the course of the slide and decided the play for the umpire.

Sheridan's View

"If all infielders were like Wallace and O'Leary you wouldn't need no umpires," said the late Jack Sheridan* on one occasion. "Them two decides the plays for you. There ain't never any doubt in your mind when Wallace or O'Leary tags a runner but Wallace is the cuter of the two by just a little bit.

'"A couple of fast steppers, them two. You never see them takin' the spikes of a runner. They always manage to get out of the way of 'em."

Cobb has been tagged out numerous times and heard the umpires call him safe. He had a habit of making the play look different than it really was. He never overlooked an opportunity. He always tried to get between the umpire and the fielder, whenever possible. He generally managed to hide the play and that made it a guess as far as the umpire was concerned. That is what Cobb wanted. Whenever the umpires had to guess Cobb was certain of getting the edge.

*Jack Sheridan (1862–1914) umpired for 30 years in organized baseball, spending 18 years in the major leagues. As a friend of league president Ban Johnson, he was known as the Dean of the American League Umpires in his 14 years with that league.

CHAPTER 26

His Methods

Use of Psychology—
Worrying Opponent s—Lou Criger Ruined.

Psychology has always been an important part of Ty Cobb's system. It played a big part in his base running. Asked one time why he was so successful in stealing base, he replied:

"Well, often I tell them I'm going to steal. I'll tell the catcher, if I'm at bat, that I'll go down on the first or second pitched ball if I get on base. Then, if I do get on he starts thinking about my going down. If he thinks I am only fooling, I get the percentage there; if he thinks I really mean it, I again get the percentage, for he's going to be over-anxious. He'll grab for the pitched ball and he'll throw hurriedly. Chances are he won't get a good hold on the ball, for he won't take time. And then he'll throw before setting himself. Chances all favor a wild throw."

There was the lean and grouchy Lou Criger, one of the best catchers the league produced. Cobb figuratively ran Criger out of major league baseball by telling him he would steal, and then stealing.

Criger Irks Cobb

Criger was a star for Boston. He was battery mate for Cy Young, and the battery of Young and Criger was the best combination of its time. Young never permitted any man but Criger to catch him. Later Boston sold Criger to St. Louis. Arriving in St. Louis during the winter, Criger was interviewed, he was asked about Cobb.

"Why, he only got fool's luck, He won't last another season. He makes a lot of crazy breaks and gets away with them. But he won't try none of his

Lou Criger (1872–1934) in 1909. Boston's Lou Criger, shown here catching as Wee Willie Keeler hits and Silk O'Loughlin umpires, was the only catcher that powerhouse Cy Young would allow to catch him. Having diagnosed Young's habit of never throwing to first after his hands met his chest during the windup, Ty Cobb was able to steal nearly at will against the pair. Salsinger writes that because of this, Cobb figuratively ran Criger out of major league baseball, taunting him over and over again by telling him he would steal, and then successfully doing it. Criger caught for five teams in his 15-year major league career. *Courtesy Library of Congress Bain Collection.*

monkey business on me. If that bird tries any of that foolish stuff, I'll make him look silly. Just let him try to run bases wild on me; I'll show him up."

The interview was widely printed. Cobb read it. The first game that Criger caught against Detroit as a member of the St. Louis team was played on a cold May afternoon.

In the first inning Cobb sauntered to the plate, swinging three bats as usual. Before taking up his position he stopped a moment to talk to Criger.

"So you're all set to show me up, are you, Criger?"

"I will if you try any of them monkey shines of yours on me."

"Well, this looks like a fine spot to help my base-stealing record."

"Not today you won't."

"Yes, I will. And what's more. I'm going to get on right now and steal on the first pitched ball, so get the old souper oiled up and cocked for a fast throw to second."

Cobb Steals Second

Cobb got on. He pranced up and down the base line, He drew a few throws from the pitcher, beat the ball back to first; and finally, the pitcher tired of trying to nab him, turned his attention to the batter. As the pitcher started to wind up, Cobb was off. Criger had asked for a pitch-out — a ball thrown out of the batter's reach — to give him added opportunity in throwing to second without interference from a swinging bat. Cobb beat the throw. The umpire called him safe.

Cobb arose and yelled to Criger!

"Well, that was a better throw than I expected to see an old gent like you make. I'll give you another chance. I'm going to steal third on the next pitch."

Once more Cobb took his lead: once more the pitcher delivered the ball; once more Criger threw with all his might. But a whirling cloud of dust arose from the bag as Cobb landed safely at third.

"Hey, Criger! I'd steal home, only you can't throw home!" yelled Cobb.

Twice after that, in the same game, Cobb reached first. Each time he made good his promise to Criger that he would steal second on a certain pitched ball. Each time he stole second, beating Criger's throw by a step, getting up and shouting to Criger how easy it was to steal on him. The last time Cobb stole, Criger threw the ball high and wide into the outfield, and Cobb scored. The enraged Criger had lost all sense of direction.

Criger, publicly rebuked and humiliated, was broken by the incident. He really never recovered from it, and soon afterwards passed from the major leagues. The hoots and jibes and boos of those who had read or heard his loud boasts were too much for him. Then he passed from the major league stage forever.

But Criger probably does not know yet that it was not the loss of his throwing speed that enabled Cobb to humiliate him that cold May afternoon, but that Cobb had found a movement of monumental significance to a base runner in the pitcher: a movement which tipped off to Cobb when the pitcher intended pitching to the batter and enabling Cobb to get a start that would have prevented any catcher in the world throwing him out. Wise as he was, Criger was humbled by a man whom he had ridiculed but who was just a bit wiser than he.

CHAPTER 27

Value of Surprise

Value of the Unexpected—
How Cobb Used It—Ty Changes Game.

Base running was revolutionized by Ty Cobb. When he broke into the major leagues he noticed that base runners, in hitting the ball safely to the outfield, crossed first base, turned to the right, passed outside the foul lines, and leisurely trotted back to the bag. They could not be tagged out as long as they turned outride the chalk line.

Also, Cobb noticed that outfielders fielded the ball leisurely and lobbed it back to the infield. That gave him an idea. Instead of turning leisurely to the outside, Cobb touched the bag and turned sharply, starting in the direction of second base. Outfielders, not used to this method, were surprised, and Cobb took advantage of the surprise and sprinted to second base.

After Cobb had gotten two-baggers on what other men would have received singles, outfielders began to change their methods. Instead of fielding the ball slowly, they would do it hurriedly and throw the ball back to the infield on a line instead of lobbing it back.

He Knew Distance

Cobb was a keen judge of a batted ball. He had a superb eye for distance and he knew his speed to the fraction of a second. He continued running in what looked to be wild and crazy fashion. But it was not as wild nor as crazy as most of his opponents believed. Cobb had studied the matter thoroughly and planned carefully.

He continued turning first base sharply on his short drives and watching the outfielders. Sometimes he made a half-turn toward first and as the outfielder's arms was raised slowly and a slow throw was started, Cobb reversed and streaked for second. Or he would come to a dead stop, and the outfielder, thinking Cobb would make no attempt to advance, would take his time. At the proper moment Cobb sprinted. He rarely ever lost on the play.

During the first few years that he ran bases in this way they said it was the "luck of a lunatic." And then, noticing his continued success, other players started copying his methods. This was especially true of the younger players, because the veterans were too thoroughly drilled in the old system to change. No longer did base runners jog beyond first and turn outside the base line and jog back to the bag. They turned sharply at first and made a start for second, ready to take advantage of any opportunity.

Changed Methods

As this style became general, the outfielders had to change their methods to meet the new style of attack. The outfielders used to play deep. That gave them a chance to get balls hit far out, and they could always come in for short flies. All outfielders find if easier to come in on a ball than to go out on one.

That is logical. That is the way they played when Cobb started his new style of base running.

The outfielders now came in much closer; they had to; it gave them a chance to cut off ground-hit balls and prevent the runner taking an extra base. It gave them a shorter throw and, again, prevented the runner getting a one-base advantage on account of a long throw.

It is so in any game. When the attack changes the defense must necessarily changes to meet the attack. Things have to equalize, or come as near as possible to equalizing.

Cobb had noticed, after entering the major leagues, that base runners circled the bags, touching the outside corner or stepping on the center of the bag in passing. He decided that he could gain a great deal more by changing this system and touching the bag on the inside corner. This would save at least three steps, and three steps mean a great deal in a stretch of 90 feet — the distance between bases.

Touched Inside Corner

Cobb practiced this. Going from the plate to first he touched the inside, corner of the bag as he made a sharp turn instead of the wide, sweeping turn. He stayed near a direct line between the two bags, and when he touched the next side it was again on the inside corner, and so on to the next one. He eliminated yards of waste running and actually lessened the distance between bases. Later on players all adopted this style, touching the bag on the inside.

In running bases Cobb was always credited with basing his attempt on the manner in which the outfielder handled the chance. That is only partly true. It is as a matter of fact, a half truth. Cobb started his dash, depending on the situation in the outfield; but after he was on his way, he depended on the infielders. And he did not judge his opportunities by the position of the infielders but by the eyes of the man covering the base toward which he was advancing. Most infielders deceive the runner by their pose. They stand in a position meant to be misleading. Often an infielder who is waiting to take a throw will stand with his hands dangling at his sides, or hands on hips. Also, he will not be standing in the direct path of the ball but turned partly sideways. The object is to lead the runner to believe the ball has not been thrown to slow him up. The runner slows. The infielder suddenly leaps into action, but then it is too late for the runner to spurt. Many runners have been caught because they were "sucked in" by the false position and attitude of the infielder. Cobb learned how to overcome this ruse.

CHAPTER 28

Nine Slides

Cobb Invented Them—
How He Watched the Ball—Confusing the Umpire

An infielder can stand in a wrong position. He can fool a base runner by his attitude. But the infielder's eyes cannot deceive.

Ty Cobb knew, of course, that to catch a ball a man has to have his eyes on the ball and, therefore, while the infielder may not be standing in the path of the ball and while his hands may not be in position to make the catch, his eyes will be following the ball and by watching the man's eyes the runner not alone can tell what direction the ball is taking, but he can also discover how near the ball is to the infielder.

Cobb decided to concentrate his attention on the eyes and pay no attention the position of the infielder. This he did. By watching the eyes of the man covering the base, Cobb discovered the direction of the ball and then he changed his course so that he came in the direct line of the ball. He ran so that he would come between the ball and the man waiting to catch it.

This plan had a double advantage. There was the chance of Cobb hiding the ball momentarily from the infielder and thus making possible a fumble or misjudgment, and there was the chance of the ball hitting Cobb. As Cobb was in the direct line of vision the infielder had to watch Cobb as well as the ball, providing he could see the ball.

None Hit as Often

Often during his career has Cobb been hit by a thrown ball. There was never a player hit as often and the reason is given in the preceding paragraphs.

Cobb traveled ahead of the ball, and if the play was close the chance was always that Cobb and the ball met.

Several times Cobb has reached a base, or scored, by kicking a ball. Five times in one season Cobb scored on a play like this. One time, in a game between Detroit and Philadelphia, with J. Franklin Baker playing third base, Cobb got in the line of the ball. The throw was a bit faster than Cobb and as he slid the ball struck the ground just ahead of him and bounded up. As the ball arose Cobb kicked. His spikes struck the ball and it rolled into the Detroit dugout. Cobb got up and walked home. Baker protested. The umpires said it was an accident, as it was impossible for Cobb to deliberately kick the ball while sliding. Baker lost his argument, but he was not convinced. He knew — so did Cobb.

By watching the infielder eyes Cobb also judged his sliding. If he thought the ball would beat him to the bag he slid in the opposite direction from the one in which the infielder's gaze was focused.

Cobb had developed nine different slides. This thing of sliding came difficult at first. Like everything else he mastered the art of sliding by long and constant practice.

"I worked at it until sliding came as second nature to me. I would always slide in a game, slide when there was no occasion for it. I did this so I would slide naturally. Nearing a base I would hit the dirt without thinking about it. I knew I would not have time to think about it. I learned to slide past fielders just as I would dodge around pedestrians if running in the street. I would dodge around them without pausing to make up my mind what to do. I wanted to slide the same way, and I learned it. I slid automatically, naturally. I first learned the ordinary, orthodox slide into a base. Then I decided I would have to improve on that to get a bigger percentage in running bases. I learned to slide on the outside and hook my toe in the corner of the bag as I passed. It took me a long time to learn it, for this slide required judgment of distance. Your take-off has to be right and your direction accurate. It means quick action. I learned to slide on the inside of the bag and on the outside, always away from the spot where the fielder would take the throw."

He perfected other slides later on, his fadeaway and other variations.

Couldn't Outguess Him

Infielders became acquainted with Cobb's slides, but to outguess him on them in order to tag him was like outguessing Christy Mathewson's delivery to hit him. And then, one day, Cobb made a slide several feet outside the infielder. He slid past the bag. The infielder lunged after him. Suddenly Cobb threw his body on the outside, away from the pursuing fielder and touched the bag with his hand. He had invented another slide.

Few men have been as supple as Cobb. He seemed like Rudyard Kipling's "Injia rubber ball." He was "quick as a cat." Few infielders have ever handled him successfully as a base runner. There never was another man as difficult to tag.

Cobb introduced the method of sliding to first. He started doing this on close plays. That was another one of Cobb's innovations that seemed foolish to his profession at first, but Cobb had his own intelligent reason for it.

"With a runner crossing first in an upright position, the umpire has the runner and the ball in the same line of vision. If the runner slides what's the result? If the ball is coming to the first baseman waist-high, as it generally is, or higher, the umpire has to look at the ball and then change his line of vision and look down at the runner. He loses either the runner or the ball; he can't see both at the same instant. And if the throw is low the runner sliding will raise a cloud of dust that prevents the umpire seeing the ball."

The majority of players now slide into first on close plays.

CHAPTER 29

Stride

Cobb Learned Stride—
Defines Its Necessity—Ty on Gridiron.

Ambitions to become a college sprinter were responsible for his later success as a base runner, according to Ty Cobb's own story.

As a boy he wanted to be a track athlete. He got all the books on sprinting that his home town library carried. These books were written by college coaches or successful sprinters. Cobb absorbed them eagerly.

He discovered that these experts laid particular stress upon stride. Without the proper stride no boy could become a sprinter. Cobb committed to memory the paragraphs on stride, and then, each morning, he ran one or two miles, sometimes more, before breakfast. All the while he was running he practiced the stride described in the books as proper. He developed stride.

"It is not speed in base-running," Cobb says. The best base-runners in baseball were successful because they had developed stride.

Stride Not Enough

"But stride in straightaway or circular track running, as college and amateur runners recognize it, will not be alone sufficient to make them good runners in baseball. Some have tried it and failed.

"You need stride in base-running, just as you need stride in sprinting, but you need stride plus something else, and the something else is a fine judgment of distance that permits you to make sharp turns and touch each base without perceptibly lessening that stride and cutting down your speed.

"Champion sprinters would be beaten by the majority of ball players in circling bases. They would have the stride and the speed but they would not have the knack of negotiating the sharp corners of the diamond without losing stride and speed. That is the trick of the thing.

"Stride is also important in fielding. There has never been a great outfielder who did not have a good stride. No matter what speed the man has, if he does not know how to get the most out of it in his stride he will not succeed. Stride is the most important thing in fielding and running bases."

Cobb Plays Football

Cobb's stride would have made him a great football player. One time, after he was successfully launched on his major league career, he visited Vanderbilt university at Nashville, Tenn., during the football season. He was invited to attend practice. Cobb watched the Vanderbilt squad practice, studied the tactics and the different maneuvers. The next afternoon he returned and asked for a uniform. He did well in ordinary practice, and when scrimmage followed Cobb asked to be permitted to engage in that. The request was granted.

Cobb played with the scrubs and soon the scrubs were down in their own 15-yard zone. Cobb asked for the ball. The scrub quarterback handed it to him on the next pass from center. All Cobb did was to run through the entire team of Vanderbilt regulars 85 yards for a touchdown. In his run he straight armed and finally reversed his field.

The same run, had it been made in a major game, would have been hailed as one of the feature plays of the gridiron season.

Cobb could not have been a failure in any sport. Harry Tathill, who trained and seconded a number of leading boxers, was trainer of the Detroit team. Cobb asked him to teach him boxing. Tathill consented. They boxed every day. One afternoon Tathill said "I'm through." Cobb wanted to know why. "I've taught you all I know; I can't teach you any more," explained Tathill.

Good at Everything

Men that have hunted in the field with Cobb, or shot at the traps with him, say he is one of the best in the country.

He has, at various times, participated in several of the events that make up a track and field program. His work compared well with that of the leading college performers.

In bowling, hand ball, basketball and in practically every other sport Cobb has tried his hand he never failed to astound experts by his showing.

In no way related to this matter was an incident that occurred during the Detroit-Chicago world series of 1908. A titled Englishman was in Chicago and expressed a desire to see the world series. He was escorted to the park and occupied a seat in a field box. In one inning Cobb stole second, finishing the attempt with a slide that carried him over 25 feet of infield soil safely to the bag. He was given a remarkable ovation, and when the noise subsided the Englishman remarked:

"But really I cawn't see why this terrific tumult. You know, ole chawp, the bloomin' beggar could never have got there if he 'adn't sat down."

CHAPTER 30

90 Feet

Cobb Mastered "90 Feet"—
Tricks and Deception — Planned Plays.

Ty Cobb was the first man to score from second base on an infield out. He used various tricks to accomplish this. He was not running and trusting to luck, for his plays had been carefully planned by him with all details taken into consideration. Some of them, of course came on the spur of the moment as the opportunity presented itself, but most of them were the result of deep study and intricate planning. Cobb often relates how, at the start of his career and after he was on his way to fame, he would lie in bed at night, awake, in the darkness, planning some new move, some new spectacular turn.

His attack was always planned according to the opposing team. His success lay in outwitting the defense of the opposition. These defenses differed and therefore Cobb's attack differed. He played according to the individual ability of the fielders opposing him. If the infield was slow then all he would have to depend upon was his speed and a good lead. He was able to get the lead because he generally knew the pitcher's characteristics. He could tell when the pitcher intended pitching to the batter and when he intended throwing to a bag. We do not remember ever seeing Cobb have a long lead when the pitcher threw to a base. He was not caught napping a dozen times during his career. Any time he had a long lead the pitcher delivered to the batter. With his long lead, his quick start and his speed, he had an advantage that no slow infield could discount.

Depending on Infield

With a fast infield Cobb resorted to trickery and deception. It was then that he depended upon cunning and ingenuity. Cobb, advancing to second or third on an out at first, would take a lead toward the next base and come to a dead stop. The first baseman, assured that Cobb did not intend going any further, would leisurely pull back his arm to toss the ball to the pitcher. Cobb realized that the first baseman could not very well fail to go through with the leisure toss after the arm motion had started, or if he did he would have to pull back his arm and "reset" for a fast throw. In either instance Cobb had the advantage, and as the first baseman started to toss Cobb broke for the next base. If the first baseman went through with the toss the pitcher would turn to take the ball, turn and throw to the base toward which Cobb was advancing. This would take so much time that it would be next to impossible to catch Cobb on the relayed throw, especially as the pitcher's throw would be hurried and probably wild. If the first baseman, seeing Cobb start, pulled back his arm second time for a fast throw, he would overhurry the throw and most always make a wild peg.

The basic principle of Cobb's base-running was to make fielders throw the ball.

Sure of an Error

"Start them throwing and keep them throwing and one of them is bound to muff the ball or throw wild. The more you hurry their throwing the surer one of them will make an error that gives you your chance."

He always tried to make them throw. And he succeeded.

Cobb's specialty was upsetting infields. With Cobb on base they would become nervous. They could never guess him. Cobb's mind, moving two and three plays ahead of the defense, was something they could not cope with. They went into a panic and before they fully recovered Cobb's teammates had taken advantage of the situation he created so while Cobb was never one of the whole but rather one apart from the whole, he was still the greatest aid to the whole because he provided the opportunities by which the team benefited. Most of the rallies of the winning Detroit teams were started by Cobb.

The distance between bases, as everyone who is interested in baseball knows, is 90 feet. That distance is the most imposing feature of the game. The success of baseball lies in that 90-foot stretch. One foot more or one foot less would make an unlimited difference in the game.

That Perfect 90 Feet

If "Father" Chadwick, the man that invented baseball, had watched the game 50 years; if he had noticed 1,000 major league players; noted carefully the opportunities of batting against pitching and the speed of the runners; diagnosed their chances to the minute fraction, and then decided on an ideal distance, he would have made it exactly 90 feet. A player must have everything in his favor to negotiate the distance safely. Ninety feet is the secret of the game. It is just far enough to make it possible but improbable, just near enough to tempt the base-runner.

Cobb's first task was to overcome the 90 feet. And Cobb is the only man in all baseball that ever developed to such a high degree that he was on even terms with 90 feet. Cobb on an attempted steal of second or third would often make the play even if the catcher's throw was perfect and if the infielder handled the ball perfectly. The late Timothy Hurst, a famous umpire, often said that anytime Cobb made such a play it was toss-up whether he was safe or out if the play was made perfectly at both the fielding ends.

But of all the men that have run bases from coast to coast, and from border to border, Cobb is the only man that ever got on even terms with 90 feet.

CHAPTER 31

Heads Up Baseball

Two Bases on a Bunt—
on Hal Chase's Arm—Ty Hears A Boast.

What is now described by the terms of "heads-up" and "on-your-toes" baseball was first introduced by Ty Cobb. He brought the "heads-up" and "on-your-toes" style of play to its highest peak. Before Cobb's debut ball teams had nearly always clung to what baseball calls the "old army game," playing in a strictly orthodox fashion. Cobb's style of base running and fielding brought about faster and quicker play. The plays he introduced and which were gradually adopted, compelled players to be alert to stay on their toes and to keep their heads up.

No player was ever as consistently or finely alert as Cobb. Recalling one play that describes this alertness:

New York used to have a giant catcher, [Jeff] Sweeney by name. In one game Cobb came to bat with Donie Bush, then Detroit's shortstop, on second base. Cobb drove through the infield. The centerfielder came tearing in on the ball, scooped it up and whipped it to Sweeney to catch Bush at the plate. Ball and runner reached home about the same time and Umpire Jack Egan called Bush safe. Sweeney jumped to his feet and protested. Egan started away from the plate, as umpires frequently do when an argument starts. But

Opposite: **George Moriarty (1885–1964) in 1914. New York's George Moriarty (here pictured with Detroit) was playing third when Ty Cobb, for the first time ever according to Salsinger, safely reached third base from first on a sacrifice bunt. In the game played the following day, Cobb repeated this feat against the Yankees twice more. Moriarty played thirteen seasons in the American League, including three with New York and seven with Detroit. He led the league in assists at third base in 1914. *Courtesy Library of Congress Bain Collection.***

Sweeney, hands on hips, with one hand grasping the ball, stayed right at Egan's side.

A Second Close One

In the meantime Cobb was slowly sauntering off third and toward the plate. The umpire, to get rid of Sweeney, walked toward the pitcher's box. Sweeney, not to be shaken loose, followed the umpire. Their backs were to the plate. There came a sudden loud roar. Sweeney, turning, discovered Cobb streaking for the plate. Sweeney could not throw the ball, as no one was ahead to receive it, so Sweeney ran for the same spot. Cobb and Sweeney hit the dirt at the same time, sliding for the plate from opposite directions, but Cobb got his hand on the plate just a fraction of a second before Sweeney's right hand, grasping the ball, touched him.

Cobb always studied his opponents. He tried to discover the weaknesses of individuals and the weaknesses of teams. It was always his aim to out think him. He studied their line of reasoning and then he knew what to do to cross them completely.

It was while Clark Griffith was manager of the New York Americans that Cobb first pulled his play of going from first to third on a sacrifice bunt. It had never been done before. The runner had always been satisfied to advance one base.

At that time Hal Chase, greatest of first basemen, was with New York and George Moriarty, now an umpire, was playing third. Cobb reached first and Claude Rossman bunted a sacrifice. Cobb, who had taken a big lead on the pitched ball, touched the inside corner of second and raced to third, the first time anyone had pulled a play like that.

Cobb Hears Boast

After the game Cobb was in the clubhouse. Next to the Detroit locker rooms were those of the visiting club. A locked door was between the two rooms, but above the door was a transom and it was open. Through this opening Cobb heard the voice of Griffith on the other side, bawling out Chase and Moriarty for letting that "crazy nut of a Cobb" show them up by going from first to third on a sacrifice.

"Never mind, we'll get this simp tomorrow if he tries any of his nut tricks on us again, won't we, Morrie?" said Chase. And Moriarty agreed that they would.

Cobb thought the matter over that night and the next afternoon, before the game, he called Rossman aside.

"Will you bunt every time I get to first?"

"Sure, if you want me to."

"All right then, bunt every time."

He Did It Twice

Cobb twice reached first base in that game and each time Rossman, coming up to the plate next, bunted. Each time Cobb streaked from first to third on the out. Each time, Chase and Moriarty, both set for just that play, failed to get him. Chase made a good throw, but the ball got to Moriarty just a fraction too late to enable him to make the play. When Cobb pulled the play a second time in that game and got away with it, Moriarty, taking two steps toward the pitcher, threw the ball on the ground and reached down to get it on the rebound. But before his hand touched the ball there came a roar of human voices. Moriarty turned and caught a picture of a human cyclone headed for the plate. He hurriedly tried to grab the ball. He did manage to get it and throw, but his throw pierced a cloud of dust at the home plate, for Cobb had beaten the ball by several feet.

Walking into the clubhouse after that game, Manager Griffith glared at Moriarty and then he glared at Chase, whose locker was several feet further on. That is all he did—glared. Neither spoke a word.

CHAPTER 32

Headlines

Why Ty Got Into Them—
The Superiority Complex—Master of the Thrill.

Ty Cobb had a way of getting into the headlines. He forced his way in by delivering in a crisis. No man ever provided as many thrills to spectators in sport as Cobb. He came through oftener than any player that ever lived when coming through meant victory.

An illustration of this was furnished several years ago. Bill Donovan finished his career as a major league pitcher soon after Cobb reached his top form as a player. Donovan became manager of the New York Americans. In one Detroit–New York game the Tigers were one run behind when they came to bat in the ninth. Detroit managed to get two men on with two out. It was Cobb's turn at bat.

Donovan turned to his trainer and said:

"Start collecting the bats; this game is over."

A Withering Look

[Frank] Gilhooley, a utility outfielder, sitting next to Donovan on the bench, remarked:

"You figure he's going to strike out Cobb?"

Donovan gave Gilhooley a withering look, and told him:

"No, he won't strike out Cobb. What Cobb is going to do is hit."

"But he hasn't made a hit today!" countered Gilhooley.

"I know he hasn't. But you can have my month's salary for yours if you want to bet that he won't hit now. There hasn't been a chance for him to pull anything today. This is the first chance he's had to win this game. Watch him."

The pitcher got two strikes on Cobb. It looked as if Donovan had guessed wrong. Then two and two.

And then—

Cobb took a vicious chop at the next one. The ball shot out on a line. Right and centerfielder started for the fence. Two runs scored. The game was over.

"That's him," said Donovan, walking toward the clubhouse through a cheering mob. "That's him all over—Cobb every time. He saves his hits until they can drive him into the headlines."

Superiority Complex

Psychology, which bobs up at every turn in Cobb's playing career, mastered the delicate situations for him. In a pinch the edge was with Cobb at all times. He had the advantage because he believed himself superior to any man that ever pitched a baseball. He was a better batter than any man he ever faced was a pitcher. Of this he was convinced.

He always had that advantage. Cobb never went to bat in a pinch, while he was at the zenith of his career, that he did not believe he was master of the situation.

Cobb coming up struck fear into the hearts of an opposing team. It put them on edge. They believed after a while that he had some supernatural power. They over-played the situation whenever it involved Cobb in a crisis. They over-strained, over-pressed.

Facing a pitcher in a pinch, Cobb knew he had it on that pitcher. He was not afraid of the pitcher, but the pitcher was afraid of him. The pitcher would over-try. He wanted to put too much stuff on the ball. This had but one result: He got little on the ball or he got so much that he did not control it and soon found himself in a situation where he either had to walk Cobb or cut down on his stuff to get the ball over.

Situations never bothered Cobb, but they bothered his opponents. He had the psychological advantage. He had them on the defense, and when you put a man on the defense the odds are all in your favor.

Master of the Thrill

Spectators marveled how Cobb came through so many times in a pinch; how he so often provided the break in the game that won for Detroit. But there is really nothing mysterious about it. With Cobb coming up when bases were empty or Cobb coming up where the score was lop-sided, one way or another, it was easy enough to handle him, for the pitcher and his supporting cast concentrated on Cobb. But when he came up in a pinch it was not easy. There was Cobb and there was the situation and all its possible angles. The defense became panicky and over-pressed. While over-pressing it blundered. The pitcher blundered or the defense blundered. It made everything quite simple for Cobb, much simpler than in any other situation. Pinches were a distinct advantage to him.

He was the master of the thrill. He knew when to cut loose. A natural showman, he realized how he could perform to the best advantage.

Everett Scott, one of the greatest shortstops the game has developed and who holds the baseball record for playing in consecutive games,* said during the season of 1921:

"The only thrill I ever got out of baseball was to see Cobb thundering down to second base. He always seemed to me like a great thoroughbred coming down the stretch. He had a rare fascination for me. It was the one thrill that baseball has given me in all the years I have played it."

*Everett Scott appeared in 1307 consecutive games between 1916 and 1925, setting the record later broken by Lou Gehrig. Cal Ripkin set the modern consecutive game record with 2632 games played in 1998.

CHAPTER 33

The Threat

Cobb Created the Threat—
Fooling the Opposition—Nothing To Chance.

There was always a reason in Ty Cobb's mind for everything he did on the playing field. Many of his plays seemed useless, needless and even foolish, but they were all in Cobb's general scheme.

He was a master of psychology and he made psychology his strongest weapon.

"It isn't what you do entirely—it's just as much what they think you're going to do that counts," said Cobb. "The idea is to make them think you're going to do a certain thing, and then if you get them to believing you're going to do that certain thing it's easy enough to pull the play you want to pull, for then you have them completely crossed up. The big thing in baseball is to do the unexpected. If you do the expected the chances are generally a trifle against you, for there are too many opposed to you. But if they can be caught flatfooted the advantage is all with you, no matter how many are against you."

To carry out this idea he created what he called the "threat." It is really it mental hazard.

How Cobb Worked

Cobb would come to bat and let the first pitched ball go by a few times without offering. Just about the time the pitcher was convinced that he never intended hitting at the first one, he would cut the plate with it to put over a strike and get an advantage over Cobb. But that was exactly what Cobb wanted him to do. The ball would not cross the plate.

In running bases he would go down on the first or second pitch quite often. He would try to impress the opposition that he had decided on a set system and just about the time this opinion became established Cobb would cross it up.

Where a game was won by a big lead or hopelessly lost and where the run would help his team either way, Cobb would set about to create these mental hazards. That is where the plays regarded as "foolish" were always made. His object was to impress the opposing team that he made the play that way. The next time they would be set for it and then he could do exactly the opposite.

At bat he used the bunt to great advantage. Cobb always believed that the bunt was the most effective weapon of the offense.

Effect of the Bunt

"If a pitcher is going good, and you are unable to do anything with him, bunt," says Cobb. "A bunt will throw a pitcher off his stride. Bunt to either side of the box. He's got to go after the ball. It's an entirely different fielding chance than those that have been offered. It doesn't make any difference whether he throws you out or whether you are safe. You've accomplished your purpose and that is to get the pitcher off his stride. Many batting rallies have been started by a bunted ball on a pitcher that couldn't be reached before the bunt was laid down."

Cobb employed the bunt to create his threat. After he bunted a few times the first and third basemen would come in. They would he drawn toward the plate by Cobb's threat to bunt again. As soon as he had pulled them toward the plate, he slashed the ball in either direction. No first or third baseman, tearing in to field a bunted ball, can field a hard drive hit at him. He can not switch that quickly.

Not alone in batting, but also in base-running, did Cobb create the mental hazard in the opposition, always with the idea in mind of having them build their defense to take care of a similar play the next time he got on; but the next time he got on he worked an entirely different play. And the opposing team was never prepared for the play he worked.

Nothing to Chance

Cobb was constantly working out new plays, new surprise moves. But he first set his stage for his drama. He, who was supposed to leave everything to chance, left less to chance than any other man in the game. He studied out every detail, he worked out his plans to the last thread. He figured out all matters with mechanical precision. He built upon his own mechanical ability, but also upon that of the men that opposed him, chiefly upon them. Unconsciously they aided him in working out his plays. Unconsciously they were instruments in his hands.

He always liked intelligent players. The more intelligent they were the better he liked them. He could always tell what an intelligent man would do under certain circumstances but no one can tell what a stupid player will do; he is likely to do anything especially in a delicate situation. The intelligent player follows a certain style, a certain system. He will do the thing he should do under the circumstances. Cobb knew exactly what should be done, and knowing the fielders, he knew what the intelligent ones would do. Knowing that, he had the key to the situation — he knew exactly what he would do.

Reviewing Cobb's career we therefore find that most of his dazzling plays were made against the smart infielders and outfielders. He could figure them to a fine point.

CHAPTER 34

Ty's Best

His Brainiest—
A Battle of Wits — Chase His Victim.

Tommy Connolly, one of the very best umpires the major leagues ever had and who watched Ty Cobb from the day he broke into the American league, says Cobb made the brainiest play he ever saw executed on a ball field. It happened during a Detroit — New York game. Cobb always played sensational ball when opposing New York; be seemed to outdo himself in those games.

In this particular contest, Cobb was on first with Crawford at bat. As Crawford swung on the ball Cobb broke for second base. Crawford hit to the shortstop. Knowing it useless to try for Cobb at second he shot the ball to Chase, at first, and retired Crawford. As Chase touched the bag and put out Crawford, Cobb rounded second and went about 30 feet in the direction of third. Then he came to a dead stop, watching Chase intently. And at first stood Chase, intently watching Cobb. There they were — the brainiest pair in the game at that time — engaged in a battle of wits that was lost on the spectators.

Opposite: **John "Schoolboy" Knight (1885–1965) in 1912. While Knight was playing third base for New York, Ty Cobb once befuddled him by scoring from first base on a single by Sam Crawford. In a typical hit-and-run play by the Cobb-Crawford duo, Cobb took a long lead off first and was nearing second when Crawford singled to left field. As Knight faced left field for the throw into third base expecting a slide, Cobb rounded the base at full speed behind him. The crowd roared, and as the surprised Knight turned to throw home, Cobb slid safely across the plate. Knight played infield for eight seasons in the American League with four different teams, Philadelphia, Boston, New York and Washington. He had a career batting average of .239 and led the League in 1907 in both put-outs and errors at third base. *Courtesy Library of Congress Bain Collection.***

Chase could not make up his mind whether to throw the ball to the pitcher, to the second baseman or to third. Neither made a move for more than a second, but it seemed like longer to the veteran Connolly.

Chase's Mistake

Suddenly Cobb lunged toward second and Chase snapped the ball in that direction. But as Chase pulled back his arm for the quick throw Cobb reversed and dashed for third. As soon as he threw, even before the ball left his hand, Chase saw his mistake for Cobb had made a false move simply to draw the throw. But it was too late then for Chase to reverse; he had to go through with the throw to second.

The second sacker took Chase's throw and relayed the ball to third. He threw hurriedly but low, keeping the ball down, for he "knew" Cobb would slide and the low throw gave the third baseman a better opportunity to make a play on Cobb, for he was in position to tag him when he took the throw. But the second sacker guessed wrong, and so did the third sacker, who made a stab to touch the sliding Cobb. The runner was not sliding. He had touched the bag while taking a sharp turn and was on his way home. The third baseman had to right himself, set, pull back his arm and throw to the catcher. His throw was hurried, but not fast enough to catch Cobb, who slid safely across the plate. Cobb scored because he knew exactly what each player would do and he built his attack to take advantage of the New York defense. He knew how fast he could move and how fast they could move. He had it figured down to a fine fraction of a second and his success proved the correctness of his calculations.

Why He Was Lucky

Cobb figured out early in his career that while the danger of his being put out would increase in proportion with the chances he took, the danger of the infield making an error also increased. The faster he went the faster they would have to handle the ball to retire him. All too frequently this fast handling of the ball resulted in a fumble or wild throw that gave him the opportunity to score. Sometimes he was thrown out, but the percentage was much in his favor. He was lucky, yes, but he was lucky because he created his own luck.

Jack Egan, who umpired in the American league for a while, related this incident. It occurred in a game where he was working:

Jack Knight was playing third for New York, Cobb was on first and started to steal. But on the pitched ball on which he went down, Crawford singled to left. Cobb was almost on second when Crawford hit. Cobb soared around like a sea gull and headed for third. The New York infield yelled to Knight to get Cobb, for Knight had his back turned to the diamond awaiting the throw from the left fielder. Knight knew that Cobb was coming from the way the crowds roared. He expected him to slide and was ready to swing down on him. But Cobb did not slide. Knight discovered that when he swung down. And before Knight could throw home Cobb had slid across the plate.

His Specialties

Cobb made a specialty of scoring from first on chances that the average player would never consider advancing more than one base. He scored from first on bunts, singles to short outfield territory, fly balls. He did not get around the bases, from first to the plate before the ball was returned to the infield, but he did get around before the ball was returned to the pitcher. It was not clean going, but it could not have been that. Someone had to make a mental or physical error to get Cobb around, but that was part of Cobb's play. He always tried to make the opposing team commit errors, mechanical or menial. He led them, one way or another, into blundering. That is where his advantage was centered — in his own mechanical ability and in the shortcomings of others.

While Cobb climbed, others suffered, but it was not a single individual that was the victim of Cobb, for he, in the words of Clark Griffith, "made monkeys out of the whole league."

CHAPTER 35

His Target

Ty Aimed at Chase and Outwitted Him—
Another Great Play.

Hal Chase was the nearest approach to Ty Cobb the major leagues have produced. Chase was as quick and as fast as Cobb. He was just as supple, as near "double-jointed." Chase also had a lightning brain. He knew baseball. He could not break into top speed as quickly as Cobb. He did not think quite as fast and he did not think as deeply, but he came nearer to Cobb than any other man ever did, and he was of the same nervous type. His execution of plays was as spectacular and as brilliant as Cobb's. While he never compared with Cobb as a base runner, he was a fellow type in fielding.

Several years ago Cobb was asked one day to describe his greatest play. He has been asked this a number of times and has named a number of plays, but of all those he relates as his best play, the one that was a duel of wits between himself and Chase was probably the greatest. At least it was the one in which Cobb look most pride.

Aimed at Chase

The play occurred during a Detroit–New York game in the early years of his career. At that time Chase was considered the greatest player in the American league, at least by far the most spectacular. Cobb always aimed to outwit Chase, making Chase the target of his best-laid schemes because he was the highest mark he could shoot at.

In this particular game the score was close. One man was out, Crawford at bat and Cobb on second base in the inning where the play took place. Crawford being a "dead" right field hitter, Jimmy Austin, who was playing third base for New York at that time, played close in; Jack Knight, the New York short stop, moved over close to second and Frank LaPorte, the second baseman, had gone far to his left and taken a position back on the grass — ready to cut off a slashing grounder from Crawford's bat; standing almost against the foul line and parallel with LaPorte was Hal Chase. The outfield had shifted in a similar manner and New York was set to take care of Crawford.

If Crawford hit to the infield the play would be made at first base, on Crawford. He hit a ball hard and he was a slow runner; therefore, easy to get as long as an infield drive could be handled. The New York infield would ignore Cobb, of course. It is a baseball rule, "be sure and get one." Getting Cobb was extremely uncertain and getting Crawford was a foregone conclusion, if he hit to the infield.

He Hits to LaPorte

Crawford sent a hard grounder to LaPorte and LaPorte threw to Chase retiring Crawford. Cobb had started with the crack of the bat. He touched third, turned and started for the plate, just as Chase expected him to do. Chase whipped the ball across the infield, on a line to Austin, to get Cobb sliding back into the bag, but as Austin whirled to tag out Cobb he found no spiked shoes trying to reach the bag. He straightened up and what he saw was the mercury-footed Cobb sliding across home plate with what proved to be the winning run.

To the spectators this appeared to be a wonderful piece of daring base running, the taking of a long chance and getting away with it. The average ball player called it "just crazy luck." But the inside workings of this play escaped players and public. Cobb treasures it because in this play he outthought Chase, who had the second fastest mind in the game during Cobb's time.

How Cobb Figured

This play, better than most of those in which Cobb created new phases, illustrates how Cobb managed to keep a step ahead of his opponents in planning. With Crawford, a slow man, at bat and Cobb on second, Cobb knew that Chase would expect him to round third as the play on Crawford would be made leisurely. Cobb always did round third in a situation of this kind and take a lead toward the plate. His quick start enabled him to do this in safety. If the play at first was perfect, Cobb could slide back to third. If the play at first included a fumble, Cobb had the scoring advantage in the lead.

Chase was no ordinary first baseman. Ordinary first basemen would not try to catch Cobb off third, but Chase would. Chase could get a ball away faster than any first baseman in the game and he threw accurately. Chase WOULD throw and Austin, a smart third baseman, would be expecting the throw, ready to tag out Cobb sliding back. Cobb also knew that if Austin took the throw he would not look around for Cobb. He would go down and dive for him. He would not find him. His hand would sweep in a wide circle, trying to touch Cobb's shooting legs or feet. He would miss. He would hear the yells and look. Then Austin would have to get up and set to make the throw home. All this would take time so much time that Cobb would have the opportunity to score.

That is how Cobb figured out the play the previous evening. The situation arose and the play was made exactly as Cobb anticipated it would he made. Knowing Chase and Austin as he did, the play would not be made otherwise. It wasn't.

CHAPTER 36

The Umpire Gasps

Scores on Hit to Left—
A Phantom Runner—An Explanation.

Most of Ty Cobb's long chances looked simple enough after he explained them. But until he stated his reasons and analyzed the play they seemed extremely foolish and risky.

In one Detroit-Philadelphia game Cobb was on first when Veach hit a single to left. Cobb had a good lead and was off like a flash. He cut inside of second base and sailed for third. In recent years Cobb rarely attempted to go from first to third on a single to left, particularly where the left fielder had a fairly good throwing arm, but in those days he always did, and the occasions when be failed to reach third were scarce, indeed.

J. Franklin Baker, playing third for Philadelphia in this game, ran to the bag when the ball was hit, knowing full well that Cobb would try for third. Baker's hands were reaching for the ball. Cobb reached the bag about the same time that the ball landed in Baker's hands. Baker thrust down the hand holding the ball to tag the sliding Cobb, but no Cobb was sliding for third. He had stepped over the hand, tickled the bag on the inside corner, turned sharply and continued on to the plate. Baker, failing to find Cobb, straightened up and snapped a throw to the catcher, but Cobb beat the throw by a fraction and Umpire Billy Evans called him safe.

Cobb Explains

As Cobb jumped to his feet the umpire nearby gasping.

"That play seemed like plain suicide." said Evans.

"Oh, no, it didn't. It was simple. Baker expected me to slide. Ordinarily

I would. But I knew that Baker expected me to slide and the way he was reaching for the ball I knew he thought he had a chance to tag me coming in. He wouldn't stop to look, he didn't have time for that. No, he would turn and plunge to the ground to nail me. Not finding me he would have to uncross his legs and set for the throw. I had it all figured out. I knew that by the time Baker did all of those things I would be scoring, and you got to admit that I did."

There was never a harder loser than Cobb. He played to win and he used every ounce of brain and energy at his command to succeed. He could never give up. There was a striking illustration of this in a game between Detroit and New York while Clark Griffith was manager of the New York team.

It was a dreary game and the Tigers were pounding the veteran Jack Chesbro, then in his last days as a major league pitcher. For some reason Griffith refused to take Chesbro out of the box. Managers do that sometimes.

Not in His Nature

It seemed that Chesbro would never get three men out in one of the late innings. Cobb singled and as he was prancing around the bag Bill Donovan, coaching at first base said to Cobb:

"Let 'em tag you out and get this game over with. That's the only way they'll be able to get anybody out."

"Yes, go on and do that! I'm getting tired myself," said Hal Chase, playing first for New York.

Chesbro heard the remark and took a hint from the conversation. He threw the ball to Chase. Chase reached over to put the ball on Cobb. The runner jerked away a few inches. Chase lunged at him to make the out and Cobb jumped away again. Chase began running after Cobb and then the excitement started. Cobb ran up and down the base line, jockeying between infielders. The entire New York infield gathered around him to participate in the rundown. The ball was thrown back and forth. Finally there was a wide throw to second, Cobb slid, out of reach of a fielder, hooked the bag with his toe and was safe.

"I just couldn't stand there and let 'em put me out without giving 'em a run for it," said Cobb later on in the way of explanation and apology.

Never Laid Down

It could never be said of Cobb that he laid down. Most every other player does, at times. Cobb always played the string out. He tried his best on all occasions.

In exhibition games, where nearly all players loaf because there is nothing at stake and the record books are closed as far as these exhibitions are concerned, Cobb played his best while he was on the field. In explanation he always said:

"Some of these people came a long way to see you. They have probably never seen you before and may never see you again. The impression they carry off with them is the picture they get of you in that game and if you want to make good on everything they have been reading about you and everything they think you are, you've got to go at top speed to keep them from being disappointed and disillusioned. Also, if you get in the habit of loafing at certain times, in games like these, you are likely to catch yourself loafing when you can't afford to loaf. The habit gets on you unconsciously. The only thing to do is to keep going at top speed while you're on the field. Always be extended. It's the best habit you can acquire." Cobb acquired it early and never got out of it.

CHAPTER 37

Comparisons

Sisler of the St. Louis Browns—
Hornsby of the Cardinals—What Rickey Thinks

Comparisons are often drawn between Ty Cobb and George Sisler or Rogers Hornsby. Some believed Sisler might overtake the Georgian but an unfortunate eye ailment cut down the brilliant career of the former University of Michigan star. Hornsby has steadily improved. Of the two Sisler most resembled Cobb.

But, returning to the matter of comparison. If there is one man who should be in position to pass judgment it is Branch Rickey. He resigned as baseball coach at Michigan to become manager of the St. Louis Americans. He took Sisler to St. Louis from the campus at Ann Arbor and saw him develop into one of the truly great players of the game. Then he went over to the National league and became manager of the St. Louis Cardinals. On his team he found Rogers Hornsby and he has seen Hornsby develop into the leading player of the National. Rickey saw much of Cobb while managing the Browns. He has seen much of Sisler and of Hornsby. Asked which of the three was the greatest player, Rickey replied:

"Cobb is easily the greatest. No one can doubt that Cobb is the greatest that ever lived. Why I believe that Cobb carried brains in his feet. He at least played that way. I saw Cobb make one play while I was manager of the Browns that I will never forget. That one play, if nothing else, would convince me that Cobb was a super player."

Cobb Against Weilman

"We were playing in Detroit and the score was tied in the ninth. Two were out. Carl Weilman, who had it on Detroit all the while he was in the American league, was pitching that day. It was Cobb's turn at bat.

"Weilman had more success against Cobb than any pitcher Cobb ever batted against. It was chiefly because Cobb could do nothing against Weilman that Weilman was able to beat the Tigers eight times in one season. But this day Cobb scored a point over Weilman.

"When Cobb came to bat Weilman started working on him. He never was convinced fully that Cobb was easy although the records show that he was, as far as Weilman was concerned. Well, there was Weilman working on him and Cobb shifting around in the batter's box and doing everything he could to disrupt Weilman. He finally managed to get a base on balls.

"As soon as Cobb reached first he took a long lead off the bag. Weilman threw to Leary, our first baseman, to catch Cobb off but Cobb easily beat the throw, sliding gracefully into the sack. Leary lobbed the ball back to Weilman and Cobb immediately dashed away again and drew another throw which he managed to beat to the bag.

"Leary lobbed the ball back to Weilman and Cobb dashed away again. Weilman snatched the ball out of the air and whipped it back to Leary but again too late to catch Cobb. He once more beat the play.

Weilman Urged On

"Right here I thought I saw a chance to retire the side by catching Cobb off first. I stood up in the dugout and yelled to Weilman:

'Do it again.'

"Weilman snapped the ball back to Leary but he had no more success than before. This time Leary, disgusted at failing to catch Cobb, lobbed the ball back to Weilman even higher than before and away Cobb went, this time for second base. Weilman snatched the ball out of the air and shot it to Johnny Lavan, who was playing second base for us. But Weilman overhurried and the ball struck the ground near Lavan's feet and caromed off into center field. Cobb rounded second and kept right on going for third.

"Now, our centerfielder had backed up the play perfectly and had the ball before Cobb was half way to third base. I figured him a dead cinch for an out at third, where Jimmy Austin stood on the line awaiting the centerfielder's throw. The ball beat Cobb by yards but Austin was over-anxious and momentarily fumbled. Right here happened something that convinced me that Cobb has brains in his feet. Either that or he isn't human.

"The ball was lying out there between Austin and Cobb for just a fraction of a second. Austin was reaching for the ball but in that instant Cobb did more thinking than the average ball player does in a season. Instead of sliding for the base he was sliding for the ball feet first and proved that his foot was quicker than Austin's hand, for before the third baseman could touch the ball, Cobb gave it a kick that sent it into the dugout and then jogged to the plate with the winning run.

"It was a clear case of interference but I couldn't make the umpires see it that way. The game was over and you aren't going to win any arguments from the umpires after the umpires call it a day. At that, it would have been a crime to call Cobb out for interference after making a play as brilliant as that.

"Yes, sir, when you're talking of the world's greatest ball player you're talking about only one man — Mr. T. Raymond Cobb."

CHAPTER 38

Then and Now

Baseball Has Changed—
Brilliance Discounted—Mitchell Tells One on Cobb.

Ty Cobb was fortunate in entering baseball when he did. Those were the days of tight pitching duels. The list of .300 batsmen each season rarely consisted of more than a dozen regular players. Those were the days before the lively ball; when teams had to fight for each run and when base running was of paramount importance in the attack. Runs did not come in clusters as in recent seasons.

Cobb's best work was done on the bases; not alone in stealing bases, but in running out hits and running on field chances. He appealed to the student of baseball, who understood his work, and he appealed to the heart of the bleacher that did not understand the inner workings of the plays but that liked to see Cobb run because he was always picturesque and spectacular.

They Play Safe Now

Because hits have been so easy to get in recent years; because teams have adopted a policy of playing safe on the bases and waiting for the hit which was likely to come (for between 50 and 75 batsmen in each major league were hitting .300 and better) the kind of base running that carried Cobb to fame has been neglected. The percentage of late has been in waiting and playing safe. Ball teams play percentage.

But, during the first 10 years of Cobb's career, he was at his best. After he was in the game a few years longer the lively ball came in and there was no longer need for the Cobb flash and daring on the bases. It was just as well for Cobb's sake. When the lively ball was introduced Cobb had slowed down enough to prevent him from making the kind of plays that gave him his remarkable reputation. He could not have done the same tricks then no matter how badly he wanted to.

He brought many innovations into the game with base running. He was the first man to score from second on a sacrifice hunt and he was the first man to score from first on a single. He got much assistance from Claude Rossman, who played first base for Detroit and who followed Cobb in the batting order. Rossman was one of the best batsmen of his day. He was by far the surest bunter in the majors. Rossman could bunt a ball no matter where it was pitched, as long as he could reach it. And he bunted any kind of delivery. Some people think fast balls are the easiest kind to bunt, but they are mistaken. It is much easier to bunt a curve ball than a fast one, but Rossman bunted anything; all he asked was a ball within reach.

With Rossman coming up behind him, Cobb could get cooperation when he wanted it. The perfect bunts of Rossman and the fact that Rossman always bunted when he signaled that he would, gave Cobb the help he needed in his spectacular exhibitions. But as a rule Cobb worked alone. He created his own opportunities, as he planned, or as the occasion arose.

Fred Mitchell, who was a catcher in the American league and later a manager in the National, describes one of Cobb's base running plays to show how he took advantage, of opportunity in a flash:

"I was catching that day against Detroit and [Frank] LaPorte was playing third for us. It was a tight game. Two men were out when Cobb reached third. I had my suspicions. I figured that Cobb would try to pull something. He made a sudden move toward the plate. I whipped the ball to LaPorte. Cobb beat the throw back.

"Once more Cobb moved off third and I again whipped the ball to LaPorte. Cobb slid back easily. Cobb got up, dusted himself off and stood with one foot on the bag. LaPorte, holding the ball in his gloved hand, took a few steps toward the pitcher. The pitcher walked toward LaPorte.

Into Instant Action

"As LaPorte moved toward the pitcher and as the pitcher moved toward LaPorte, Cobb sauntered toward the plate. LaPorte, as players often do, tossed the ball a foot or two in the air and caught it. He was talking to the pitcher. Cobb apparently was paying no attention to them. He seemed to be looking toward his own dugout.

"LaPorte again tossed the ball into the air and caught it. He took another step nearer the pitcher, still talking. Now the pitcher talked to LaPorte, who, while listening, tossed the ball up again. And at that instant Cobb made a break for the plate. I never saw a man in my life spring into action so suddenly. He was going top speed.

"There was shouting and confusion. I was yelling madly for the ball. LaPorte, startled, failed to see Cobb. He did not realize what was going on. By the time LaPorte had realized the play and had set himself and thrown the ball to me, Cobb had slid safely across the plate and was standing up, brushing the dust off his uniform."

Opportunity never knocked more than once at Cobb's door. Opportunity never had to knock more than once. Cobb even anticipated the knock and answered in a flash.

CHAPTER 39

Spiking

Ty Accused of Spiking—
Cobb's Contention—Cutting Down Baker.

During the height of Ty Cobb's career there were frequent accusations made against him charging that he intentionally spiked infielders while going into a base. Most of these charges were unearned although Cobb's career is not entirely free from intentional spiking. According to his own stories he spiked only two men intentionally during his entire career.

According to baseball rules the runner has the right to the base paths. Cobb insisted on that right. He insisted that the fielder keep out of his way and that a fielder blocking the line, was open to spiking which could not be avoided.

Cobb had his rows with players He was never an easy man to get along with. He made a great many enemies but he never set out to "get" any man without giving him warning. If Cobb spiked a man the victim had himself alone to blame.

Few Blocked Him

Few men ever blocked the base lines with Cobb on the paths. They learned it was poor policy. Cobb never took particular care to prevent spiking a man and he was within his baseball rights there. He was entitled to the line and the man who tried to block him had his own safety to look out for.

The most famous spiking incident of Cobb's career occurred during the days when Detroit and Philadelphia were the leading baseball rivals of the American league. Connie Mack was building his superb machine. J. Franklin Baker, a former butcher of Trappe, Md., was playing third base for Mack.

Connie Mack (1862–1956) in 1911. Salsinger describes hearing Connie Mack lament the fact that his 1914 world champion Athletics drew only one-third the fans drawn by sixth-place Detroit when on the road. When Salsinger asked why, Mack replied: "You'll find the answer in center field." Connie Mack managed the Philadelphia Athletics for an amazing 50 years, including 7,466 games with 3,582 wins, nine pennants and five World Series. Mack hired the 40-year-old Cobb in 1927 and 1928, his last two seasons in baseball. Connie Mack was elected the Hall of Fame in 1937. *Courtesy Library of Congress Bain Collection.*

Later on, when the Athletics met the Giants for the world championship and beat them, Baker was Mack's strongest offensive weapon and by hitting home runs off Mathewson and Marquard earned the nickname of "Home Run" Baker: the title clung to him the remainder of his career, although in recent years a dozen players in each league have made more home runs annually than Baker did in his best season.

During those days of Detroit-Philadelphia rivalry, every game between the two teams was a bitter contest. A feud existed between the teams and this broke out in some scene during every game.

Cobb Spikes Baker

Cobb, tearing into third base, found Baker blocking the bag. Cobb came in, spikes shooting high and glittering in the sunlight. Baker had the ball waiting for Cobb. The spikes struck Baker in the forearm, penetrating the flesh. The game was held up while Baker had his arm bound up.

Connie Mack gave out bitter interviews that evening. These were broadcast. Cobb was described as a man with qualities undesirable in sport, a man who stopped at nothing to gain his end.

Cobb replied to these accusations and the feud grew intense.

A newspaper photographer happened to be at third base in that game and he was fortunate in snapping the play. It was a clear photograph, showing Cobb coming into the bag and Baker's hand holding the ball, a foot or so away from his body.

The photograph was used to show that Baker was clumsy. That he had deliberately gotten in the way of Cobb's spikes. He had tagged Cobb and failed to jump to one side. That was also Cobb's contention — that Baker did not get out of the way but purposely got into the path of the spikes.

Philadelphia replied that the photograph, instead of showing that Baker had tagged Cobb, really showed Baker in the act of reaching for Cobb. The position of the hand in the photograph could be interpreted either way. Baker, they said, had not yet tagged Cobb and could be in no other position. Cobb, seeing that he was caught, was deliberately throwing his spikes into Baker.

Threats, Police Escorts

There was a long newspaper controversy — indulged in generally in all parts of the country — on the merits of photographs as evidence. It seemed the final conclusion that this particular photograph could serve either side for its own purpose. The shutter snapped while Baker's hand was in the air, near the body, but it proved nothing. While the camera did not lie in this instance it surely did not speak a specific truth, for Baker might be in the act of touching Cobb or he might be in the act of pulling back his arm after touching him.

There was much ado over this incident. Feeling ran high. Soon after the Detroit team played in Philadelphia. On arrival Cobb received several letters. One of them read:

"I'll be on the roof of a house across the street from the ball park with a rifle and in the third inning I'm going to put a bullet right through your heart. Just a warning."

Cobb received similar letters. When the team took the field that afternoon the outfield was rimmed by policemen. They escorted Cobb on to the playing field and they escorted him off the field. Not a person touched Cobb or tried to. All they did was to hiss and boo, but Cobb was used to that. He would have been lonely if they hadn't hissed and booed.

CHAPTER 40

Fielding

End of the "Rainbow"—
Depended on Speed—Hooper's Humiliation.

Ty Cobb was a good outfielder and an intelligent one, but never great in the senses that were such men as Fielder Jones, of Chicago, and Tris Speaker, of Boston and Cleveland.

Jones was a marvel in several ways. He was a star outfielder when Cobb broke into the league. He played centerfield for the Chicago White Sox and his right fielder and left fielder, both below the average in mechanical skill, had little to do. Ball players used to say that Chicago was the only team in baseball that used two fielders on the foul lines. They played closer to the chalk marks than any right or left fielders since. The Chicago outfield was composed almost literally of Fielder Jones — so wide was his range. He played center, but he also played left and right.

Tris Speaker also covered a wide range, but not as wide as Jones, because Speaker always had one or two good men alongside him in the outfield and there was no need to stretch his area.

Shifted for Batters

These outfielders, Jones and Speaker, always shifted for the batsmen. They depended upon keen judgment plus mechanical ability, to get the ball on outfield drives.

Cobb was unlike them in the main. He, too, covered a great deal of territory, not quite as much as Speaker or Jones, but still more than the average outfielder. But where Jones and Speaker played the batter and stationed themselves in the spot where the batsman was likely to hit, Cobb did not play position; he depended upon his quick break and speed to get him to the spot where he could make the play. Jones and Speaker played the batsman first and then the ball. Cobb played only the ball.

When he began playing for Detroit as a regular he was the Tygers' right fielder. Sam Crawford played center field. Later on they were shifted. Crawford going to right and Cobb taking Crawford's place in center because of Cobb's superior speed. But most of Cobb's best out-fielding was done while he played right field.

Before Cobb entered the league outfielders always "rainbowed" the ball back to the infield on singles. In other words, the outfielders lobbed the ball back. Cobb, by turning first base sharply, forced these "rainbow" returns out of existence. Also, he moved them deeper into the discard by his defensive play in right field. He introduced some new methods in outfielding and these were adopted where the player had the mechanical ability to accept and use them.

Unsuspected Outs

Cobb proved to baseball that a snap throw from an outfielder to the infield could produce many outs, the possibility of which never had been suspected.

When Cobb began developing and playing the outfield regularly, base runners were forced to change their methods. Cobb compelled them to stay on their toes, to play heads up baseball.

One of his big days occurred in a game where Boston opposed Detroit. Harry Hooper, an excellent hitter and a smart player, was with Boston. Hooper will probably remember the day, for Cobb stole two hits from him that afternoon; and if there is one thing more than anything else that will impress itself upon a ball player's mind, it is the loss of a base bit. Hooper was a right field hitter; be rarely hit in any other direction. Cobb decided to take a chance on him and for once he changed his position, coming close toward the infield. Hooper, an excellent lead-off man, headed the Boston batting order. He waited out the Detroit pitcher as usual and when the count became three and two Hooper offered at the next ball which was over. He drove it into right field, a low line smash that struck on the grass and bounded on a direct line toward Cobb. The Detroit first sacker, Claude Rossman, had been instructed by Cobb to run to first and cover the bag in case Hooper hit safely into right. As the ball shot between first and second Rossman ran to the bag. Cobb tore in on the ball, scooped it up and made a snap throw to Rossman. Hooper was out by a full step, and in those days Hooper was by no means a slow base runner.

Did It a Second Time

The next time at bat Hooper grounded to the infield and when he came to bat a third time that day Cobb was again playing close in, at least closer than ordinarily. Once again Hooper smashed through the infield. Cobb again streaked in on the ball, scooped it up and made a snap throw to Rossman. Hooper was once more out by a step.

Cobb had the same success against other players. He saw his opportunities so he played a shorter right field than any other man handling the position. He depended on his speed in doing this. Breaking quickly as he did and having a great deal of speed once under way; also, being a fairly good judge of a fly ball by this time, Cobb decided he could go back and get any kind of chance in right field that was possible to get. By playing close he could always come in on ground-hit balls and have a chance of getting the runner at first. He at least would make a snap throw that prevented the runner from venturing off the bag or taking any kind of lead toward second. If the man cut inside of first and started for second. Cobb was sure to have him caught off base. He caught quite a number that way.

CHAPTER 41

Ingenuity

Plays He Invented—
Had 'Em Either Way—Ty Describes One.

It was while playing right field for Detroit that Ty Cobb invented his "cross" play. With a runner on first and a fly ball hit to right, not too deep, Cobb would pretend to be set for the catch. He really was set for the catch, hands cupped and feet firmly planted on the ground. Seeing that Cobb apparently intended catching the ball, the runner on first would hang close to the bag to prevent Cobb making a snap throw to the first baseman and executing a double play. The man who hit the ball would generally come to a dead stop on his way to first or would turn out entirely, giving up hope. Just as the ball was about to land in Cobb's cupped hands, he would pull the hands away, let the ball strike the ground and then catch it on the rebound. A fast throw to first base and a quick relay to second would complete a double play.

He also worked this play with reverse English. He would come tearing in on a ball and then feigning an attitude that he could make the catch, would set himself to catch the ball on a first bound. The runner on first, sure the ball would fall safe, would dash madly for second. Then Cobb suddenly reversed, jumped forward, made the catch and whipped the ball to first base for a double play. Cobb had a double play ahead of him either way he made the play and, in the language of the sport, "he had 'em going and coming."

Moved to Center

Later Crawford became too slow and Cobb was shifted to centerfield. He no longer had the opportunity of making the same plays in centerfield and he had to change his tactics. The throws from centerfield were too long and the same situations did not present themselves. It was mechanically impossible to do the sensational work he had delivered in right field.

But, no matter where Cobb played, he found opportunity to do the spectacular. He was a born showman, and showmanship with him was a fine art. He learned to dive for balls, a play not made successfully by many outfielders and bungled by all except the most expert. It requires the keenest kind of judgment of batted balls to make diving catches of the kind Cobb made repeatedly. Such judgment he gradually developed. He had the dexterity, the suppleness and the quickness to execute them guided by his keen judgment.

As an outfielder Cobb was spectacular rather than thorough. He knew how to put the dramatic touch to his work. He never used two hands where he could give a plausible impression that he had to use one. He never stood under a fly where he had any chance to take the ball while running. He always picked the most difficult way to do things, but while difficult there had to be a thrill involved. He knew the heart of the gallery better than any man that ever played baseball, and he knew how to reach that heart better than any man in the game. He made a study of the matter. No actor better loved applause than Cobb.

Describes Greatest Play

One time he was asked to name the best fielding play he ever made and he replied:

"It was during a Detroit-Boston game at old Bennett park in Detroit. It was a hot Saturday afternoon, as I remember it. We had a comfortable lead when the ninth inning opened but Boston suddenly made one of those rallies. With nobody out, they got runners to first and second. Jake Stahl, a reliable batter, was up. Stahl drove a low liner over second base. It looked like a sure hit. Both runners were off sprinting at top speed. So was I. Then I noticed that my only chance was in making a dive for the ball and I dived, arms outstretched. I extended my gloved hand as far as possible and was lucky enough to stab the ball just off the grass. It took only an instant to jump to my feet and toss the ball to Jim Delahanty, who was playing second base for us at the time. Jim relayed the ball to first and completed a triple play, ending the game. The runners who were on base when Stahl hit the ball had advanced so far that I could have really made the triple play unassisted if I had cared to."

Improved on Others

Not all the tricks that Cobb used in the outfield were new. Tommy McCarthy, a great fielding outfielder of the past, had some of them and Hughie Duffy, another great fielder whose career preceded Cobb's, had some of them. But neither Duffy nor McCarthy had the bag of tricks that Cobb carried. Neither of them did his stunts as impressively as Cobb and neither could make his work as effective as Cobb. He had the knack of getting the most out of every opportunity and they lacked it. He gave more science to outfielding than they had given and he elaborated upon their lines of endeavor. They introduced certain features of outfielding and Cobb extended these features, broadened them and added to them.

Cobb was once asked how he learned to play the outfield and he answered:

"By watching the best men who played the outfield positions when I started in the majors and by what I heard of the play of other outfielders. I tried to copy the best points of these men, their strength, and, I guess, I got to be a composite of the leading outfielders of my time. At least that is what I tried to become."

CHAPTER 42

20 Years

Cobb at Top Speed—
The Prophets Err—Why Ty Lasted.

Physically, Ty Cobb has always appeared like a superman. Ball players have said of him: "The guy just ain't human."

He went through 20 seasons of the most strenuous competition that any man has ever known in baseball. For twenty years he spent six months each year going at top speed, setting a nerve-racking, muscle-tearing, tissue-destroying clip. And twenty years is four times as long as the most optimistic gave him.

When he started his career and players realized his style they said he could not go at that pace more than a year or two — no man could go longer. They did not think it was possible for a human being to do it.

Their "Consolation."

College sprinters burn themselves out in a few years. Cobb did more sprinting in one year than a college sprinter does in a lifetime. The pace he set was beyond the imagination. He threw his body into the breach, risked limb day after day in desperate running and sliding. He took long chances as far as bodily risk was concerned. And his competitors, whom he overshadowed, had the consolation that it could not last long. Cobb would burn himself out, or break a leg or an arm and that would be the end of their troubles; for Cobb was a constant, source of annoyance to them — he "hogged" the headlines. They did not like it. He had all the spotlight.

But Cobb did not burn out. He outlasted them by years and years. He went double the distance given the exception among big leaguers. The average major league career stretches over six seasons. An exceptional career lasts ten. Those that hang on longer than ten are the real stars of the game and their number is extremely limited. And Cobb, who extended himself more each year than any three men in the game, has enjoyed one of the longest, careers on record. In the twentieth season of his career he was numbered among the leading five batters of his league.

But Cobb had studied out the entire thing years ago. He had method in his baseball madness; his carelessness was studied and fully comprehended.

Cobb realized the dangers of sliding as well as anyone. But he also knew how to discount the dangers. A man sliding always takes the risk of straining or spraining an ankle, often of breaking it. Nearly every player has at some time or other suffered a strain or sprain in sliding. Not a few of them have ended their careers with broken legs. Cobb has suffered less injuries than any player in the game, or any player of his time. The only serious leg injury he ever suffered was a sprained ankle a few years ago. He received this in a game played on a fresh diamond. It was the game that opened the new playing field and the base lines were filled with holes and bumps. Cobb struck one of these bumps while sliding and twisted his ankle. He was out for weeks.

Cobb never received a serious leg or ankle injury on big league playing fields. Early in his career he studied out a method to prevent accidents of this kind. He started his slide while going at top speed. He hurled his body into the air and toward the ground at an angle. As soon as he left his feet his body went limp. He relaxed completely until he was straightened out on the ground, sliding toward the base. Then he resumed control of the muscles so that he could throw his body in any direction. But he remained partly relaxed. There was no tenseness. Therefore, there was no injury.

He had learned, or figured it out, that most injuries in baseball come to players who fail to relax. They hesitate a moment before starting their slide. Then they are uncertain about hitting the dirt. They are tense; the legs are generally stiff; the feet hit the ground; the body is carried with little speed; the speed is not enough to carry the feet and legs forward rapidly—the feet stick and the weight of the body is thrown on the ankles, causing strains or sprains.

This fault in running bases has brought the careers of many players to a premature close. By failing to relax and by hesitating in their take-off when sliding, the players continually throw their weight on the ankles and this constant strain wears out the ankles and slows up the player. The legs are the most important part of any competitive athlete and when the legs go the athlete goes. Few players know how to take care of their legs; Cobb did. While Cobb seemed to be reckless, risking his legs in desperate attempts to reach bases, he was doing it in a manner that insured against injury and his record is the best proof of this.

At bat he was rarely hit by a pitched ball. Only once in his career, late in August of 1921, was Cobb hit in the head by a pitched ball. Jack Quinn hit him over the right ear and knocked him unconscious. Cobb's peculiar stand at the plate always enabled him to duck balls pitched on the inside. He was able to get out of the way quickly. He had that in mind when he adapted that peculiar stance.

CHAPTER 43

Keeping Fit

Six Months' Idleness—
Why Cobb Lasted—Ty and His Dogs

Ty Cobb took precautions to save his legs and ankles and to prevent being hit by pitched balls, but these were only part of the system that carried him through 20 seasons of terrific competition where he was forced to play at top speed always to win a batting and baserunning championship, to defend it or to try and regain it.

Many players have had their careers curtailed by being hit by pitched balls. Cobb was hit fewer times than any other player. When he was hit it was generally because he wanted to be hit to reach first. It was sometimes fine baseball policy to get hit. Most of the times when a pitched ball struck Cobb it was because he managed to stop the ball with his body. But he never intentionally stopped one that might in any way injure him. He was too intelligent and clever for that.

Other Precautions

Still, to last as long as he did, Cobb had to take other precautions. One of the most important was food and of just as much importance was the off season, the weeks between the close of one baseball calendar and the start of the next. To keep muscles from going flabby a man must continue to work them. A ball player, who exercises every day through seven months of the year, goes into absolute idleness during the other five. He takes no exercise. What is the result? The muscles become flabby and as soon as that happens they begin to deteriorate. Players that loaf between seasons find it harder and harder to get into playing shape. They slow down rapidly and find an untimely end to their careers. Cobb argued the matter out and decided that he would have to do something through the winter months. He decided to hunt.

The idea may not have been original with him. He had two fine examples in the leaders of his profession when he broke in. There was Honus Wagner and Larry Lajoie, both "lasters," the sports term for men that remain active over a long stretch of years. Neither of these two remained idle between seasons. Wagner retired to the woods as soon as the season closed and spent his time hunting and fishing. Cobb decided he would spend his vacation periods hunting. That would keep him in the open air and also provide the necessary exercise.

Dogs His Hobby

He became interested in dogs. Down where he now lives, and lived at that time, in Augusta, Ga. one finds a hunter's paradise. Nowhere in the country can more quail be found than in that part of Georgia. Nearly everyone in the section where Cobb lives owns a pointer or setter.

Cobb favored the setter over the pointer and he took to setters. He obtained some good ones. The pride of his kennel is Cobb's Hall and rightly so for Cobb's Hall was the greatest field trial performer of the setters of his time. The greatest field trial dog the country has produced was Mary Montrose, a pointer, owned by the millionaire sportsman William F. Ziegler. Mary Montrose retired undefeated in field trials and the only time she came close to losing was in a race with Cobb's Hall. This setter ran a dead heat with Mary Montrose, the champion of the field trials and a run-off was necessary to decide the American championship at Grand Junction, Tenn. Mary Montrose was given the decision over Cobb's Hall in the run-off but it was a close verdict.

As soon as the season closed Cobb retired to his home at Augusta and started hunting. He would take his setters to the woods day after day. Setters in the south work much faster than in the north. The sportsmen down there follow them on horseback. Cobb followed his setters on foot. Sometimes he walked 10 miles a day, rarely less; often twice that far. Men that have hunted with Cobb will tell you that he really does not walk but trots.

Legs, Heart, Lungs

No track athlete ever performed more faithfully or trained harder during his season than Cobb trained during his off-season. He kept his legs in shape and he called on the heart and lungs. There was no chance for his muscles to become flabby.

He gave the same attention to his food. No trainer ever took greater care of the menu that he arranged for athletes than Cobb took of his personal bill of fare. He drank great quantities of milk and ate many eggs. He claimed that milk and eggs contained the best food properties obtainable for building muscular tissues and for the nerves. He did not eat much red meat, particularly through the winter season.

When he entered the major leagues he ate three meals each day. Then he decided three meals too much. A man could not do his best after eating a full meal. The less he ate just before competition the better he performed. So Cobb cut down on his noon meal, limiting his menu to a plate of soup and sandwich or simply to a double order of ice-cream. And then, one day, he decided that as he got along fairly well with little he could get along better with nothing at noon so he eliminated lunch and limited himself to a morning and evening meal. He drank coffee with both meals. In the morning he always ate generously of fruit. He continued his eating program through his major league career and in that is one of the reasons why Cobb lasted over such a remarkably long stretch of intensive competition.

CHAPTER 44

His Battle

The Cleveland Stabbing—
Clubhouse Fights—Butcher Shop Row.

A volume could be written on "The Battles of Tyrus Cobb." He had a violent temper when he broke into the game, a temper that he has learned to control to some extent since his debut. He has become involved in many misunderstandings, disputes, arguments and fights. Often he became frantically aroused over a slight matter that would pass unnoticed with all but few people. A slight wrong, or an imagined wrong, could start a violent fit of anger.

Cobb's lack of self-control has brought him into embarrassing scenes. It has led him into courts and, on at least one occasion, it required great political influence to save him from serious consequences.

He figured in embarrassing scenes in three different hotels. In a hotel mixup in Cleveland, Cobb was charged with seriously stabbing the night watchman. A warrant was issued for his arrest the next day but he was spirited out of town before it could be served. The matter went to the grand jury and Cobb was placed in a delicate position. Political power finally rescued him.

Fights with Schmidt

He had several fights with players, the best known of which were his two fights with Charlie Schmidt, veteran Detroit catcher. One of these fights took place on the clay diamond of a southern ball field in the presence of the Detroit team. Players separated the two after Schmidt had Cobb thoroughly beaten.

In 1914 Cobb engaged in an argument with William L. Carpenter, a Detroit butcher who ran a shop near Cobb's home. The butcher had sent three perch to Cobb's house. The perch cost 20 cents. There was a dispute regarding the freshness of the perch. Cobb went to the butcher shop and after he and Carpenter had come to an understanding, Howard Harding, a 20-year-old helper in the shop, took up his employer's quarrel. Cobb and Harding went outside and fought on the sidewalk. Cobb got young Harding down and in trying to punch him, missed the boy's head and struck the sidewalk, dislocating his thumb. Cobb was hauled to police station in a patrol wagon and was out of the game for some time because of the injured thumb.

Wide Publicity

The fight was given a vast amount of publicity at the time, but most of Cobb's other rows did not receive the same airing.

One time he was fined in police court for striking a negro street worker who had asked him not to step on freshly poured asphalt.

Claude Lueker in 1912. Lueker was the New York heckler who shouted obscenities and insults at Ty Cobb on May 12, 1912, resulting in Cobb's entering the stands to attack him. This resulted in Cobb's ejection from the game and suspension from the team, and ultimately to the first wildcat strike in baseball as Cobb's Tiger teammates, who felt he was justified in his actions, refused to play while Cobb was suspended. This incident was widely reported in the press at the time, with much of the coverage favorable to Cobb and his actions. Even in today's press, this incident is often cited as evidence that Cobb was a rowdy. But writers almost never mention that Babe Ruth entered the stands to attack a spectator on two different occasions, once after being ejected from the game and punching the umpire and once after throwing sand the umpire's face. *Baseball Magazine.*

In May of 1912, Cobb got into a row in New York and this fracas came near causing a break in the American league, although few blamed Cobb for the incident. In a Detroit–New York game a spectator continued abusing Cobb after Cobb had asked him to stop his tactics. Cobb finally went into the grandstand and struck his tormentor. Later it was found that the victim of Cobb's assault was a cripple, a fact Cobb did not know when he attacked the man.

President B. B. Johnson of the American league suspended Cobb for this incident. The Detroit team went from New York to Philadelphia and here the players rallied to Cobb's support. They had demanded his reinstatement and when it was not granted they went on a strike in Philadelphia—the famous players' strike of 1912. Manager Jennings was compelled to go out and recruit a team of amateurs and semi-pros to play the Athletics and protect the Detroit franchise. Jim McGuire and Joe Sugden, veteran coaches, were the only two men on the Detroit payroll who participated in that game which, in many ways, was the most unusual ever played in the majors. Philadelphia won by an overwhelming score.

Strike Is Settled

Frank J. Navin, owner of the Detroit club, President Johnson and other baseball leaders rushed to Philadelphia to settle the strike. This they finally succeeded in doing. Cobb remained suspended and the players went back to work.

In the spring of 1917 Detroit and New York were playing a series of exhibition games. The Giants, notorious for their "riding" tactics, made Cobb the target of their abuse. The most abusive was "Buck" Herzog, later a manager. Herzog took Cobb to task for his "airs" in reporting for spring practice; charged him with being "swell-headed," and so forth. Cobb told Herzog to save his comedy for the minor leaguers and threatened to "get him" if he did not "lay off."

The two teams played in Dallas the next day. Herzog resumed his tactics. Near the middle of the game Cobb reached first. He went down on the first pitched ball. Herzog, ten feet inside of second, took the throw. Cobb sailed into him, spikes high. Cobb cut Herzog on the thigh. Herzog punched Cobb. They rolled on the ground, fighting. Finally they were separated. The umpires made a mistake in chasing Cobb and letting Herzog remain. That evening Herzog sent word to Cobb that he would appear in Cobb's room and fight it out. He appeared. Cobb outweighed Herzog by about 40 pounds. He did not land any blows on Herzog, but roughed him up considerably in the scuffling. After five minutes of wrestling Herzog said he had enough. Cobb quit the team the next day and the tour continued without him, both clubs losing heavily in gate receipts because of Cobb's absence from the lineup. Cobb rejoined the Detroit team at Toledo, just before the season opened.

CHAPTER 45

Ty Cobb, the Man

A Dual Personality—
Polish, Culture, Suavity—Temper and Self-Interest.

The make-up of Ty Cobb is complex. His is a dual personality. In him we find a man who at times has the polish, the gloss, the culture, the bearing and supreme suavity of a George Bryan (Beau) Brummell* and, at other times, when he loses his temper and lashes into a wild fury, he resembles the Bill Sykes† of Charles Dickens' Oliver Twist. His composition is of Jekyll and Hyde construction.

There is no middle ground with Cobb, no in-between, no temperance and no modifying. He is one extreme or the other; at times he is a supreme optimist. Always is he a creature of varying moods.

A recruit, who had just met Cobb, told a veteran player that he regarded Cobb as the finest gentleman he had ever met.

"You'll say different after you've felt the lash at Simon's whip."

"What Simon?" asked the recruit.

"Simon Legree‡ Cobb." the veteran informed him.

Mellowed — Slightly

The passing years have in a measure tempered Cobb, mellowed him. He has become more and more of a philosopher but the temperamental fires still flare although not as frequently as of yore.

*Beau Brummell (1778–1840) was a well known 18th-century English gentleman, and a "dandy" who dressed lavishly and set the trend for men's fashion at that time. He is credited with introducing and establishing as fashion the modern man's suit, worn with a tie.

†Bill Sykes is the most vicious character in Dickens' *Oliver Twist,* who is portrayed as a rough and barbaric man who is prone to sudden bursts of extreme behavior.

‡Simon Legree was the fictional, Northern-born slave owner in Harriet Beecher Stowe's anti-slavery novel *Uncle Tom's Cabin* who had Uncle Tom flogged to death.

In his long career his disposition has always been of a truculent nature. He never was able to stand reverses with good grace. He often expressed a selfish nature and too frequently lacked sympathy.

Cobb has always been a student. His mind is one of the keenest in his native land. He was quick to grasp, to understand any subject. He has an inquiring mind, a thirst for knowledge of all kinds.

He can discourse on any favorite subject of the drawing room. He can talk intelligently on the various arts and on sciences. He knows a great deal about finance and business. He knows much about manufacture. He knows a good deal about literature, about music.

Knowledge of Art

A friend was showing Cobb a portrait of one of his forebears.

"That's a Stuart." said the friend and after a pause, he added in explanation: "I mean the canvas was painted by Stuart."

"Yes. I know what you meant, but personally — well, while Stuart, is a good portrait painter. I personally prefer Sir Thomas Lawrence. I think Lawrence was a great painter," replied Cobb.

Yes. Lawrence was a good painter an excellent one. But so were Joshua Reynolds, Romney, Gainsborough, Rubens, Van Dyke. And there was a Spaniard — "

"A Spaniard by the name of Velasquez." interrupted Cobb.

"Yes. Diego Rodriguez Velasquez de Silva, a great painter," agreed the friend.

"He was a great painter and to many painters he was the greatest painter. He was in fact, the painters' painter," added Cobb and the friend agreed.

Cobb knows the old masters and the modern. Knows Corot and Turner, Whistler and Degas, Millet and Diaz, Melchers and Sargent.

And Cobb knows music. He knows the classical in music. He is acquainted with the works of the great composers, the French, Italian, German and Russian.

Surprises Musician

One evening Cobb sat in a famous restaurant. The orchestra was offering that evening a program of classical selections. During the intermission the conductor came to Cobb's table and was introduced. Cobb invited him to sit down. The composer asked Cobb how he liked the orchestra and Cobb criticized certain phases of the rendition. The orchestra leader, a really gifted musician, immediately tried to corner Cobb in a technical discussion. The attempt failed utterly for Cobb dazed the leader with his knowledge of the technique of orchestration. The conversation drifted to the violin for the orchestra leader was a noted violinist and analyzed the merits of the various leading masters of the instrument, supporting each statement with a brilliant collection of facts. A stranger, bearing the conversation, would have experienced difficulty in choosing the musician if told that one man was a musician and the other was not.

He has a knowledge of sculpture. He knows Rodin and admires the work of the great French master. The ruggedness, virility, power and force of Rodin's sculpture appeals to Cobb more than that of any other man who works in stone, wax, clay or bronze.

He has a knowledge of precious stones. He knows diamonds, pearls, rubies, emeralds, sapphires. He knows the history of many gems. He is a judge of diamonds and the nativity of the different diamonds, their cut, their value.

The man who thinks he can sell Cobb a modern Oriental rug for an antique will soon discover his mistake. Cobb has studied rugs. He knows his Bokhars, Shiraz, Daghestan, Karmunshah, Saraband, Kabistan, Mosul, Kazak, Senna, Ghiordes, Kulah, Ladik, Beluchistan and others. He has studied pattern, weaves, color, history of rugs. He found certain fascination in them as he has found fascination in most of the things of life.

CHAPTER 46

His Nature

Things Cobb Appreciates—
Window-Shopping—A Psycho-Analysis.

The nature of Ty Cobb is in many ways poetic. The beautiful things in life have a fascinating appeal for him. He is highly intellectual, highly sensitive; art appeals to those as sensitive as he. He is always attracted by a painting well done, by a car of artistic design, by a well made animal, an etching, a rug of fine design, a statue, a precious gem, fine china ware, rare cut glass, fine linen, silk wall paper of rich pattern—all hold his attention.

Whenever Cobb is in New York he never fails to spend hours strolling along Fifth Avenue, "window shopping." He pauses and inspects that which is beautiful, rich in color, artistic in design, articles that show craftsmanship.

A Friend's Comment

One day a friend accompanying Cobb on a "window shopping" hour, remarked to him:

"My ambition in life is to have so much money some day that I can walk along this Street and stop in shop after shop. To say to a clerk, 'Here, my boy, what is the price of this bronze?' And the clerk will name the figure. I will say, 'Here is your money. Express it to this address.' And I'll say to another clerk. 'What is the price of this picture? And of that one and that one?' pointing out all the pictures in the gallery that strike my eye. And I will give him a check covering the total cost and tell him to express them.

"And so down the street, shopping wherever the eye arrests attention, picking these treasures and obtaining them, where now I can only look at them through a window pane. That would be a grand feeling, wouldn't it?"

Cobb thought a moment before he replied:

"No, you're wrong. You are very wrong, You are far richer now and happier than you would be with money to buy all those things. Here you are looking through the window panes desiring this and desiring that. You appreciate all these fine things. But you wouldn't appreciate then any longer if you had them. Your wouldn't appreciate them if you could own them. Your greatest pleasure comes in wanting a thing. To obtain it removes that pleasure. If you bought all these things that you have been admiring, or if you could buy them, you wouldn't be happy over them. They would have become common place to you. This is the curse of being in a position where you can have all you want."

An Army Analysis

Several years ago W. J. Borland, former psychological examiner of the United States Army, made a test of Cobb and gave a psycho-analysis of the player.

"Cobb has genius without the usual neurotic trend," read Borland's report. Further on, the Borland analysis states:

"Cobb never was, is not now, and never can be an egotist. True, the ego, or the psychological equivalent for soul, is highly developed, but the soul of Cobb is never expressed through the medium of egotism. One single trait in his character proves, beyond the possibility of doubt, that egotism can no more be expressed by Cobb than the Iliad of Homer by the Wild Man of Borneo. That single trait is bashfulness.

"On the emotional side. Cobb has that indefinable quality in personality that infuses others with faith, confidence, enthusiasm and zest for the task at hand, and it is the 'aura' as psychologists call it that would carry Cobb to the pinnacle of fame as a leader of men in whatever endeavor he chose to follow.

"Extra effort, the drawing upon potential or subconscious reserve, is responsible for outstanding success in every line of human endeavor. It is this quality, whether conscious or not, that has made Cobb the player that he is."

Never an Egotist

That is the opinion of one psychologist. Others might differ in some details, but they would agree in the main.

Cobb has never been an egotist. He has a bashfulness unusual in men. Until a few years ago it was impossible for him to talk in public. He would stutter and stammer. Only when among a few that knew him well was he at ease.

He disliked talking about himself or his accomplishments in baseball. He never talked baseball unless there was no escape. He gladly discoursed on any other subject, particularly if the men with whom he talked could give him some new knowledge on the subject.

And still Cobb, when introduced in a stranger, was the most courteous and gracious of men. He would make his new acquaintance feel that an unprecedented honor had come to Cobb, that he could now call his life complete, something which it never would have been but for the introduction. Easy and graceful in conversation, he never failed to leave a deep and favorable impression, regardless of the social status of his new acquaintance.

CHAPTER 47

Ty's Hobby

A Love for Dogs—
Their Attachment—His Own Great Dog.

Dogs have been a hobby with Ty Cobb for several years. It is said that the attitude of dogs toward a man indicate the kind of man he is. Dogs will shy from a man lacking in good qualities. If this is a true test then Cobb must rank far above par; dogs always take to him. Strange dogs follow him. Dogs known as vicious and not to be trusted will readily trot up to Cobb, tails wagging and barking in friendly manner.

He loves dogs, not in the manner of the regular dog fancier who likes in dogs the show points. The dogs for which Cobb has the greatest affection are dogs that would "get the gate"' in any show ring; he never looks for the show points but the soul of the dog.

A noted dog judge interviewed Cobb one day. This man, wise in kennel affairs, knowing every breed listed by the American Kennel Club (and there are more than 75), asked for an interview on dog shows and show dogs, also on field trials.

His Praise of Dogs

"I know nothing of show dogs nor dog shows, but I have studied dogs" said Cobb. "I believe dogs are among the greatest things in the world.

"Dogs are little understood but they are nearer human than anything outside of human beings.

"I honestly believe that dogs have souls. You would agree with me if you studied them as I have. They really have souls.

"A dog will live with you and he will die with you—yes, sir, the dog will die with you. How many dogs have followed their masters to the grave and died there? How many dogs died soon after they passed out?

"You will find qualities in a dog that you can not find in a human being. No man ever had a friend as honest and faithful as a dog. There never lived a human being as sincere, frank and honest, as a dog.

"I have gone out hunting with my dogs. The dog on the hunt has not the advantages that you have. Your feet are protected by heavy leather and thick sole. The dog has no such protection. He will hunt until he drops, his feet raw from burrs and thistle and underbrush, and then, dragging himself home after you, the dog will wait until you yourself are comfortable; then he will come and he at your side, look up at you and lick your hands. He is tired, exhausted, bruised and sore, but still ready to limp out and serve you."

A Genuine Emotion

Cobb, lacking in sentiment in some ways, is one of the most sentimental of men in others. His love for dogs, his admiration, respect and esteem for them, is deep and sincere.

He has remarkable power over dogs. Had he himself trained and handled the pride of his kennels, America would have had another champion. This dog, Cobb's Hall, was a straight-bred Llewellyn English setter, by Rigoletto out of Mouna. Rigoletto is by Prince Rodney and Mouna was a litter sister to Momoney. Both Prince Rodney and Momoney were national field trial champions, so that Cobb's Hall had almost perfect breeding for field trial competition. Cobb trained the dog during the winter months, shooting over him, but when he came north in the spring he had to turn the dog over to a professional handler during the baseball season. The field trials were held at Grand Junction, Tenn., in the autumn, and Cobb's Hall and others were pitied against Mary Montrose, the undefeated champion and the greatest field trial performer America has produced. She was a pointer. Under the professional handler Cobb's Hall did not behave well. He lacked the fine finish that he showed when Cobb handled him, but even at that he finished a dead heat with Mary Montrose and an extra heat had to be run to decide the championship. As related in a previous chapter, in this extra heat the decision went to Mary Montrose. It was the nearest the famous Mary ever came to defeat, and she would have been beaten over the Tennessee field at the trials if Cobb could have had charge of his star.

"No Finer Companion"

"Dogs are a great thing for boys," says Cobb. "There is no truer companion than a dog and a boy in the company of a dog is in good company. If he observes the dog, which he will do naturally, he can learn a great deal that will be helpful to him.

"Dogs are among the world's greatest instructors. Few of us realize that, but if you are around dogs and study them you will soon discover this to be a fact. For one thing, dogs are much more moral than men. They have their own code and it is the only perfect one. In other ways are dogs superior to the human being. If we studied dogs more and copied some of their virtues we would all be better off. What a precious human being a man would be who had the loyalty, the honesty, the frankness, the honor and the deep sincere friendship that we find in the dog!"

CHAPTER 48

A Bad Loser

Defeat a Disgrace—
Faults That Made Him—His Earning Power.

Sports never saw a more colorful performer than Ty Cobb. Individually he brought more money into the box office than any other single performer. Only two men have ever come near being possessed of the drawing power that he had. One of these is George Herman (Babe) Ruth, playing in the same league that Cobb is in and, like Cobb, always having played in the one major organization, and the other is Jack Dempsey, champion of boxing. Ruth, of course, drew more money into the box office during his best three years than Cobb did during any three years of his career, but Cobb played over a much longer stretch and therefore will total more in gate receipts than Ruth.

When color is analyzed in human beings it is proved that color consists mostly of what the world looks upon as weaknesses and faults. In Cobb color was a combination of spectacular play and a fiery temper that brought him into unpleasant situations which resulted in much newspaper notoriety. But, while many of his acts have led to criticism, they never diminished his drawing power; on the contrary, they augmented it.

Some He Didn't Like

No other player ever knew better the value of publicity. Of course there are various kinds of publicity and there are certain kinds that he did not relish but he appreciated the value of this advertising.

Among these things which helped make Cobb a great ball player and a national figure were some of the faults that have been subject to criticism.

It required a certain amount of selfishness to develop ambition such as Cobb had. He was always a bad loser and regardless of how small the stake was and how immaterial the result. If the decision went against him he never took the reverse gracefully but almost always created an unpleasant scene. This was a fault that most men found unforgivable but at the same time this fault helped Cobb to the highest peak in his profession. Nothing so hurt him as to lose and he has sat in his room after a losing game and literally wept.

Men that gain the heights are men that cannot endure defeat. Some of them mask their inner feelings better than others, but Cobb with his fiery disposition, could not wear the mask. He lost complete control of himself. To be beaten meant to be disgraced. He fought all the harder against defeat, risking everything to win.

The Difference

After the New York Yankees lost their second consecutive world series to the New York Giants in the autumn of 1922 Colonel Tillinghast Huston, half owner of the American league team and one of the most ardent baseball fans in the land, came over to the Waldorf-Astoria, where John J. McGraw had his headquarters, to congratulate the manager of the Giants on his victory. On his way out a friend stopped Huston, patted him on the back and said:

"Colonel, 'you lost. But there's one thing they're saying about you that's worth more than winning the series — they say you are the best loser in the country. I want to congratulate you on that."

Huston thanked him, walked a few steps and turned to an acquaintance:

"That man makes me feel like a rotten hypocrite, an awful four-flusher. Good loser! That is to laugh. Show me the man who is a good loser! All of us are bad losers. We all hate to lose. It hurts us. The difference is that some of us can hide it. We are what they call the 'good losers.' Others of us can't hide it. We frankly show it. And they are the 'bad losers.' The difference between a good loser and a bad loser is that the good loser is dishonest about it and the bad loser is honest."

So the fact that Cobb is known as a bad loser is at least, according to

Colonel Huston's definition, more to be admired than the men who pride themselves on being "good losers."

Made Him Great

The temperament that brought many unpleasant incidents into Cobb's career was probably his most valuable asset. Without that temperament Cobb could never have been the player that he was. The trouble with the majority of ball players is that they lack temperament; they are too phlegmatic; they take matters as they come. Cobb never did. He always tried to make matters come as he wanted matters to come. He created his situations.

Cobb could never have plunged ahead, jumping into plays and into situations had he lacked temperament. It was the fiery, unquenchable temperament that gave him the drive. There was only one way for him to go and that was ahead. He never knew retreat.

He has his faults as all mortals have, but he has his virtues as well. Physical courage is one of them. None ever doubted Cobb's courage. No matter how bitter his enemies were, what they charged him with, he was never accused of being a coward. He was in many ways a bully, but not a bully in the full sense of the word, for he was also a man of supreme courage, and not many bullies are that.

CHAPTER 49

Ty's Views

His Opinions Change—
Two Interviews—His Pet Subject.

The opinions of Ty Cobb are subject to change. Consider his opinion on pitching, for instance. In an interview given in 1921 Cobb made this statement:

"Many good pitchers have been curved out of the league. One of the worst mistakes a pitcher can make is to use too many curves. They spoil the pitching arm. I think a good fast ball with a hop is far more effective than a curve and there are some pitchers who could do much better if they would rely on their fast one instead of prematurely ending their careers because they prefer the curves."

Now consider his opinion on the same subject as uttered in an interview given in the year 1924.

"The trouble with pitchers is that they don't use enough curve balls. They're afraid to curve the ball. They think it spoils their arms and cuts down their career. That is where they are all wrong. Nothing is so good for a pitching arm as throwing curve ball. If you doubt it look at the pitchers that had long careers that lasted over long periods. You will find that practically all the good curve ball pitchers were men that pitched curve balls a lot. The more curves they pitched the longer they lasted. The curve ball strengthens the arm. When you find a pitcher complaining about sore arm it is 10 to 1 that he is a fast ball pitcher who doesn't use a curve much. If he used a curve a lot he would not have a sore arm."

Those That Are Fixed

However, some of his opinions will not be changed. He said, some years back:

Cobb in 1924. On May 10, Ty Cobb was honored at pre-game ceremonies in Washington, D.C., by more than 100 dignitaries and legislators, mostly from Georgia and Michigan. Cobb, known to be an avid reader, was given a set of 21 books representing his years of service in professional baseball. *Courtesy Library of Congress Bain Collection.*

"Baseball is an open game. If anyone had ever found a recipe for winning ball games there would be no more baseball, as all you would have to do would be to buy the recipe and use it. The success of the game will continue as long as its uncertainty lasts."

On another occasion he said:

"Criticisms hurt a ball player more than any fan realizes. Success in baseball is two-thirds ability and one-third confidence and concentration. Criticism destroys confidence and concentration and therefore reduces the playing value of a man at least 33⅓ percent.

"That also explains why so many ball clubs do a great deal better on the road than at home. The player expects criticism abroad and never pays any attention to it. The criticism hurled at him while he is at home is the criticism that destroys his value."

Speaking of psychology and its relation to baseball he said:

"Psychology plays a big part in baseball. If you have a pitcher in the box who is going along fairly well but none too good, and have a man warming up in the 'bull pen,' the fact that the pitcher in the box sees the man warming up in the 'bull pen' is likely to cause him to weaken. A man who is pitching has all he can do to keep his mind on the batter. He has to concentrate on him and how can the man in the box concentrate on the batter when every time he winds up he sees out of the corner of his eye a teammate warming up in the 'bull pen' and getting ready to relieve him. He gets to thinking that the manager believes he isn't good enough to stay in the box and he'll get to believing that he isn't and then suddenly he won't be.

"Now, on the other hand, if your pitcher happens to be going a bit wobbly in a close game and he sees a pitcher come out of the visiting team's dugout and start for the opposite 'bull pen' to warm up for relief duty, you can immediately see a change in your pitcher. He sets the motion that the other team has come to the conclusion that he is unbeatable and is getting ready to send in a relief for the man opposing him in the box. He takes courage immediately and pitches his head off.

"That is plain psychology working in different directions."

Cobb on Hustling

Cobb often talks on his pet baseball subject, psychology. It applies to every angle of the game. Here is one:

"Hustling is infectious. If you take a lazy player and put him next to a hustler, one who plays 'heads-up' baseball and is on his toes all the time, you will soon note a change in the lazy player. He begins showing energy. The hustler causes the change in him. Get several men on your team that hustle and you will find the rest hustling. The more one hustles the more the others will hustle."

That is not always true though, a fact that Cobb has discovered and admitted. The hustler can cause to hustle only those who have it in them to hustle. Some men do not happen to have the ability to hustle and they would not change their tactics regardless of who played alongside of them. Cobb has found that out, for a few that have played alongside of him never hustled and there is no denying that Cobb could not find a better hustler anywhere in baseball than himself.

CHAPTER 50

The Dynamo

Comparing Cobb, Wagner and Lajoie—
Where Comparison Stops.

Frequent comparisons are made between Cobb and other great players of past and present. They all fall short of Cobb chiefly because they lack his competitive spirit. There probably never lived another man in sports who had it as highly developed as Cobb. They fall short of him, too, because they lack his magic brain. No two men are alike, nor any two people of either sex. There are, therefore, no two brains exactly alike. The brain of Cobb happens to be the singular exception—a brain so made that it gives more rapid action to thought than the brain of any other player; it is a machine of rare intelligence and superior cunning, this brain of Cobb's.

All men must be judged by comparison. Cobb is the greatest ball player of all time by comparison. Other men have had as much mechanical skill and some had more, but none of them ever put it to the extraordinary use that Cobb did. None ever thought so rapidly nor acted so quickly.

Compare the Two

Consider Hans Wagner. He is considered by some to be Cobb's superior. He was a great fielder and a great hitter. He knew baseball, but he never knew it in the deep sense that Cobb did. He did everything well, but he never did it with the consummate skill that was Cobb's. Wagner lacked the extra touch, the spark, the flame; there was no fire to Wagner; he was phlegmatic; he was thorough. But Wagner lacked, above all things, imagination. He was not possessed of the inventive mind that was Cobb's. Cobb at play in his greatest moments was the very soul of baseball.

Take Napoleon Lajoie. Here was poetry of motion on the ball field. The Frenchman had perfect form. Easy, graceful, polished, finished to a decimal. Lajoie was the perfect type, mechanically. He never took a wrong step, never made a false move, never wasted energy; but he, too, lacked competitive genius. He had power but no dash. He had strength, but lacked the springy quickness that was Cobb's. The fire was lacking in Lajoie. He was a model. Cobb a whirling dynamo.

Sam Crawford was also of the phlegmatic type, easy going, powerful, lacking in speed; thorough, but never brilliant; reliable, but never daring. He was conventional and strictly orthodox. But Lajoie and Wagner were also thoroughly orthodox. They did the conventional a great deal better than others.

The Great Anson

Adrian C. Anson, powerful hitter, intelligent first baseman,

Napoleon Lajoie (1874–1959) in 1913. Nap Lajoie was the leading American League batter from 1901 through 1904. After Ty Cobb won the first of his many batting titles in 1907, an annual competition between Cobb and Lajoie was underway. This rivalry peaked in 1910 when the St. Louis Browns intentionally allowed Lajoie to bunt safely seven times in the season-ending doubleheader. Despite the help, Lajoie finished at .384, a point behind Cobb. Browns manager Jack O'Connor and coach Harry Howell attempted to bribe the official scorer to change an error to a hit and thereby give the batting title to Lajoie. A furor arose when the official scorer refused the bribe and reported the attempt, resulting in O'Connor and Howell being kicked out of baseball for life. Seventy years later, modern historians scoured the records of the entire 1910 season to find two questionable hits that had been awarded to Cobb that year, and advocated that Cobb's 1910 batting title be retracted and his lifetime batting average be reduced from .367 to .366. Major League Baseball has not officially made such a retraction. Lajoie finished his 21-year career in 1916 with a career batting average of .338, thirty points below Cobb's. He was elected to the Hall of Fame in 1937. *Courtesy Library of Congress Bain Collection.*

was of the Crawford type. He lacked the finish, the gloss, the polish of Lajoie. He, much like Wagner, depended upon physical power. He was not exceptional in mechanical skill.

The players that climbed to fame in Cobb's own league during his sweep of conquering seasons were George Sisler, Tris Speaker, Eddie Collins, Joe Jackson and Babe Ruth. There were others who went a distance up the ladder, but in the entire field the players named here were foremost and the outstanding player of the group is of course, Ruth.

Since Ruth became the master slugger of the baseball ages, much time has been spent comparing him with Cobb, and — while many say there is no comparison — let it be understood that Ruth is a great deal better player than he has been given credit for being. Ruth is more than the general public believe him to be — a great slugger. He is one of the best outfielders in the game, and he was the best in the American league during 1924. He is fast, has a fine pair of hands, is a sure catch of a fly ball, plays the batter well, goes a long way to get them and gets any gettable ball; and he has the most accurate and best-throwing arm in the league. On bases he lacks the speed that Cobb and others had, but he runs with excellent judgment. He has a thorough knowledge of baseball, though not as much as Cobb. He does not throw to the wrong base and he does not make the wrong play; and those are the standards on which ball players judge the ability of ball players.

What Ruth Lacks

Ruth pleases the eye; Cobb pleased the mind and eye. Ruth lacks the speed, the quick start, the lightning-like brain of Cobb. He lacks the genius of imagination that Cobb has, but he is more than a mere slugger, although of a type removed from the Cobb type.

George Sisler, quick fast and supple, came probably nearer the Cobb standard of play than anyone else. One reason is that Sisler made Cobb his model, and tried to copy him as much as possible. Sisler is one of the greatest batters that ever lived. Had he escaped the injury to his eyes it is quite likely that Sisler would have outclassed Cobb as a batter and would have outclassed him by using the Cobb system at bat. He was a batter of exactly Cobb's type. He had a quick start, although he did not break as quickly as Cobb, but he ran as fast. As a fielder he played strictly according to the Cobb style.

He lacked Cobb's imagination and the fiery spirit of Cobb, but, as we have explained, all others players lacked it in the degree that Cobb had it. Comparisons with Cobb always stop when it comes to a comparison of mental activity and competitive spirit.

Speaker was a much better fielder than Cobb and not far behind him in batting. Also, he was an exceedingly intelligent player, but he did not compare with Cobb as a base runner.

Collins, while excellent in all departments and the best second baseman his league showed, fell short of Cobb on attack. Jackson was a great hitter and nothing else.

CHAPTER 51

The Old Days

Longs for Ye Old Days—
For "A Schaefer"—For "The Old Gang."

No player ever had more trials and tribulations in trying to break into the major leagues than Ty Cobb. He was harassed on all sides. Veterans of the rough and tumble school, the men that knew how to give and take, were the kind that he went up against. He was sensitive, hot-tempered, sharp-tongued; he was the type of player that invited "riding" and the boys were accommodating—they "rode" Cobb. They would steal his shoes and part of his uniform. They even made kindling wood out of his pet bats. They would lock him out of the clubhouse after a game so that he could not get in to take a shower. When he did get in they made him stand aside and wait until all had their baths.

They had not won any pennants when he joined them and they did not threaten to win any. They were just a ball team playing out the schedule after July 4, with no place to go, as they say in baseball. They helped fill out the league muster.

Jennings the Diplomat

The third season that Cobb was with the team Hughie Jennings was manager. And Jennings found the type of players that he desired, the fighting, hard-boiled variety of scrapping ball players. They had the stuff in them and it took a man with the diplomacy and leadership of Jennings to mould them into a machine. Instead of being nine units, each bound in a different direction, they became a whole with one purpose.

Cobb led this fighting attack. Behind his fine exhibition of competitive spirit the others fell in and fought on. The men that had been his chief tormentors, the very players that had tried to close the door to him and break him, became the beneficiaries of the skill they could not smother and the spirit they could not dampen.

Cobb has forgiven them for their attitude and many times after they passed he longed for them.

"If we only had some of the old gang here now," he has often mused. "If we only had a 'Germany' Schaefer, a Claude Rossman, a Charley O'Leary, a Matty McIntyre and Davey Jones—What I'd give to have them on the team now. Yes, and a Charlie Schmidt and Bill Donovan. And a George Mullin."

"They Had the Stuff"

"Those were the boys, let me tell you. They were the boys that had the stuff. You don't see it any more. They don't seem to be turning out their type these days. They were the fellows that had the old fight. They had the dash and ginger. They were game, those boys. Imagine that crew laying down the way these fellows do! Imagine what they would do! 'Come on at 'em and tear 'em up,' is what they used to yell and that's just what they did. They battled everybody. You couldn't beat them because they wouldn't let you They were a rip-roaring and tearing lot. Lord, if I could only get about six players like those of the old days when we had a fighting team."

The attitude that Cobb first encountered when he reported to the Detroit management had its beneficial results. Cobb at that time made up his mind that if he ever got the opportunity he would lend a helping hand to a recruit. He would do all he could do for them. He would see that other recruits did not undergo the same humiliation, torture, embarrassment and mental agony that he did.

Cobb kept his promise. He has always befriended the recruit. Any time he got the opportunity he gave helpful advice to youngsters breaking into the big leagues, or trying to. He never failed to encourage them; to give them hints on hitting, fielding: he told them how they could improve themselves.

If They Took It

Any recruit who took Cobb's advice and followed it sincerely was certain to continue getting it, particularly if he showed any improvement.

"I am getting old," said Cobb a few years ago. "I'm getting to that stage where it will soon be the bench for me. The old legs and arms won't respond the way they used to. We all reach that stage sooner or later. I'm near it now.

"I used to get a great deal of pleasure out of doing things myself. Now I get my pleasure out of getting others to do them. There is more satisfaction, I find, in seeing a recruit develop under the advice and training you give him than in accomplishing something yourself. At least I'm getting more pleasure out of it than I used to get out of my batting and base-running and fielding. Doing things through others holds a far richer reward."

There is one thing at which Cobb draws the line and that is having a recruit dispute him. As soon as one of his pupils questions his opinion on anything concerning baseball Cobb immediately resigns as instructor. His word and his opinion must be final and beyond question or argument as far as the recruit is concerned.

CHAPTER 52

His Moods

Kaleidoscopic Changing Moods—
Heights of Optimism—Depths of Pessimism.

Ty Cobb has always lived in moods. He would change from the happy and gay to the gloomy and morose. Sometimes he was a mate for Pollyanna, at other times a fit companion for a hypochondriac.

There were times when he wondered what it was all about and what use it could be. On one of these occasions he said:

"If I had my life to live over again I would be a surgeon instead of a ball player. I think I could have done a great deal of good in surgery. I would then have been of some deep use to humanity."

At other times he decided he would quit baseball. Often, in the last five years, did Cobb seriously consider leaving the game. He intended to settle down, fish, hunt, read and enjoy life.

Changing Moods

"Down south we know how to live," he would say. "Down south there is not the hustle, the bustle, the tear and wear that you find in the north. We get something out of life down there. We know what home is and where; in the north, most people believe that an apartment of a few rooms is sufficient; we would never think of such a thing down south. We know food down there and we know how to relax. There is not the battle and strife for the dollar that you find in the north. Tell me, what do they get out of life—these people that are fighting for fortunes that few of them ever get? They grow old and helpless long before their time and when they have passed their usefulness what have they got? What do they get out of life even if they do succeed in getting money? By the time they accumulate their fortunes they don't know how to enjoy the money."

At other times he would say:

"When I quit baseball, which will be very soon now, I shall depart with one deep regret, and that is that I have done no real good to humanity. I suppose everybody will have forgotten me in a few years' time."

In recent years he often tired of baseball, as this observation by Cobb shows:

"I am fed up with this continual strain. I am tired of it all. All the ambitions I had when I broke into professional baseball down in Augusta in 1904 have been satisfied. Yes. I have achieved more in baseball than I set out to achieve. Now I can go back and settle down and get something really worth while out of life."

Year after year he made up his mind to quit. At the age of 32 he said it was his last year. Then another season and another farewell resolution. But he was still playing daily six years after his first resolve to quit.

"Thirty-five is the age limit for professional baseball men in the big leagues," he said at 32. "When a man reaches that age he loses his ginger, his pep and his speed. I am not at top form now. Since 1914 I have gradually let down.

"After a ball player reaches 30 he becomes methodical, I have become methodical and today I find myself doping out each play before I make it with a view to conserving as much energy as possible.

"Most of the success I am having is due to psychology. I apply it constantly. For instance, when the Tigers are leading and the opportunity presents itself, I often take chances, making a freak play or stealing a base when there is no necessity for it. I create a series of mental hazards for the opposing team that causes the player to fumble nine times out of 10 on a similar play that may follow.

"When I was in the flush of youth I could play all day and all night without tiring, but now I find that as the years creep along my stamina weakens. I can no longer make the plays I used to make."

Grows More Difficult

Fire belongs to youth, and even with Cobb, in whom the flames burned longer than in the average mortal, it became more and more difficult to stir the embers.

"Baseball is a hard, nerve-racking life when you play the game for all it is worth. There is no rest when you are weary and the travel is tiresome."

He wanted to have time to read. He likes books, as he likes pictures and music and other works of art. In books he appreciated fine phrasing. The play of words has a fascination for Cobb.

And he likes biography. He has read nearly all the biographies of Napoleon. He has engaged in reading the biographies of the illustrious Bonaparte during the winter seasons. The greatest character in the world's history, in Cobb's opinion, was Napoleon, with Julius Caesar next. And it would be difficult to say that his biographical study did not have powerful influence over Cobb's career. He probably would be the last to say that it did not.

CHAPTER 53

Rest

Cobb's Ideas of Rest—
Plans for Future — Clarke's Experience.

Throughout his career Ty Cobb devoted study and attention to physical welfare. He studied foods and got to know their nutritive values. He studied the science of work and the science of rest.

Cobb experimented with himself, learned how much rest he needed and saw that he got it. He shaped his daily program so that he would be at maximum physical ability when he took the field in the afternoon. He recharged his nerve and muscular batteries between games so that he would be in perfect condition for the mental and physical test that from two to three hours competition would demand.

Several years ago Cobb told a newspaper editor that he owed his long and strenuous career to 12 hours sleep of each 24. He spent one-halt his life sleeping. Before that Thomas A. Edison had said that he slept four out of 24 hours and worked 20. A famous French scientist, years before Edison, slept 20 hours out of every 24 and worked four. Cobb had discovered that some people need more sleep than others and decided that be needed more because he went to greater speed and spent much more nerve and muscle tissue than the vast majority of people. Cobb spent more in two hours than the average ball player spends in a week.

What Cobb Meant

It was a good newspaper story, that one about the 12 hours sleep each day, but Cobb did not mean it exactly that way. Still, it served well for publicity purposes and Cobb got a great deal of publicity out of it. The question of sleep is ever an interesting one and newspapers hopped to the idea with Cobb giving it new impetus.

What Cobb really meant was that he managed to rest 12 hours out of each 24. Not the entire 12 was taken up by sleep, part by lounging. But for 12 hours in every 24 Cobb aimed to give his body perfect relaxation. And in this relaxation is found one of the chief reasons for Cobb's long career.

As he protected his career and prolonged it, so Cobb plans to protect himself when his playing days are ended. He has decided on a system that will insure him for future years.

Men that indulge in strenuous athletics and who quit suddenly invariably pay the heavy price. Lung or heart trouble usually descends upon the man who retires from sport. Cobb intends to protect both heart and lungs.

An Enlarged Heart

A few years ago Cobb was examined by an expert in Atlanta Ga.

This man discovered Cobb had unusually large veins and an enlarged heart. Cobb had exercised for years, ever since early boyhood. The condition was a natural result of that exercise. The doctor told him there was no immediate danger but warned him of serious consequences if he ever quit playing.

Fred Clarke (1872–1960) in 1910. Fred Clarke was manager of the Pittsburgh team that beat the Tigers in the 1909 World Series. Clarke was player-manager with Pittsburgh for 15 years between 1900 and 1915, winning 1,422 games, losing only 969, and winning four National League pennants and a World Series. During this time he also managed the Pirates to five second-place and three third-place finishes. He was elected to the Hall of Fame in 1945. *Courtesy Library of Congress Bain Collection.*

On the day Cobb quits active play he will start a course of daily exercises to prevent a "collapse" of the veins. He intends to continue these exercises.

Cobb told his plan to Fred Clarke, who managed Pittsburg the year that the Pirates beat Cobb and the Tygers for the world championship. Clarke then related his own experiences to Cobb.

Clarke quit exercising when he quit baseball and soon after his heart began troubling him. He consulted a physician. The doctor told him his heart was bad. He told Clarke to report for daily treatments but after a week Clarke's heart was not improved.

Clarke's Experience

The doctor's office was three blocks from a car line and the doctor was always at his office promptly at nine o'clock so by being in the office before nine Clarke was assured of being first called and avoiding waits in the office.

One morning it was exactly nine o'clock when Clarke got off the car. Not wanting to be late he ran to the doctor's office. Examining Clarke a few minutes later the doctor exclaimed: "Your heart action is perfect this morning. My treatments must be doing you a lot of good." So each morning for a week Clarke ran three blocks to the doctor's office and was told that his heart action was perfect. One morning he walked and the doctor discovered Clarke's heart was bad again, just as bad as the day he came to him. So Clarke told the doctor what he had been doing and the doctor prescribed a set of daily exercises for Clarke. His heart trouble disappeared, permanently.

Men who engage in sports enlarge the heart because of the action demanded of the heart. And they naturally enlarge the veins. The same is true of the lungs. The more the athlete exercises and the greater demand made on the lungs, the larger they become. When the athlete retires the heart, veins and lungs collapse because only the normal parts of each organ are used. The result of this collapse is often fatal.

And Cobb is prepared to escape the same fate.

CHAPTER 54

Cobb's Selections

The Greatest Team—
Greatest Pitcher—Praise for Plank.

Cornelius McGillicuddy's Philadelphia Americans of 1910 and 1911 formed, in the opinion of Cobb, the greatest team he ever saw. They appealed to him mostly because they were intelligent. On that team was what they called in those days "the $100,000 infield." This sounds funny in the light of recent, baseball history. The Philadelphia infield of 1910 and 1911, coming to the top 10 years later, would have been called "the million dollar infield." Imagine four players like "Stuffy" McInnis, Eddie Collins, Jack Barry and Frank Baker, going for $100,000 at a time when one recruit infielder, Wille Kamm, a player who had never played on a major league field, brought $100,000 alone!

"I believe that the Philadelphia team had the smartest second-base combination the game ever produced. They were better, in my opinion, than Joe Tinker and Johnny Evers, and while the 'Tinker-to-Evers-to-Chance' line received much publicity, I believe that Barry to Collins to McInnis, while the line did not suit the purpose of rhyming, was a combination much more valuable to baseball.

Power on Attack

"The Athletics were not alone a great defensive team, but they had remarkable power on attack. They were intelligent at both ends of the game, more so than any team I have ever seen.

"Before the Athletics developed to their top form, a simple signal system was used by pitchers and catchers. The catcher would point one finger in his glove and the pitcher would throw a fast ball. He would point two fingers and that meant a curve ball. But the Athletics made that system obsolete and compelled teams to adopt combination signals.

"The Athletics 'stole' signals. This was not done illegally, but in a legitimate manner. They would get a man on second base and he would watch the catcher. The batter would make the catcher waste a few balls. The runner would get the signals. Then he tipped off the batter.

"Then the Athletics, coming to bat and knowing the signals, would get in position where they could watch the catcher signal. They would tip off the batter to what the pitcher intended throwing."

Long Time Solving

"It took teams quite awhile to discover why the Athletics were hitting so well. When it became known, all teams were compelled to change their systems. The catcher would use three or four signals. Only one would mean anything. It might be the first, second or third signal. The others would be used to confuse the opposing team. And then the catcher could call off whatever signal he had given by tossing dirt in front of him or behind him and switch the signals.

"Besides a great infield, the Athletics had a splendid pitching staff with Coombs, Bender and Plank leading. They had a good outfield and a fairly good catching staff. They were a balanced team; a smooth-working machine, highly intelligent, highly powered, mechanically skilled."

The greatest pitcher?

Cobb believes Ed Walsh, of the Chicago White Sox was the greatest the league produced. He gives Eddie Plank a place close up. He also names Denton T. (Cy) Young. These three — Walsh, Plank and Young, in order named — are his choice.

Never Names Weilman

He never names Carl Weilman, who had more success against him than any pitcher Cobb ever faced. Although Weilman was Cobb's master, he never considered him a great pitcher, and Cobb is correct in that.

Plank was intelligent. He knew how to pitch. He had a cross-fire that few have used with anywhere near the success that Plank achieved. He had everything.

"Plank had marvelous control for a left-hander," says Cobb. "He had a fine drop ball and a deceptive curve and he delivered from almost any angle, making it extremely difficult to judge his delivery. He nearly always had the batter in a hole. And after he lost his fast ball he still stayed in the big leagues. This is a feat since a left-hander 'must' have a fast ball to be successful. But Plank worked until he developed a good slow ball to take the place of the fast one he lost, and I want to say I never saw a better slow ball.

"Cy Young has a record that will probably not be touched unless it is by Walter Johnson. But I don't consider Young greater than Johnson or Plank because Young pitched for a team that fielded well and that nearly always made a lot of runs for him. He won more often when he was hit hard than any pitcher I know of."

Cobb's mind is set on teams and pitchers, but on other players he has shifted his opinion frequently. Cobb's judgment is a matter of likes and dislikes, rather than ability. His ranking of players is ruled by sentiment chiefly and is open to reversal.

CHAPTER 55

In His Wake

A Different Game—
A Sport Remade—His Opinion of It.

Ty Cobb will leave baseball a different game than it was when he entered the sport. He revolutionized the game, gave it new life, new speed. He brought about a change at a time when the game had gotten into a groove; when it was an orthodox thing; when it was cut and dried and to a degree that was monotonous. He brought it out of this condition gave it a polish and a gloss, a sparkle and new zest. He made something more out of the game than it was—and the rapid development of baseball, its astounding growth and dazzling spread in popularity, can all he credited to Cobb's vision; to his speed of limb and a brain that worked in perfect coordination and spirit. He injected into the same a powerful personality that was felt gradually throughout the sport.

"He did more for baseball than any single individual that ever lived." said Byron Bancroft Johnson on one occasion. "Baseball owes more to him than the game realizes."

Disapproves Lively Ball

And what does Cobb think of the game today? Not as much as he thought of baseball five years ago. The lively ball, introduced a few years back, changed the entire aspect of the game. Cobb never liked the lively ball; he opposed it from the start and his opinion never changed as far as the ball was concerned. He said often in the past few years:

"The lively ball has robbed the game of its finesse. The art has been taken out of baseball. A premium has been placed upon brawn instead of brain.

'The object of the lively ball is, of course, to produce more hits. The owners believe the public likes hits better than anything else in baseball. The public does like hits, but there can be too much of anything. Too much hitting causes overbalance. The public will tire of too much of anything in any sport. You can have even too much of such a good thing as extra base hits.

"What the lively ball has done to baseball is to spoil much of the strategy. After the lively ball few players bunted any more and few stole bases. It was not profitable to bunt or try to steal. Why? The percentage was all against you. Maybe you stood an even chance in trying to steal, but that would advance you only one base. You stood almost as good a chance to be advanced two bases on a hit and probably score, particularly if you were on third. Stealing

Byron Bancroft Johnson (1864–1931), circa 1910. Ban Johnson was the founding president of the American League in 1901, and was arguably the most powerful man in baseball for the next decade or more. Ty Cobb and Johnson were often at odds, with Johnson suspending Cobb in 1912 for entering the New York stands and attacking an abusive spectator. Regardless of the tension between them Johnson realized the profound impact that Ty Cobb had on the national pastime. Salsinger quotes Johnson as saying about Cobb: "He did more for baseball than any single individual that ever lived. Baseball owes more to him than the game realizes." Ban Johnson was elected to the Hall of Fame in 1937. *Courtesy Library of Congress Bain Collection.*

third was folly; it became a bone-head play. The outfielders had to get out so much farther. They played from 20 to 30 feet farther out than when the old style ball was in play. Their new position made it simple to take two bases on a hit. A runner on second was almost sure to score on any kind of a hit to the outfield. So, why steal third?

"Science Is Gone"

"Why take a chance at all in stealing? The thing to do, with the lively ball in play, was to stay anchored to a base and wait for the hit that was almost sure to come. There was no percentage in base-running. That was passe. They waited for the hit; they got runs in clusters; teams no longer played for a run, but they played for RUNS.

"The best thing to do was to play the infield back, aim to get one man, keep the other team's run total as low as possible, and trust to getting more runs yourself.

"The science of batting has been fairly well lost. The idea seems to be to stand up and take a healthy poke at the ball. You don't have to hit it a mile, although you generally do when you get hold of it. But a ball hit on the ground will do as well most of the time. The lively ball, hit right, goes so fast over the ground that it generally has speed enough to get by the infielders.

"A damper has been put on inside baseball by the lively ball. It has been put temporarily on the shelf. Inside baseball was used chiefly to produce one run at a time. One run is no good in these days, except in rare instances. You've got to get them in clusters, get three and four at a time, sometimes (yes, quite often) more. Big rallies, that's the thing that counts today.

Outfielders' Assist

"The fast defensive work in which the outfields participated is gone. The outfielders are out too far to get into the play. How many men have you seen cut off at the plate on direct assists from the outfielders in recent years? Nearly all the assists outfielders get are on relayed throws in which an infielder or more gets credit for an assist also.

"The law of the manager today is safety first; take no chances; wait for the wallop. The manager takes his cue from the batting averages. They show the percentage is in favor of the batter hitting as against the base-runner trying to steal. The hit gets you so much more.

"But baseball moves in cycles. When I first broke into the league the craze was pitching. All kinds of freak deliveries began to appear, the shine ball, the emery ball, the spit ball and all the other freaks. Then, suddenly, there was complete reform. All freak deliveries were made illegal. Pitchers could not apply dirt or anything else to the ball. Baseball went from one extreme to the other. No temperance. The sky is the limit or there is absolute prohibition. That is how the cycle moves. This is the day of the slugger. And tomorrow — who knows?"

CHAPTER 56

The Dollar

The Dollar's Effect on Game—
The New Generation—A Business Now.

In many ways the players who are now coming up in the major leagues, the new generation of ball players, differ from the old. There is little resemblance between the general type 20 years ago and the general type today, Ty Cobb believes.

"There is not the same love for baseball among the average players today that existed between the average 20 years ago," says Cobb.

"One reason is the dollar. Salaries have gone up tremendously."

Cobb knows this from his own experience. When Cobb was at his best his salary was $9,000 a year. He was the highest-paid player in the big leagues. Today there are players—players who would have had a hard time getting a regular job at the time Cobb broke in—drawing as much money as Cobb received when he was at his peak. Today Cobb and Ruth, the highest-paid players in the game, draw more than $50,000 a year each. That salary, of course, covered Cobb's playing as well as managing.

Reduces Efficiency

But the dollar, Cobb believes, has cut into the efficiency of players and consequently into the quality of baseball.

"When I broke in ball players had a love for baseball. The salaries were small, compared to the salaries of today. They were but a fraction of what they are now, the pay was not the attraction but the game was. The salary is the magnet that draws men to baseball now—the promise of a small fortune to be gotten out of the game if they make good.

"When I broke in we had ball players; today we have business men. The money is the main object today; the game was the goal 20 years ago.

"But, while the ball players of 20 years ago were better ball players, as a whole, and more enthusiastic ball players; while they were men who played the game mostly because they loved to play it, the players of today keep in much better condition than they did at that time.

"You used to see men report for spring training in the worst condition imaginable. They paid absolutely no attention to training or diet during the winter months, and most of them, at least those inclined to take on weight, reported in the spring "hog" fat.

For Business Reasons

"They take better care of themselves now. They pay stricter attention to diet and they keep regular hours. This is not because they love baseball for itself, but because baseball is the means to the money end. They have learned that the man who loses all semblance of condition during the winter months does not last long. If their careers are cut short then their earning capacity will cease abruptly; so they pay attention to what they eat and what they do. The longer they last the more money they will receive. So it is the dollar again that has brought a change in the baseball, but in this instance a change that is an improvement.

"There is lacking today, however, that whole-heartedness, that burning desire to win that I sensed in baseball as soon as I started playing. The whole thing is a business proposition with the average player of today. He is paid to give so many performances a year, and he gives so many. His object is to get them over with as soon as possible. What does he care about the result? He will draw his money just the same, win, or lose or draw."

Some Other Reasons

There are some other reasons why baseball is not played the same as it was 20 years ago, Cobb points out:

"Most of the recruits that are sent to the majors now are not quite ready for big league baseball when they come out of the minors. There is a scarcity of baseball material, and the majors demand new blood. The boys that come up out of the minors are not prepared for the big league stuff. Nearly all of them need two or three years more in minor league company.

"The chief trouble with these boys is that, as soon as they join a major league club they believe they are made. In my day a youngster had to go through a grueling preparatory course in the minors and then sit on the bench for a few years in the majors before he got his chance. Study the careers of all the veteran stars in the game and you will find this to have been true. But not any more. They pick them before they are ripe and the grief is that the recruits can not realize they are still green. You can tell them little, generally nothing. Nobody is going to improve them, for they know it all already. The result is that their development stops right there. They don't improve one iota. They never get any better and, if anything, they get worse.

"Many of the players today are recruited from the semi-pro field, from amateur ranks and the college diamonds. They do not learn much after they are taken up by a big league club."

CHAPTER 57

Records

19 Years a .300 Hitter—
200 Hits a Year—Base Stealing Record.

Through 20 years of campaigning Ty Cobb has gradually smashed record after record. In recent years he has been shooting at Hans Wagner's goal mostly, the great Honus having the best lifetime records until Cobb swept down the final laps of his career.

Cobb shows the best lifetime batting average and it is doubtful if his mark ever will be touched.

In 19 consecutive seasons in the majors he batted better than .300, another record.

In nine seasons of his career he made 200 or more hits, beating the record held by "Wee Willie" Keeler, who in eight reasons got 200 or more.

In three years Cobb batted .400 or better, a record for modern baseball, although Jesse Burkett performed the feat in a past generation of baseball.*

He set a modern base stealing record when he stole 96 bases in 1915.†

In 1911 he was credited with an official batting average of .420, a mark that George Sisler beat, by the minutest fraction of a point later on.

Bad Luck in 1916

He led his league in batting during 12 seasons of his career and was the batting champion for nine consecutive seasons, from 1907 to 1915. He had

*Rogers Hornsby matched this record at St. Louis in 1925.

†Maury Wills broke this record and set the modern single-season record at Los Angeles with 104 stolen bases in 1962.

a great deal of bad luck in 1916, and Tris Speaker beat him in spite of a heroic finish by Cobb. In 1917 he was again the batting leader of his league and continued to be that for three consecutive seasons, bringing his total to 12.

He hit safely in 40 consecutive games but Sisler later beat that record.

He played more games than any man in the American league and more years.

He holds the baseball record for total number of hits, making more than any man that ever played baseball.

He holds the record for total bases on hits and extra bases.

In 1922, when Cobb was given an official average of .401, setting a record for modern baseball by hitting .400 or better in three sea-

Cobb in 1913. Ty Cobb swings hard and misses the ball during batting practice. By some measures, Cobb was a power hitter in his time, leading the American League in home runs in 1909, in triples in 1908, 1911, 1917 and 1918, and in doubles in 1908, 1911 and 1917. The 38-year-old Cobb announced to the press on May 5, 1925, that he intended, for the first time in his career, to swing for the fences. In that day's game and the next, Cobb hit five home runs, just to prove he could, and in doing so tied Cap Anson's 1884 record for most home runs in a two-game series. *Courtesy Library of Congress Bain Collection.*

sons of his career, a protest was made by the Baseball Writers' association.

Protest Over Hit

One of the hits admitted into Cobb's record was a disputed chance in a game played in New York on May 15. The unofficial box scores on that day credited Cobb with two hits while the official scorer gave Cobb credit for only one. The game was played in a drizzling rain, and Cobb drove a grounder to Everett Scott, the New York shortstop, early in the game. Scott had to go well to his left for the ball. While he got his hands on the ball he was not able to make the play. The majority of scorers thought it was a hit as Scott could not make the play. The official scorer thought Scott should have made the play and gave Scott an error and a time at bat to Cobb.

President B. B. Johnson had changed the score on the grounds that the majority ruled it a hit and because the official score of that day was unsigned, and had one or two other errors. The writers' body protested and demanded the official score stand as sent into the American league offices.

There was a spirited discussion and the vote among the writers was split but it was decided by a narrow margin to ask Mr. Johnson to strike out the hit. This was never done and the official averages stood as first announced. Cobb is in the record books with an average of .401 for 1922. Had Mr. Johnson ruled out the hit as requested, Cobb's average would have been only .399.

All Batting Records

Cobb holds all records for batting average, for total number of hits, total number of runs and total or stolen bases.

There have been comparatively few hitless games in Cobb's career. His average for hitting safely in games is a bit better than .700.

He had two banner days at bat. On July 10, 1912, with Detroit, playing the great machine of Connie Mack, Cobb faced [Boardwalk] Brown and [Herb] Pennock in the first game of a double-header and made five hits in five times at bat. He got three singles and two home runs. On May, 7 1922 in five times at bat against Urban Shocker, of the Chicago White Sox, he got five hits, three two-baggers, a single and a home run. This game, coming late in his career, was the best batting performance of his career.

His poorest day at bat was on July 16, 1909 in one of the greatest games in history. Detroit and Washington played 18 innings to a scoreless tie. "Kickapoo" Summers pitching for Detroit, and Bob Groom and "Dolly" Gray for Washington. Cobb went to bat seven times against these two pitchers without reaching first base.

Only three outfielders in history, Fred Clarke, Tris Speaker and Ty Cobb, were offered 5,000 or more fielding chances. Two of them are still going. Clarke had 5,211 chances.

Cobb's best day in the outfield was on September 20, 1911. He made 10 putouts in centerfield that afternoon.

P. S.—Cobb made his first home run on September 25, 1905. He had to wait until April 26, 1906, to make a three-base hit.

CHAPTER 58

100,000,000 Know Him

People Know Him—
"Who's Who" Does Not—So, What Is Fame.

Ty Cobb is the most important figure in the most important game in the most important country in the world. He is the greatest player that game has produced. He holds the majority of the records in the books dealing with that game. He completely revolutionized the style of play in that game. He has become, as the greatest player in the most popular sport of his native land, a man whose name is known to probably 100,000,000 of the inhabitants of the country of his birth. He has received more newspaper space than any American. He has carried the headlines of the newspapers oftener than any man that ever engaged in sport in any country. He has become, through the spread of baseball, an international figure.

A "Guide to Fame"

There is published in this country a book entitled "Who's Who in America." It is supposed to contain the name of everyone who is worth while in the United States; it is the directory of the Hall of Fame; the guide book of achievement.

This book is one of the thickest ever published. It contains, besides the introductory notes, indexes and a few pages devoted to advertising matter, 3,712 pages. It contains a total of 25,357 biographies. Not one man can name 10 per cent of that number of prominent people so it may be said that the list of 25,357 includes everyone of the least consequence in the United States.

There are listed in "Who's Who in America" 24 persons by the name of Cobb. The list is headed by Andrew Jackson Cobb, whose occupation is given as that of a judge and who lives in Athens, Ga., the home state of Tyrus Raymond Cobb.

Next in the list is Bertha Browning Cobb, an author, and she is followed by Calvin Cobb, who is a publisher — a Republican and a Presbyterian of Boise, Idaho.

Fourth in the list of Cobbs comes Carolus Melville Cobb, a physician of Lynn, Mass. He is followed by Charles Wellington Cobb, a lawyer, and Collier Cobb, a geologist, who discovered the Enfield horse in St. Mary's (Upper Micene) deposits of North Carolina.

Cleric and an Author

Ebenezer Baker Cobb, a clergyman of Elizabeth, N. J., comes next and is followed by Ernest Cobb, another author, who wrote "The Hen at Work," "Around the World With Father Time" and other books.

Florence Etheridge Cobb, described as a lawyer and suffragist, home in Wewoka, Okla., is next in the line of Cobbs.

Frank Irving Cobb, an editor, follows and then comes Henry Evertson Cobb, a clergyman and author of "The Victories of Youth," home at 370 West End Avenue, New York City.

Reading on down we find Henry Ives Cobb, architect, Herbert Edgar Cobb, a professor of mathematics and author of the "Elements of Applied Mathematics."

And then Irvin (Shrewsbury) Cobb, an author who was born at Paducah, Ky. Most everyone has heard of him and if he has not it is because one does not read the magazines or attend lyceum lectures. One of his accomplishments is listed as "shorthand reporter."

James A. Cobb, a lawyer, also delegate to the Republican national convention in 1920, lives at 1925 Thirteenth Street, N. W., Washington, D.C. John Blackwell Cobb is a capitalist. So is John Candler Cobb, who lives in Boston, Mass. John Nathan Cobb is an author and a naturalist who helped in the investigations of the shad fisheries of North Carolina in 1906.

Doctor and a Politician

Joseph Pettee Cobb is a physician, who has been professor of physiology, embryology, histology and pediatrics. Nathan Augustus Cobb is a scientist and educator, author of about 200 pamphlets and books, mostly the result of original research. The occupation of Rufus Willis Cobb is given as "ex-governor" and Stanwood Cobb is another Cobb who is educator and author. He wrote "The Real Turk," "Ayesha of the Bosphorus," "Simla, a Tale in Verse," and other books. William Henry Cobb is a librarian.

The occupation of William Titcomb Cobb is also given as ex-governor, but he is also described as being a manufacturer and while he was born at Rockland, in the state of Maine, he is now living at Bath, which is in the same state.

Now, among these 24 Cobbs that are listed in "Who's Who in America," one is widely known. He is Irvin (Shrewsbury) Cobb, but the man who has made the name of Cobb known to the literate and the illiterate; he whose name is familiar probably to more people than the name of any other man of his time, has never been mentioned in "Who's Who in America." He is not included among the 25,357 Americans listed as worth while.

"In a few years they will have forgotten me," Cobb has said on several occasions.

He was in one of his moods of depression when he talked that way, in the mood of Macbeth:

"Life's but a walking shadow, a poor player
That struts and frets his hour upon the stage
And then is heard no more."

Fate plays queer pranks with mortal man. The mighty brain of Tyrus Raymond Cobb, directed to the science which was his first love, surgery, might have made him world famous. The driving, ruthless, pushing, restless soul of him would have carried him to great heights no matter what role of life he had essayed: such is the belief of all who have studied him, from the psycho-analysts and the great business leaders and lawyers with whom he has come into intimate contact, to his fellow players.

He has lived his strangely fascinating and fiery life, as always a law unto himself.

"Who's Who" may not list him among the worth while, but compile your own "Who's Who," remembering:

This man re-made a nation's sport.

PART TWO

"Which Was Greatest — Ty Cobb or Babe Ruth?" (1951)

CHAPTER 1

The Greatest of the Great

In any all-time rating of players, Tyrus Raymond Cobb stands alone. He was the greatest of the great, a fiery genius and the game's outstanding individualist. Brilliant and unorthodox, he made baseball history for more than two decades. He dominated the game.

He gained his pre-eminence not because he was the fastest base-runner, nor the best base-stealer, nor the fleetest fielder or the leading hitter but because he had the nimblest brain that baseball has known. He had the ability to perceive a situation and take full advantage of it before his opponents became aware of it. He was a keener student of the game than his contemporaries and understood the game better than they did. What is more, he understood them better than they understood themselves. He knew their playing faults and weaknesses and he also knew their strengths.

He was baseball's greatest player because he out-thought them, kept a play ahead of them. He was not the greatest fielder, since there were several better. He was not the greatest place hitter since Wee Willie Keeler was admittedly better. He was not the greatest slugger since more than a dozen players could hit the ball farther. He was not the fastest man in the game since several others were just as fast and a few probably faster.

His wide edge over the field was mental. He thought more quickly than any rival and he put his mechanical skill to more uses than they did. Many of his hits were attributed to superior speed but the explanation does not hold since several others were as fast but they did not cause fielders to overhurry the way Cobb did. They did not cause them to fumble and make wild throws the way Cobb did. They did not upset infields the way Cobb did.

Bernie Wefers was one of the great sprinters of all time. One club owner decided that Wefers' speed would make him a terrific ball player. Wefers was willing to play, but he never made good. The world's fastest human of his time did not know how to utilize his speed on a ball field. In baseball, having speed and knowing how to apply it are two different things.

In running bases, Cobb's lighting brain worked as fast as his legs. He continuously crossed up infielders. He would break unexpectedly and fail to break when they expected him to run. Every move he made was carefully planned. Going into a base, he knew what the infielder would do and suited his own action to the fielder's. He developed different slides, including the hook, the fadeaway, the fallaway. He would go straight into a bag or to the outside or inside. He would purposely slide wide, past the bag, then hook the outside corner with his toe.

He was not a natural hitter and when he entered professional baseball he could not get a foul off a left-hander. By the time he was established in the American League he was able to hit left-handers better than right-handers.

He could not slide when he started playing, but he became the most expert slider in history.

He studied infielders, outfielders, pitchers and catchers and made mental note of their individual playing habits. Nothing escaped him. The mechanical moves of an infielder, the peculiarities of an outfielder, the unconscious give-away signs of a pitcher or catcher were known to Cobb.

Cy Young never understood why Ty had such an easy time stealing bases when Cy pitched. Cobb had discovered that Young never threw to a base after his hands touched his chest. While he held his arms out, he was likely to try to pick off a runner, but once he pulled in his arms and pressed his hand against his chest, he was concerned exclusively with the batter. No catcher could possibly have thrown out Cobb with the long lead he got on Old Cy.

Young was one of the few pitchers whose hands Cobb watched. With most of the others he watched their feet, explaining: "No pitcher can throw to a base without first turning his feet in the direction of the base. I make my move as soon as the feet start to turn."

He used no mystic powers, had no occult gifts. Some of his plays looked downright stupid, but they were anything but that. He would let himself be caught flatfooted between bases. Then the rundown started. Nine times out of ten Cobb would advance. "All you've got to do is make them keep on throwing the ball," he explained. "Sooner or later some one is sure to make a wild throw." Someone generally did.

Ty upset batteries and infields. He was responsible for more wild throws

Cobb in 1924. Cobb beats the throw and slides safely into third on a triple on August 16, 1924, demonstrating his classic fade-away slide technique. He recorded 295 triples in his 24-year career, still second in the modern record books behind Tigers teammate Sam Crawford. *Courtesy Library of Congress Bain Collection.*

than any other player in history. He constantly harried pitchers. "When I'm up there at the plate," he used to say, "I know the pitcher is under a lot more pressure than I am, especially in a close game. I've got a psychological advantage over him."

He scored from first on singles, streaked from first to third, or scored from second on sacrifice bunts and infield outs. The delayed steal was one of his favorites. He would turn first base on an outfield single, come to a stop, and when the outfielder pulled back his arm to lob the ball to the infield, Cobb was off. He knew the outfielder would have to change position to make a fast throw to second.

He was so far ahead of the field that comparisons seem odious. When he retired in 1928 after 24 years of major league competition, he left behind him enough records to convince even the most skeptical of his rightful place at the top of the all-time ranking.

Cobb finished with a lifetime batting mark of .367, the highest in history. He jointed Detroit in August, 1905, played in 41 games before the season closed and batted .240, the only time that he failed to hit better than .300. He won his first American League batting championship in 1907 and repeated for the next eight years. After failing to win the title a tenth straight time in 1916 when Tris Speaker hit .386 and Cobb .371, Ty bounced back in 1917 with his tenth championship and repeated the next two years, a total of 12 times in 13 years, a record that may never be equaled.

Ty led the league in total hits for seven years and tied in 1919. In eight seasons he made more than 200 hits per season. When be batted .420 in 1911 he collected 248 hits in 591 times at bat. From 1910 to 1913, inclusive, his batting average was .4027. His lifetime record shows 11,429 times at bat, 2,244 runs, 4,191 hits for 5,863 bases. He hit 3,052 singles, 297 triples, stole 892 bases (96 of them in 1915). He played 22 years with Detroit, two with Philadelphia.

Until Babe Ruth began setting home run records, Cobb was the game's leading drawing card. Back in 1914, when the Athletics ruled baseball and were acclaimed one of the wonder teams of all time, I was talking with Connie late in July. His team seemed certain to finish first again. Mr. Mack admitted it looked like another pennant for his club and added: "But we don't seem able to draw many people. Detroit is outdrawing us three to one on the road and Detroit is in sixth place." I asked him how he explained the fact that the Tigers were outdrawing his team three to one and he said: "You'll find the answer in center field."

Crowds booed Cobb and jeered him, hooted him and stoned him, but they came in great numbers to see him; and since he batted in the No. 3 slot and was therefore certain to appear at the plate in the first inning, the customers were always on hand by game time so they would miss no part of Cobb's performance.

Cobb was undoubtedly the greatest competitor any sport has known, the fiercest. He was at his best when the pressure was on. He gloried in the clutch. His most brilliant plays generally came when the odds were heavily against him. He was one of the worst losers anywhere and his bitter dread of defeat made him a spectacular winner. He could endure almost anything but failure. There was no amount of drudgery he would not undergo to reach his goal.

Socrates remade the mental processes of the world by his incessant questioning. Galileo got an idea the earth was running around the sun and not the sun around the earth and remade the story of the heavens. Napoleon believed in the red star of destiny he saw shining for him at night in the heavens and he remade the art of warfare, and for his brilliant hour dominated the world. And so it has ever been in the history of man. Men spring up from obscure places, flash their genius upon their stage, drive, inspire, dominate—and fade away, but they leave their imprint impressively on a remade world.

An Edison arises to dominate with dynamos, a Ford ordains a new industrial era, a Pasteur remakes the field of medicine, a Bach changes the course of music. They live their lives, these men, and pass on while a world of endless generations, fascinated by their deeds, seeks a key to the riddle of their baffling personalities. There is no answer, for of the world's great, each in his chosen way has been a law unto himself, refusing always to conform and daring always to sail out on uncharted seas.

Baseball also has its lonely figure sitting on the Olympian heights. There is but one, Tyrus Raymond Cobb, and the game will never know his like again. While others have changed the destinies of peoples, the ways of living and the means of life, Cobb revolutionized and remade the sport of a nation.

His is the story of a mighty brain and the driving force of genius that made him great when other men, superior in physical strength and natural ability and speed, remained mediocre.

CHAPTER 2

Babe Pleased the Eye— Ty Pleased the Mind and the Eye

It is generally conceded that the three leading players of all time were Cobb, Honus Wagner and Babe Ruth. They were unlike in build, style and temperament.

Some men rate Wagner ahead of Cobb. Honus was undoubtedly the best infielder of all time, a great hitter and base-runner. He knew baseball, but never in the deep sense that Cobb did. He lacked the extra touch, the spark, the flame; there was no fire to Wagner's play; he was sound and thorough, but phlegmatic. Above all, he lacked imagination. He did not have Cobb's inventive mind. In his greatest moments Cobb was the very soul of baseball.

Ruth had more batting power than any player before or since his day. He was the Goliath of the game, the Samson, but he was more than a great slugger. He was one of baseball's best lefthanded pitchers before he concentrated on knocking the ball into the next county and when he quit pitching he developed into an outstanding outfielder. He was fast enough, had a fine pair of hands, was a sure judge of a fly ball, played batters well, threw with speed and exceptional accuracy. He lacked Cobb's speed on the bases but ran with fine judgment. He never threw to the wrong base and almost never made a wrong play, and those are the standards by which ball players judge their fellow players.

Opposite: **Honus Wagner (1874–1955) in 1911. Honus Wagner won the National League batting title eight times between 1900 and 1911. The meeting of Ty Cobb and Wagner, the batting champions of the two leagues, in the 1909 World Series produced a media frenzy as writers and fans of each predicted that their favorite would outshine the other. The 22-year-old Cobb was clearly outdone by the veteran Wagner, who batted .333 in the series to Cobb's .231. Wagner finished his 21-year major league career in 1917 with a lifetime batting average of .328. He was elected to the Hall of Fame in its inaugural 1936 class. *Courtesy Library of Congress Bain Collection.***

Cobb in 1910. Here Cobb poses in his classic batting stance, with the bat off his shoulder and his hands spread apart. Cobb used the split grip so he could adjust his grip for each pitch thrown, allowing him to place hits to any field. In the 1909 World Series against the Pirates, Cobb discovered that Pirates star Honus Wagner, the leading National League hitter, also used this unique split grip. ***Courtesy Library of Congress Bain Collection.***

Ruth pleased the eye, while Cobb pleased the mind and eye. Ruth lacked the speed, the quick break, the lightning-like thrusts of Cobb. He lacked his imagination. He was an entirely different type.

The players that climbed to fame in the American League during Cobb's sweep of conquering seasons were George Sisler, Tris Speaker, Eddie Collins, Joe Jackson and Ruth.

Sisler, quick, fast, sure, came closer to Cobb's style than any of the others since he made Ty his model and tried to copy him as closely as possible. Had he escaped injury to his eye, Sisler might conceivably have finished his career with a higher lifetime average than Cobb. He was a great hitter. In the three years prior to the time he was stricken, Sisler batted .407, .371 and .420, a fraction of a point under .400 for the three years that he swung against the lively ball. He was nearing his peak when disaster overtook him.

He modeled his batting style after Cobb. He had a quick start, although he did not break as quickly as Cobb, but he ran as fast. He was an exceptional base-runner, a graceful fielder, next to Hal Chase the best defensive first baseman the league has known. He lacked Cobb's imagination and fiery spirit, but, as I said before, other players also lacked it in the degree that Cobb had it.

Cobb excelled because he studied every angle. He was a skinny youngster when he arrived in Detroit. He lacked the weight and power of batsmen like Nap Lajoie, Sam Crawford and others, and a bat felt much heavier in his hands than it did in theirs. To overcome the handicap of weight, Cobb started carrying three bats to the plate. While waiting his turn at bat, he swung them like a pendulum and kept swinging them until the pitcher got on the rubber. Then he tossed away two of the bats and the one in his hands felt only one-third as heavy.

Ty was the first player ever to carry three bats in going to the plate, but today it is done by nearly all players.

He disdained the orthodox stand at the plate. Instead of planting his feet apart, flat and firm, he introduced what was considered a freak stance. His feet were close together and he was on his toes as he crouched over, his hands gripped the handle of the bat only a few inches apart. By using this particular grip he discovered he had greater control over the bat. With feet close together and on his toes, he was able to shift with the pitch.

Cobb was the only lefthanded batter who could ever line an inside pitch into left field just inside the foul line. Curious to know how Ty did this, Jean Dubuc, a very smart pitcher, kept studying him closely in practice and discovered that when the ball left the pitcher's hand Cobb would shift around and be facing the third baseman when he hit the ball.

Ty used a snap swing, a quick chop, and therefore did not have to set himself. Able to shift quickly, he could meet any kind of pitch, high, low, inside, outside, and with the snap swing, or chop, he was able to meet the ball squarely, even when shifting.

Cobb's style enabled him to hit in any direction. Fielders found it impossible to play him accurately. He had no specified lane. He repeatedly hit to center, right and left fields on three successive times at bat. He could place a ball better than any man of his time.

He tried to pull infielders out of position, then hit through them. He always directed his attack against weak points. If the opposing team had an outstanding first baseman, Cobb never hit in his direction. It is a fact that Hal Chase never fielded a ball off Cobb's bat. Ty took good care to hit balls out of Chase's territory.

Cobb could hit any ball that he could reach. Some pitchers stopped him for a while, but soon or later he mastered them. Infielders became nervous whenever he stepped to the plate. He nearly always crossed them up. He bunted when he was expected to hit, hit when he was expected to bunt.

Ty introduced the tactic of swinging hard at a ball, intentionally fouling it off or missing it altogether, driving infielders back, then bunting. Or he would reverse the order, fake a bunt, pull the infield in, then hit hard.

Because of his batting style, Cobb was not a distance hitter and never pretended to be one. The hullabaloo over Ruth's batting might and the rest of it finally nettled Cobb. That was in 1925. He declared it was not a great feat to hit home runs and if he concentrated on hitting them he could produce a sizable number.

The Tigers were playing in St. Louis and Cobb promised to give a demonstration of home run hitting. He did. He hit three on May 5 and two on May 6, tying a record that Cap Anson had set and that had stood for 41 years. It also has been tied since by Tony Lazzeri and Ralph Kiner.

While Cobb hit five home runs in two successive games, only bad luck kept him from having seven. He changed his batting style completely, took a firm stance and a full swing and pulled every pitch to right field. Two of his drives barely missed the top of the right field fence and dropped for doubles.

After demonstrating that he could hit home runs if he set out to hit them, Cobb returned to his accustomed style. Incidentally his home run total for 1925 was 12. He never hit more than 12 in any season, but he was the home run champion of the American League in 1909 with a total of nine.

He was 42 years old when he finished his major league career with Philadelphia in 1928 and he hit .323 that year, his twenty third consecutive season of .300 plus hitting.

CHAPTER 3

"Be a Success or Don't Come Home"

Cobb's boyhood ambition was to become a surgeon. He planned to enter the University of Georgia. He wanted to engage in football, baseball and track.

He was born at Narrows, in Banks County, near the Carolina line. Before he learned to walk, his parents moved to Royston, near Augusta. His father was superintendent of public schools and one of the most highly regarded educators in the state.

When Ty was old enough to go to school he began playing baseball. He was careful never to accept any money for playing; he wanted to be a simon-pure amateur when he reached the college campus.

He was ambitious to become a sprinter and he read all the books on sprinting that he found on the shelves of the Royston public library. He noticed that the coaches who authored the books laid great emphasis on stride. Without proper stride no boy could ever succeed as a sprinter. Cobb committed to memory all the paragraphs relating to stride and each morning he ran one or two miles, sometimes farther, before breakfast, practicing stride.

"It's not the speed in running that counts," he said years later, "but the stride. You need stride in base-running just as you need it in sprinting, but you've also got to have something else and that is judgment of distance that permits you to make sharp turns and tag a base on the inside without losing speed. That's the main thing.

"Stride is equally important in fielding. There has never been a great outfielder who did not have a good stride. No matter how fast he is he will never succeed unless he knows how to get the most out of his speed in his stride."

Cobb's stride would have made him a great football player. One fall, after he was firmly established in the major leagues, he visited Vanderbilt University at Nashville and attended football practice. The next afternoon he returned and asked for a uniform. They gave him one and Cobb participated in the usual drills. A scrimmage was scheduled to follow and Cobb asked permission to engage in that. He was cast with the scrubs and after the kickoff the scrubs lost ground on two plays and were on their 15-yard line, third down and 14 to go.

Ty asked the quarterback to hand him the ball on the next play. He took the ball and ran 85 yards for a touchdown through the Vanderbilt varsity, straight-arming his way and reversing his field.

Cobb's thoughts were far from professional baseball until his closest friend left Royston and joined a Southern Association club. He returned in the fall with glowing tales of the life he led as a professional ball player. It was a soft life.

That got Cobb interested in baseball. He began reading baseball news and his interest grew. He finally decided that he would rather become a ball player than a surgeon and in the spring of 1904 he wrote letters to two clubs in the Sally League asking for trials.

He received a reply from the Augusta club promising him a trial if he paid his own expenses. He bought a ticket to Augusta and sought Con Strouthers, the Augusta manager. He was told to report for practice the next morning.

Ty worked out with the Augusta squad. The season was close at hand and one of the regulars, an outfielder, had played outlaw ball after the previous season and was under suspension. Strouthers told Ty that if the outfielder was not reinstated by opening day, he would have Ty substitute for him in center field.

Came opening day and the suspension had not been lifted, so Cobb made his debut as a professional player. The date was April 26. He made two hits, a home run and a double. He did not do so well the next day, but still managed to get a single. After the game, Strouthers told him he would like to see him in his office.

Thinking he was to be offered a contract at a good salary, Ty hurried to the office as soon as he had changed to street clothes.

Strouthers was waiting for him. He did not ask the boy to sit down and without a preliminary remark, told him: "You're released."

Cobb was stunned. He blurted out: "You mean I'm being let out here? You're letting me go?"

"That's right," said Strouthers. "I'm letting you go. You're a free agent. My regular out fielder was reinstated this afternoon and is reporting tomorrow so I won't need you. You can join any club you like."

Ty's father did not want him to play professional baseball. When the boy insisted he told him:

"All right, but don't come home a failure You've decided on professional baseball and so go and show that you can be a success at it. Do your best and don't come home until you succeed."

And here he was out of a job. He had lasted two days. He finally decided to call his father and tell him the bad news, but the elder Cobb was unmoved. His son had chosen his bed so let him lie in it. He reminded him again not to come home until he succeeded. It was probably the best decision ever made for Tyrus.

He went to Anniston, which was in the Southeastern League. He managed to join the club and was soon leading the league in hitting. People in Augusta read about his sensational batting and were reminded that Strouthers had unceremoni-

Eddie Cicotte (1884–1969) in 1917. Cicotte played at Augusta, Georgia, with Ty Cobb in 1904 and was one several players that the Detroit Tigers considered when purchasing Ty Cobb. Four days after Cobb's August 30, 1905, debut, Cicotte was brought up by the Tigers and pitched his first game in the majors. He pitched a total of 18 innings in three games for Detroit before being returned to the minors for the 1906 and 1907 seasons. In 1908, he was brought up by the Red Sox, remaining with Boston until he was traded to the White Sox during the 1912 season. Cicotte led the American League in wins in 1917 with 28 and again in 1919 with 29. He is best known for having been banned from baseball for his part in the 1919 Black Sox scandal. *Courtesy Library of Congress Bain Collection.*

ously discharged Cobb after two games. They demanded his return. Strouthers called up Cobb and told him he would like to have him back. Ty replied:

"I'll never play for you again, in Augusta or anywhere else."

Strouthers soon after was deposed as manager and George Leidy named in his place.

He wired Cobb an offer, guaranteeing him fine treatment and assuring him that Strouthers was no longer connected with the club in any way. Cobb came back to Augusta. He had played 22 games with Anniston, hitting .370. He got into 37 games with Augusta and hit .237 but Leidy was not disappointed. "You'll hit .300 next year sure as you live," he told Ty at the end of the season.

Detroit trained at Augusta in 1905. Frank J. Navin, who had served as the club's bookkeeper for several years, became part owner and decided to go to Augusta to see for himself how a big league club trained.

The hub of Augusta's downtown section was the Albion Hotel, long since burned down, and when Navin entered the lobby he met Wild Bill Donovan, the Tigers' ace pitcher, and Germany Schaefer, his second baseman and the league's leading comedian. Schaefer told him:

"We've got a big laugh for you. There's a kid working out with the local nine and he's a scream. Wait till you see this baby run. You'll laugh yourself sick but don't let him see you laugh or you'll spoil all the fun. We've been having a swell time kidding him along. If you talk to him, tell him you think he's a great ball player."

Navin had his first look at Ty Cobb the next day. Ty was unlike any other player he had ever seen. Navin noticed that he was extremely fast, that he broke quickly but that he needed considerable polish. He had raw ability and ran like a wild colt.

George Leidy, who finished the previous season as Augusta's manager, was no longer in command. Andy Roth had succeeded him, but Leidy was still a regular in the Augusta outfield. Navin talked to him about Cobb.

"I'll admit he needs a little polishing," said Leidy, "but as soon as the boy gets used to a bridle you're going to see the world's greatest ball player, nothing less."

The Tigers had used the Augusta ball park for training and in lieu of rent, Navin told William J. Croke, the owner, that he would loan him a player for the season and Croke promised Navin that he could have the pick of Augusta club for $750. They agreed to that.

The player whom Navin turned over to Augusta was Eddie Cicotte. He weighed 135 pounds at the time and was under medium height. Navin did not like small pitchers. He maintained that batters had no respect for a small pitcher while they did have respect for a big one. He wanted only big ones and the bigger the better.

The Tigers started north to open the major league season and they soon forgot about the screwball kid in Augusta who imagined himself a ball player.

CHAPTER 4

Small-Town Boy Learns of the Big Time

Augusta played Savannah in the opening game of the Sally League season of 1905. Ty Cobb was in center field for Augusta and an estimated crowd of 3,000 was in attendance.

Eddie Cicotte beat Savannah, 2 to 1, and missed a shutout because Cobb was eating popcorn in center field. Savannah's only run was scored on a hit past Cobb. Being preoccupied with the popcorn, Ty started late after the ball and just missed catching it.

Andy Roth was catcher-manager of Augusta and he took a dislike to Ty. The recruit outfielder did not take kindly to managerial orders and disagreed with Roth on points of strategy. Repeated arguments culminated in the sale of Cobb to Charleston for the sum of $25.

Roth acted strictly on his own in selling Cobb to Ed Ashenbach, the Charleston manager. When William J. Croke, owner of the Augusta club, heard about the sale, he canceled it.

Croke appreciated Cobb's latent ability. He was paying him $90 at the start of the season. His play rapidly improved and after two months Croke increased Ty's salary to $125 a month.

The one man who understood Cobb was George Leidy, the veteran outfielder who played alongside of him. Leidy had predicted in the spring that Cobb would become the greatest player in history and he set out to help him along.

Leidy realized that it would be useless to try to instruct Cobb, since Ty would be his own teacher, so he worked on his imagination.

Cobb was a stranger in Augusta and one day Leidy asked him what he was doing that evening. Ty said he had no engagement and Leidy proposed they visit a summer amusement park near Augusta where the working class sought relief and recreation on summer nights. It had the usual summer park equipment: Ferris wheel, merry-go-round, cave of the winds and so forth. To this place Leidy took the recruit and after walking around for a while, Leidy suggested that they sit down and rest.

As they set on a bench, Leidy commented on the amusement offerings. "You ought to see what they have in the big cities. This is nothing. Why, in New York, Boston, Detroit, Cleveland, Chicago and all of them big league cities they got parks that would swallow a dozen the size of this one. You've heard of Coney Island, haven't you? Now, Coney Island—"

Leidy followed with a vivid word picture of Coney Island. He went into minute detail and as he noticed the concentrated interest of his listener he called upon his own imagination to supply added features.

They were there again the following evening, Cobb and Leidy. Again they sat under the tree on the old iron bench and, while the barkers shrieked their wares and the merry-go-round organ squealed its cracked notes, and the youth of Augusta made merry, Leidy gave Cobb further word pictures of the big cities, the hugeness of them, their vastness, the fascinations of the metropolis. He opened the gates of Cobb's imagination.

After spending several evenings describing theaters, restaurants, the waterfronts, the avenues of the wealthy and points of historic interest, Leidy began describing the major league ball parks. "They're vast stadiums, built of stone and concrete, enormous places like palaces. They're just like those vast amphitheaters that the Greeks and Romans used for sports events, just like the big arenas where the lions used to fight and where the famous gladiators battled hand to hand until one of 'em was dead.

"You think we had a big crowd out today? Why, in them big league parks up north a crowd like that couldn't be seen. If they didn't have no more people than that out to a game, they would not even open the gates. There's more people out to one game up there than there is in the entire city of Augusta."

Then he told Cobb of the fame that came to major league stars, how the metropolitan newspapers ran their pictures, how writers devoted columns to them. A baseball star, according to Leidy, was much more important than the President of the United States.

He told him of the immortals of the game and how they become immortals. He gave a detailed account of the base-stealing ability of some of the old stars and after a moment's reflection—"But I think, Ty, that you've got more speed than any of them fellows had."

He spoke of the great hitters—Anson, Delahanty, Wagner, Lajoie—and added: "But I'm sure you could become a better hitter than any of them fellows."

And so, evening after evening, the plain and unassuming Leidy fired Cobb's imagination and fueled his ambition. He became more and more convinced that Cobb had all the latent talents and the only thing lacking was incentive. Leidy supplied that. He began showing Cobb the way to greatness, saying:

"Christy Mathewson is a great pitcher, but he wasn't always one. When he started out he had very poor control, so he'd go to the park early and take along a catcher. He'd have the catcher hold his glove in one position and try to hit the hollow of the glove with every pitch. In the winter he cut a hole about twice as big as a baseball and about the height of the average man's waist in the side of his barn, and he'd pitch for hours trying to throw the ball through the hole. That's how he got control. You gotta keep pegging at one certain thing until you get it down pat."

Another time Leidy spoke of Honus Wagner, the top star of the National League at that time. "This Wagner used to be a poor fielder. He was an outfielder and he wanted to be an infielder. They kept him in the outfield because they didn't think he could play on the infield. Wagner would get up early in the morning and go to the ball park. He'd get some kids to hit grounders. He found he was slow getting started. He couldn't get the jump going after a ball. So he took off his shoes and played in his stocking feet. He dug trenches around the short field and he'd set himself in these trenches in his stocking feet to get a quick start. He kept this up for weeks and the infielders couldn't figure out what made the ground so rough at shortstop, until one day one of them got to the park early and saw Wagner dig those little trenches. But he learned to make a quick start.

"All them fellows that made big reputations in baseball got their start that way. They practiced for hours, days and weeks and months."

Cobb decided to do likewise. There was sliding. He could not slide. He borrowed an old and torn base bag from the grounds-keeper. In one corner of the field he spaded up the ground. He set the bag at one end of the spaded plot. He practiced sliding early in the morning and late in the afternoon, after the game. His hips were raw. Sometimes he came back to the clubhouse with his uniform soaked with blood. But he learned to slide and after he mastered the conventional slide he discovered other slides. After a few years in the majors he could slide in eight different ways.

Cobb had started as a shortstop on the sandlots of Royston. Now he was playing in the outfield, and he was not sure on fly balls. He decided to master fly catching. He had Leidy bat fly balls to him by the hour, short flies and long flies, flies to the right and flies to the left, Leidy so placing the ball that Cobb just managed to reach it after a hard sprint. His greatest trouble was in learning to judge accurately a fly ball hit directly at him. That is the most difficult for any center fielder. Cobb mastered this most difficult of center field plays. After a few years he never misjudged one, but it took him a long time to learn.

CHAPTER 5

The Big Persuasion— or How the Tigers Got Ty

Cobb continued developing at Augusta in the season of 1905. Leidy, who worked with him daily noticed he was changing his style at bat, that his base-running was taking on a definite form, that he had a purpose in everything he did and his confidence was rapidly increasing. His fielding was improving. He was making fast progress.

The Sally League season was drawing to a close. While Detroit had the pick of any player on the Augusta roster, the Tigers failed to make a selection.

William J. Croke, the Augusta owner, was afraid that Cobb would be drafted and since the draft price at that time was $350, he would much rather send Ty to Detroit for $750.

Clyde Engle was a member of the Augusta team and Frank J. Navin, president of the Detroit club, was interested in him.

Bill Byron, who later gained distinction in the National League as the singing umpire, was working in the Sally League in 1905. He advised Detroit to buy Cobb. Leidy was recommending him strongly and Bill Armour, who managed the Tigers at the time, favored Ty over Engle.

Armour had a tough time convincing Navin, but he finally won his point and Navin completed the purchase. One week after the sale was made, four clubs claimed Cobb in the draft.

Cobb made his major league debut on August 30, 1905, at old Bennett Park in Detroit. The Tigers were playing the New York Highlanders and Jack Chesbro was pitching for New York.

Dick Cooley, the Tigers' regular center fielder, was ill, and Armour substituted Cobb. He batted fifth, right behind Wahoo Sam Crawford.

In the first inning Matty McIntyre, leading off, doubled. Lindsay, next up, singled, McIntyre scoring. Schaefer sacrificed Lindsay to second. Craw-

MILES
Philip
DOELGER
FIRST PRIZE
BEER

ford grounded for the second out and up came a tall, gaunt, almost gawky looking boy who seemed to be extremely nervous.

There were less than 1,200 fans in the park that day and few of them had ever heard of Cobb. His appearance was not impressive.

Chesbro, then at the peak of his career, fired a high, fast ball and Cobb swung and missed. A high, fast ball is the one pitch the majority of players in the minor leagues can't resist. While Cobb had seen many high, fast balls in the Sally League, he had never seen one as fast as the one he missed. Chesbro followed with a waist-high curve that Silk O'Loughlin, the plate umpire, called "st-r-r-r-r-r-ike two." Chesbro figured that Cobb would expect another high, fast one and decided to cross him up. He would pitch a fast one, but waist-high instead of chin-high. So he threw the fast one waist-high and Cobb stepped into the pitch and lined it past the center fielder, whose name was Hahn. Cobb, streaking to first, turned sharply without lessening his speed and slid safely into second. The following day one of the Detroit newspapers reported:

"Cobb hit .326 in the South, leading the Sally League. Of course, he does not expect to hit anything like that up here. If he can hit .275 he will be more than satisfied, and so will the fans."

Before the end of the season Cobb was considered a regular. He was at bat 150 times, scored 19 runs, made 36 hits, stole two bases and had an average of .240. It was the only season in his major league career that he failed to hit higher than .300.

Cobb was fortunate that he was Bill Armour's choice over Engle, whom Navin wanted to buy instead of Cobb. Had he been bought against Armour's wishes, the chances are that he would not have held his place in the lineup. The manager would have been prejudiced.

Managerial favor did not make Cobb's path an entirely smooth one. At

Opposite: **Matty McIntyre (1880–1920) in 1912. Matty McIntyre, who led the American League in runs scored for 1905, was the Detroit center fielder whose position was jeopardized by the arrival of Ty Cobb. McIntyre organized a group of Tigers who hazed and harassed the head-strong young Cobb. By 1907, the first full season Cobb played, McIntyre played in only 20 games. He returned to the lineup in 1908 and led the league in both plate appearances and singles. He remained with Detroit through the 1911 season and finished his career with two years with the Chicago White Sox. *Courtesy Library of Congress Bain Collection.***

that time veterans resented recruits and they made life as unpleasant as possible for them. No recruit ever found the going rougher than Cobb. Everything was against him. He was taking over the job of a veteran and his unorthodox style attracted more attention than any of the other players got. He had a fiery temperament and was not an easy individual to team with. They did everything to harass him and his resentment mounted.

Ball players 46 years ago were a different type from the players of today. They were a hard, rough and ready lot as a whole. They battled on and off the playing field.

A man had to win his place in the lineup in those days by proving he could take it.

They were a clannish lot, the veterans. They held as a common enemy any recruit who tried to break in, did everything to handicap him. They made him the butt of coarse jokes, bullied him.

The Tiger veterans deeply resented Cobb. He had broken into the regular lineup as soon as he arrived, instead of warming the bench for a season or two. They could not forgive him for that.

When the 1906 season opened, Cobb was in center field. He had a certain amount of success and this reacted against him in the clubhouse. Few of his teammates spoke to him except to hurl some fresh insult. This treatment made him all the more determined to succeed. He would show them.

He started to hit and the day after he made three in four times at bat he discovered that his favorite bats were missing. He had brought them with him from Augusta — two black bats — and had used them ever since he joined the Tigers the preceding August.

He hunted for the bats everywhere in the clubhouse, but they were nowhere. The clubhouse attendant tipped him off that he could find them outside the fence. There he found them — in splinters. Some of his teammates had hacked them to pieces. They believed that by destroying the bats they would ruin his hitting, since it is an old belief in baseball that certain bats hold more hits than others. If a player has luck swinging a bat, he treasures it above everything else. He credits the bat for the base hits he gets.

When Cobb found his bats in splinters, he returned to the clubhouse and slumped down in a corner chair, in despair. Charlie Schmidt, Detroit's regular catcher, had watched the destruction of the bats. He walked over to Cobb and handed him one of his own bats, saying:

"Here, kid, you can have one of mine. There's just as many hits in this one as the bats they broke up. Use it. If anyone tries to chop up that one, they will reckon with me."

No one cared to reckon with Schmidt. He was the toughest, rough-and-tumble fighter in the American League.

Cobb used Schmidt's bat that afternoon. He made two hits. He made two more the next day. He used the bat for a week and then two bats that he had ordered arrived at the park and he returned the loaned bat to Schmidt. Nobody attempted to hack up the new bats. Cobb having demonstrated that he could get hits with a strange bat, they were convinced it would be wasted effort to wreck any more.

That season, as well as several that followed, witnessed a succession of feuds. Cobb, the tempestuous, found it difficult to get into the ways and habits of his teammates. He did not like them and they detested him. He was left pretty much alone.

Cobb was beginning to find himself. The spark of ambition that Leidy had lighted in Augusta flamed secretly. Cobb had faith in himself, but this was not shared by his teammates, and Manager Armour, who had selected him, also had little confidence in Cobb's future.

Although batting .320 for the season, Ty had not convinced Armour that he was a sound hitter and one day Armour used a pinch-hitter for Cobb, the only time this ever happened.

Detroit was playing Chicago and Doc White, a talented left-hander, was pitching for the White Sox. When it came Ty's turn again, Armour sent up Freddy Payne, the Tigers' second-string catcher, in Ty's place. A few years later Payne was out of the major leagues.

CHAPTER 6

"He'll Be the Greatest Player"— Hugh Jennings

The turning point in Ty Cobb's career came in 1907. Bill Armour had been released as manager and Hugh Ambrose Jennings was his successor. The Tigers had power, but what they lacked was leadership, and Jennings, a graduate of the Baltimore Orioles school of baseball, was expected to bring out the dormant qualities in the players.

There probably never lived a keener judge of diamond talent than Jennings and he had few equals. He had heard about Cobb and he was eager to see him. After watching him a few days in training Jennings formed his judgment. He watched him another week and then ignored him entirely.

Cobb noticed the slight and mentioned it to a friendly baseball writer. The newspaperman told Jennings that Cobb was hurt because he was ignoring him. Incidentally, he asked Jennings why he did not pay some attention to Cobb since the boy showed a certain amount of promise.

Jennings promised to take the matter up with the player. In the meantime he wanted to assure the writer that he had in no way neglected Cobb. He had fully observed the young man and his mind was made up as far as he was concerned. That same evening Jennings took Cobb aside and told him:

"My boy, you may think I've been overlooking you, but I've done nothing of the kind. I've been watching you closely and I want to tell you this: There isn't a thing about baseball that I can teach you. Anything I might say to you would simply hinder you in your development. The only thing for you to do is go ahead and do as you please. Use your own judgment. You can teach yourself better and get along faster than by the aid of any man I know. Just go ahead and work things out in your own way and do what you think best and I'll back you."

"Do you think he has the makings of a good ball player?" asked the writer.

Jennings took him by the arm and answered slowly:

"Listen to me! He has the makings of the greatest ball player that ever lived and that's exactly what he'll be within the next three years. Mark my words and play that as strong as you like. You can't possibly go wrong."

The newspaperman took Jennings at his word. He played his prediction under an eight-column banner line. He did not go wrong.

Jennings adhered to his decision. He permitted Cobb to attend to his own development. He never gave him orders, permitting him to run wild.

There has never been another player who was as much a law unto himself as Cobb, never another one who had as little coaching.

No other manager would have handled him as Jennings did and it would have been impossible for Cobb to develop under another man as he did under Jennings. Another would have tried to make Cobb part of a machine and Cobb could never have developed as part of a whole; to develop he had to be one, all alone and separate from the whole.

Jennings, a great judge of playing talent, realized this. He also realized that Cobb, permitted to be a law unto himself, would be far more valuable than Cobb as a spoke in a wheel, figuratively speaking. He would let Cobb play his own game and create opportunities from which the entire team would benefit.

Hughie studied Cobb from the standpoint of psychology as well as from mechanical playing standards. He knew that Cobb being what he was, could not work with other men. He could not shape his play to conform with that of the others, for no one else resembled him and no one could fit into his system. He was immersed in his own style, his individual system and other players were not, either mentally or mechanically.

The perfect freedom that Jennings gave Cobb enabled him to cut loose. Having only himself to consider, Ty was not hampered by team play or signals. He did engage in a certain amount of team play, but never when it interfered with his own individual style.

He was never subjected to the rules that applied to other men. He rarely showed up for morning practice and rarely did he ever engage in the spring training exercises. He did his own training, at home, and when the season opened he was in much better condition than any of the players who had spent from six to eight weeks getting ready.

Cobb never went to bat with instructions. He could use his own judg-

ment, bunt or hit, as he saw fit. He was not subject to the signals of the coaches at first and third base. He ran as he pleased.

While this method enabled Cobb to develop into the game's greatest player, it made Jennings' position extremely delicate. Other players could not understand why they had to report for spring training when Cobb was permitted to stay at home. They could not see why they had to get up in the morning and go to the ball park and practice when Cobb did not. They did not understand why Cobb was permitted to stay away from the park as long as he liked, showing up half an hour before game time and later, at times. There were days when he was not in uniform when the game started and a substitute had to play center field in the first inning. These protests often reached Jennings and he had but one reply:

"What's YOUR batting average?"

While his mates were grumbling about the drudgery of spring training and criticizing his absence, Ty trained harder than any of them. Where they sat around all winter and accumulated surplus poundage, Cobb was spending his time in the fields and woods. He generally walked from ten to 20 miles daily and also did considerable running. He would trot a hundred yards, sprint a hundred yards, trot the next hundred, and so on.

Ty realized early in his career that a ball player lasts only as long as his legs and he took good care of his legs. He had lead plates made that a shoemaker fitted into his shoes and he wore these all winter. He explained that the lead weights strengthened his leg muscles. He would not remove the plates until he started his season's play. He invented the lead plate for the same reason that he started the style of carrying three bats to the plate. He tossed two away and the one he used felt only one-third as heavy as before.

Opposite: **Hugh "Ee-Yah" Jennings (1869–1928), circa 1910. The hiring of Hugh Jennings in 1907 to replace Bill Armour as Tigers manager was the turning point in the developing career of Ty Cobb. Jennings was an excellent judge of baseball talent and quickly recognized that there was little that he could teach Ty Cobb. Jennings' approach to managing his rising star was to give him nearly complete freedom to play the game as he pleased, setting his own practice regimen and deciding his own hitting strategy. Although this caused friction with and jealousy among Cobb's teammates, Jennings defended his approach to Tigers management and to the press, and the result speaks for itself. Jennings managed the Tigers form 1907 through 1920, when Cobb took the helm. Under Jennings, the Tigers won the American League pennant in 1907, 1908 and 1909. *Courtesy Library of Congress Bain Collection.***

So with the weighted shoes. When he got into baseball shoes they felt light as feathers.

No track athlete ever trained harder during the track season. He gave his muscles no chance to become flabby.

He gave the same attention to food. No college trainer ever studied diet more carefully. Cobb drank great quantities of milk and ate many eggs. He claimed that milk and eggs contained the best food properties for building muscular and nervous tissues. He ate little red meat, especially between seasons.

Ty was eating three meals a day when he arrived in the major leagues. Then he decided three full meals were too many. A man could not do his best after a full meal. The less he ate before a game, the better he played. He cut down on his noon meal, limiting himself to soup and a sandwich or a double order of ice cream. Then he decided that since he got along well by eating little at noon, he would probably get along better if he did not eat at all and so he abolished lunch and limited himself to breakfast and dinner. He drank coffee with both meals and in the morning he had generous helpings of fruit. He continued this eating program until the end of his major league career.

He studied the science of work and the science of rest, experimented with himself to discover how much rest he needed and saw that he got it. He arranged his daily program so that he would be at maximum physical ability when he took the field in the afternoon. He recharged his batteries between games.

One day Cobb told a newspaper editor that he managed to sleep 12 hours out of every 24. Before that, Thomas A. Edison said that he slept only four hours out of every 24 and years previously a famous French scientist slept 20 hours out of every 24. Cobb had discovered that some people need more sleep than others and decided he needed more than the average, because he expended so much more muscular and nervous energy.

It was a good story and the editor gave it full play. Cobb got a great deal of publicity out of it. The question of sleep is ever an interesting one and newspapers hopped to it when Cobb gave it fresh impetus.

What Ty really meant was that he rested 12 hours out of every 24. Not the entire 12 was taken up by sleep; he spent part of it lounging. For 12 hours out of every 24 Cobb relaxed and this relaxation was partly responsible for his long career.

CHAPTER 7

A Youngster Remakes the Game

Cobb's meteoric career got its real start under Hughie Jennings in 1907. In that season he won the first of his 12 batting championships by making 212 hits in 150 games for an average of .350. He stole 49 bases and his brilliant play enabled the Tigers to win the pennant.

What is more important to baseball, Cobb began revolutionizing the game that year. He introduced a new style of batting and base-running that others began copying so that the attack gradually changed. When the attack changed the defense also had to change.

After the 1907 season, there were still many players who looked upon Cobb as a morning glory and flash-in-the-pan. Cobb was unorthodox and baseball loves the orthodox. Players are extremely suspicious of new ideas. They explained Cobb's success by calling it the "luck of a crazy man." The veterans of the game especially disliked his style and could not understand why the public took a fancy to it. As Ty's star ascended they became insanely jealous of him. They belittled him wherever possible and sought to discount his achievements. But they failed to stop him on the field.

Even as wise a baseball man as Wild Bill Donovan predicted that Cobb would not repeat his 1907 successes.

"He won't finish in the league next year," said Bill, who had befriended the boy on many occasions. "He plays contrary to all baseball law and he can't last. He's a wild man. Next year they'll just throw the ball to home plate and wait for him to get there. These freak players never last because they play contrary to the law."

But Donovan, wise as he was, did not understand. Few did. Cobb was not going contrary to the laws of the game, he was creating new laws. He was making over the game.

To lead the league in hitting was not an easy task. There were some good hitters in those days, including Napoleon Lajoie and Cobb's teammate,

Sam Crawford, the reformed barber of Wahoo, Nebraska, who was known as "Wahoo Sam."

Since Lajoie and Crawford were two of the leading hitters, their batting style was considered the one to adopt and it was generally adopted.

Lajoie and Crawford, as well as the others, never varied their style. They would step into the batter's box, plant their feet firmly on the ground, set themselves and await the pitch.

When they elected to hit they would throw their shoulders behind the swing and follow through. They stood flatfooted so they could get their full weight behind the swing.

Cobb, lacking the weight and power of Lajoie and Crawford, had to invent a style that would offset their physical advantages. Furthermore, he had to invent a style that would enable him to hit to all fields.

Cobb discovered that a man with Crawford's stance could hit only in one direction. Crawford was a dead pull-hitter and whenever he came to bat the fielders shifted to the right, using practically the same shift that Lou Boudreau introduced in recent years to try to stop Ted Williams.

Cobb developed a style that would enable him to change his position to suit the pitch. Instead of spreading his legs and planting his feet firmly on the ground, flatfootedly, he stood with feet close together and balanced on the balls of his feet. In this position he was able to switch instantly and assume any desired position when the ball left the pitcher's hand. With the stance he adopted, Cobb struck his first revolutionary note in baseball.

What is described in the "trade" as "heads-up" baseball was brought to its highest development by Cobb. Before his debut, teams played what was called the "old Army game." Cobb's style of batting, base-running and fielding was responsible for quicker and more alert play. No player was ever as consistently or finely alert as Cobb. Recalling a few instances:

New York had a giant catcher named Sweeney. Cobb came to bat with Donie Bush, the Tiger shortstop, on second. Cobb drove a grounder over second. The center fielder rushed in on the ball and threw to Sweeney in an attempt to nail Bush at the plate. Ball and runner got there about the same time. It was a close play and Umpire Jack Egan gave the decision to Bush.

Sweeney jumped to his feet and protested. Egan walked away, Sweeney following him, hands on hips and his right hand grasping the ball. To get rid of Sweeney, Egan walked toward the pitcher's box.

In the meantime, Cobb had sauntered off third base, apparently taking no interest in the argument. Sweeney and Egan had their backs to the plate. The argument was suddenly interrupted by a yell from the crowd. Sweeney, turning around, discovered Cobb streaking for the plate. Sweeney could not throw; he had to run. Cobb and Sweeney hit the dirt at the same time, sliding from opposite directions, but Cobb, who veered to the outside, got his hand on the plate a fraction of a second before Sweeney put the ball on him.

It was while Clark Griffith was managing the New York Americans, then called the Highlanders, that Cobb first went from first to third on a sacrifice bunt. It had never been done before; the runner was always satisfied to advance one base on a sacrifice.

Hal Chase, one of the greatest of all first basemen, was with New York at the time and George Moriarty was the team's third baseman. Cobb walked and Claude Rossman, who followed him at bat, laid down a bunt. Ty, who had taken a big lead, touched the inside corner of second base and raced to third, beating Chase's throw.

The Tigers' dressing room adjoined the visiting clubs' locker room. There was a con-

Hal Chase (1883–1947) in 1911. New York's Hal Chase was playing first base when Ty Cobb successfully reached third from first on a sacrifice bunt three times in two straight games, much to the dismay of New York manager Clark Griffith. Chase would be a prominent player in what Ty Cobb later described as his greatest play, when Cobb was able to reach home from first base on a infield force-out at first. Chase played for fifteen seasons in the majors, including two in the Federal League, and retired in 1919. *Courtesy Library of Congress Bain Collection.*

necting door, always locked, and a transom over the door that was always open.

Cobb's locker was near the door and through the open transom came the voice of Griffith, bawling out Chase and Moriarty for letting "that crazy nut of a Cobb" go from first to third on a sacrifice.

"You're a fine pair to let a bird like that show you up," declared Griffith.

"Never mind about today," said Moriarty. "We'll get that tramp tomorrow if he tries another of his screwy tricks, won't we Hal?" Chase agreed that they would.

Before the next day's game, Cobb took Rossman aside.

"Will you bunt every time I get on first?"

"Sure, if you want me to."

"All right then. Bunt every time."

Cobb twice reached first base in that game and each time Rossman bunted and each time Cobb sprinted from first to third while Rossman was being retired. Chase made a good throw each time but the ball reached Moriarty a fraction of a second too late to enable him to make a play on Cobb.

When Cobb got away with the play the second time that afternoon. Moriarty walked toward the pitcher's box, bounced the

ball on the ground, as players often do, but when the ball hit the ground a mighty roar went up and Moriarty turned and saw a human cyclone headed for the plate. He made a hurried grab for the ball. He threw into a cloud of dust, made by Cobb as he slid over home plate, beating the throw by several feet.

When he entered the clubhouse after the game Manager Griffith glared at Moriarty and then he glared at Chase, whose locker was four "doors" away. That is all Griffith did—glared. Neither said a word.

CHAPTER 8

Like a Thoroughbred in the Stretch

Cobb was fortunate that he entered baseball when he did. He made his debut in an era of tight pitching duels where one run had far greater value than it has today when teams go after clusters of runs.

Base-running was of vital importance. Today the percentage lies in waiting for a base hit instead of advancing by theft. Cobb was not alone the best base-runner of them all but the most spectacular.

"He gave me the greatest thrills I got out of baseball," said Everett Scott, who did the shortstopping for the Boston Red Sox and later the New York Yankees. "Tearing along the base line, Ty always reminded me of a great thoroughbred turning loose his last burst of speed in the stretch. He fascinated me."

He introduced many innovations with his base-running. He was the first player who scored from second on a sacrifice bunt or sacrifice fly, the first to go from first to third on a sacrifice and the first to score from first base on a single.

Ty received much assistance from Claude Rossman, who followed him in the batting order. Rossman was not alone one of the leading hitters of his day but the best bunter in the American League. Rossman could bunt a ball, no matter where it was pitched, just as long as he could reach it, and he bunted any kind of delivery.

Cobb got cooperation from Rossman whenever he requested it and Rossman never failed him after flashing the bunt sign. As a rule Cobb worked alone. He created his own opportunities.

Fred Mitchell, who was a catcher in the American League and later a manager in the National, described one of Cobb's base-running plays to show how he took advantage of an opportunity in a flash.

"I was catching that day and Frank LaPorte was playing third. It was a tight game. Two men were out and Cobb was on third. I figured that he would try to pull something. He made a sudden move toward the plate. I whipped the ball to LaPorte but Cobb got back safely.

"Cobb moved off third with the next pitch and I again fired the ball to LaPorte but Cobb got back in time. He got up, dusted himself off with one foot on the bag. LaPorte took a few steps toward the pitcher, holding the ball in his glove hand. The pitcher walked toward LaPorte.

"As LaPorte moved toward the pitcher and as the pitcher moved toward LaPorte, Cobb sauntered off the bag. LaPorte, as players often do, tossed the ball a foot or two in the air and caught it. He was talking to the pitcher and Cobb apparently was paying no attention to him. He seemed to be looking toward his own dugout.

"LaPorte again tossed the ball into the air and caught it. He took another step toward the pitcher, still talking. Now the pitcher talked to LaPorte who, while listening, tossed the ball again and at that instant Cobb made a break for the plate. I never in my life saw another man spring into action so suddenly.

"There was shouting and confusion. I was yelling for the ball. LaPorte, startled, didn't see Cobb and didn't realize what was happening. By the time LaPorte awoke to what was going on and threw the ball home, Cobb had slid across the plate and was standing up, brushing off his uniform."

Opportunity never knocked more than once on Cobb's door. Opportunity never had to knock more than once. Cobb even anticipated the knock and responded in a flash.

Chase was the quickest thinker among Cobb's contemporaries in his earlier years and he took particular pride in outwitting him. Chase not alone thought fast but he moved fast. He was a great fielder and thrower and one of the best hit-and-run experts the league has known.

Ty was asked several times what he considered his greatest play. I don't remember that he ever mentioned it for publication but privately he said that the one that pleased him most and in

which he took the greatest pride was a play where he beat Chase in a duel of wits.

In this particular game the score was close. In a late inning Cobb was on second base and Crawford at bat. Since Crawford was strictly a pull hitter,

Jimmy Austin, the New York third baseman, came in on the grass; Jack Knight, the shortstop, moved to second; LaPorte, the second baseman, shifted over toward first and played back on the grass, while Chase stood parallel with LaPorte. The outfield shifted in a similar manner and New York was set to take care of Crawford. If Sam hit to the infield, the play would be made at first base. Crawford hit a ball hard but he was a slow runner and easy to retire as long as an infield grounder could be handled. The New York infield would ignore Cobb since there would be little chance of throwing him out at third.

Crawford hit a grounder straight at LaPorte, who tossed to Chase for the putout. Cobb had started with the crack of the bat. He tagged third and broke for the plate, just as Chase had expected him to do. Hal rifled the ball across the infield to Austin, hoping to get Cobb as he slid back into third. Austin whirled and shoved his glove hand down to tag Ty but found no spiked shoes heading back into the bag. He straightened up and what he saw was a mercury-winged Cobb sliding across home plate with what proved to be the winning run.

This play illustrates how Ty kept a step or more ahead of his opponents in planning.

Everett Scott (1892–1960) in 1916. Up to 1924, Everett Scott was one of the greatest shortstops the game had ever developed. He led American League shortstops in fielding percentage each year from 1916 to 1922, with an average for those years of .969. Scott said during the season of 1921: "The only thrill I ever got out of baseball was to see Cobb thundering down to second base. He always seemed to me like a great thoroughbred coming down the stretch. He had a rare fascination for me. It was the one thrill that baseball has given me in all the years I have played it." ***Courtesy Library of Congress Bain Collection.***

With Crawford, a slow man, at bat and Cobb on second, Ty knew that Chase would expect him to round third as the play on Crawford would be made leisurely. Cobb always did round third and take a lead toward the plate in situations of this kind and Chase figured he would outsmart him with a quick throw to Austin. If the play at first was perfect, Cobb was always able to slide back safely, but if an error occurred at first, he managed to score because of his lead off third.

Chase was no ordinary first baseman. An ordinary first baseman would never have tried to catch Cobb off third; he would refuse to take a chance on making a bad throw.

Chase could take that chance. He was able to throw quicker, faster and more accurately than any other first baseman of his time.

Austin, a smart third baseman, would be looking for the throw and hoping to tag Cobb as he slid into third. Ty also knew that if Austin took the throw from Chase he would not go looking for him; he would dive down to tag him. He would sweep his glove hand in a wide circle, hoping to put the ball on Cobb's foot or leg. His attention would be distracted by the yelling from the stands. He would then have to straighten up and set himself for the throw home. All this would take more time than Cobb needed to sprint 90 feet.

That is how Cobb figured out the play the previous evening. The situation arose and the play worked out precisely as Cobb had anticipated. Knowing Chase and Austin as he did, the play would not be made in any other way, and it wasn't.

CHAPTER 9

Creating the Mental Hazard

There was always a reason in Ty Cobb's mind for everything he did on the playing field. Many of his plays seemed useless, needless and even foolish, but they all belonged to Cobb's general scheme. He was a master of psychology and he made psychology his strongest weapon.

"It isn't what you do, entirely, it's just as much what they think you're going to do that counts," he explained. "The idea is to make them think you're going to do a certain thing and then if you get them to believing that you're going to do that certain thing, it's easy enough to pull the play you want to pull, for you'll have them completely crossed up. The main thing is to do the unexpected. If you do the expected the chances are somewhat against you for there are too many opposed to you, but if they can be caught flat-footed the advantage is all with you, no matter how many are against you."

To carry out this idea he created what he called the "threat." It was really a mental hazard. He would be at bat and let the first pitch go by without offering. He would do the same thing the next time at bat, and the next and the next. By that time the pitcher was convinced that Cobb had no intention of swinging on the first pitch and he would groove the first one to get ahead of him. That would be the pitch Cobb had been waiting for.

In running bases he would go down on the first or second pitch, the same pitch three or four times in succession, until he impressed the opposition that he had decided on a set system and just about the time this opinion became established Cobb would cross them up.

When the Tigers had a long lead or when they were hopelessly behind, and where a run would neither help nor harm

the team's chances, Ty would establish mental hazards. That is where the plays that were called foolhardy were always made. He wanted to impress the opposing team that he made the play that way. The next time they would be set for him and he could do the exact opposite.

He always believed that the bunt was the most effective weapon of attack. It upsets pitchers and infielders.

"If a pitcher is going good and you are unable to do anything with his delivery, start bunting," he always said. "A bunt will throw a pitcher off his stride. Bunt to either side of the box. He's got to go after the ball. It's an entirely different fielding chance. It makes no difference whether he throws you out or whether you beat the throw; you've accomplished your purpose and that is to get the pitcher off his stride. Many batting rallies have been started by a bunted ball on a pitcher who couldn't be touched before the bunt was laid down."

Cobb used the bunt to create his threat. After he bunted a few times and the first and third basemen moved in close when he faked another bunt, he would slash the ball directly at the first or third baseman. No first or third baseman, running into field a bunt, can handle a hard-hit ball coming directly at him. He can't shift that quickly.

Not alone in batting, but also in base running, Cobb created mental hazards. His purpose was to have them arrange their defense to take care of a similar play later on, but the next time he got on base he worked an entirely different play and the opposing team was rarely ever prepared for the play he used.

Cobb was constantly working out new plays, preparing surprise moves. He first set the stage for his drama. He was supposed to leave everything to chance, but he left less to chance than any other player in the game. He studied every detail, worked his plans to the last thread. He figured out all matters with mechanical precision. He built upon his own mechanical ability and also upon that of the men who opposed him. Unconsciously, they aided him in executing his plays. Unconsciously they were instruments in his hands.

He always liked intelligent players; the more intelligent the better he liked them. He could tell what an intelligent man would do under certain circumstances, but no one can tell what a stupid player is likely to do. The intelligent player follows a certain style, a set system. He will always act as expected in various situations. Cobb knew precisely what the intelligent players would do. Most of his brilliant plays were made against smart infielders and outfielders. He could figure them to a fine point.

An infielder can stand in a wrong position. He can fool a base-runner by his attitude, his pose, but his eyes can't deceive. Cobb knew, of course, that to catch a ball a fielder must have his eyes on the ball. While he may be standing out of the line of a throw, with his hands dangling idly at his sides to slow down the runner, his eyes will be following the ball.

Ty ignored the position of the fielder and his pose. He watched his eyes. By observing the eyes he discovered the direction of the ball, then changed his course and came in the direct line of the ball. He ran so that he would come between the ball and the infielder waiting to take the throw.

This plan had a double advantage. There was a chance of Cobb momentarily hiding the ball from the infielder and thus making possible a fumble, and there was the chance of the ball hitting Cobb. As Ty was in the direct line of vision the infielder had to watch him as well as try to watch the ball.

During his career Cobb was often hit by thrown balls. There was never another player hit as often. Cobb traveled ahead of the ball and if the play was close the chance was that Ty and the ball would meet.

Several times Cobb reached a base or scored by kicking the ball. Five times in one season he scored as a result of accurate kicks. One time in a Tigers-Athletics game, with J. Franklin Baker playing third base, Cobb got in the line

Frank "Home Run" Baker (1886–1963) in 1914. Salsinger relates how on five occasions Ty Cobb reached a base or scored by kicking a ball while sliding into base. One incident involved Philadelphia third baseman Frank Baker, when Cobb reached his foot up for a thrown ball that short-hopped to Baker at third and kicked it into the dugout. Cobb then got up and trotted safely to home as Baker protested to the umpire to no avail. Ty Cobb was also involved in a widely publicized spiking incident in which Baker was cut in 1910. Athletics manager Connie Mack alleged that the spiking injury was intentional, but detailed analysis of a photograph of the incident showed that Cobb was actually trying to avoid a collision with Baker. Baker played thirteen years in the American League, seven with Philadelphia and six with New York. He led the league in home runs four times (1911–1914) was elected to the Hall of Fame in 1955. *Courtesy Library of Congress Bain Collection.*

of the ball. The throw was a bit faster than Ty and as he slid the ball struck the ground just ahead of him and bounced up. He kicked the ball and it rolled into the Detroit dugout. Cobb got up and walked home. Baker protested, but the umpires said it was an accident since no player could deliberately kick a ball while sliding. Baker lost his argument with the umpires, but he was not convinced. He knew—and so did Cobb.

By watching the infielder's eyes Cobb was also able to judge his slides. If he thought the ball would beat him to the bag he slid in the opposite direction from the one in which the infielder gazed.

Speaking of sliding, he said: "I worked at it until sliding became second nature to me. I would always slide, whether or not there was any occasion for it. I did this so I would slide naturally. Nearing a base I would hit the dirt without thinking about it. I knew I wouldn't have time to think about it.

"I learned to slide around fielders just as I would dodge pedestrians if running in the street. I would dodge around them without first making up my mind on what to do. By constant practice I got so that I slid automatically, naturally."

Infielders became acquainted with Cobb's different slides (he had nine of them) but guessing just how he would come into a base was another matter; there were too many different possibilities.

Few players have been as supple as Cobb. He seemed like Rudyard Kipling's "Injia-rubber ball." He had feline quickness. Few infielders handled him successfully. There was never a more difficult man to tag with his use of tricks.

Cobb introduced the slide to first. He started doing this on close plays. It was another of his innovations that his contemporaries called foolish, but Ty had a definite reason. He explained:

"With a runner crossing first base in an upright position, the umpire has the runner and the ball in the same line of vision. If the runner slides, what happens? If the ball is coming to the first baseman waist-high or higher, as it generally is, he has to look at the ball and then change his line of vision and look down at the runner. He loses either the runner or the ball; he can't see both at the same time. And if the throw is low the runner sliding will raise such a cloud of dust that the umpire will be prevented from seeing the ball."

CHAPTER 10

When Ty Outguessed Rube and Won the Flag

Cobb will always remember September 30, 1907. One of the tightest pennant races in history was entering its final stage. All summer long it had been a four-team struggle, with Chicago, Cleveland, Detroit and Philadelphia fighting for the lead and taking turns heading the standings column. Chicago and Cleveland gradually dropped back in the stretch run and it was now a two-team race with the Athletics in first place by half a game when the Tigers arrived in Philadelphia on September 27 for a three-game series.

The Athletics had won the pennant in 1905, but lost the World's Series to Christy Mathewson and the Giants. The Tigers, who finished sixth the previous season, had become the sensation of the league under their new manager, Hughie Jennings.

Connie Mack had a great pitching staff including Rube Waddell, Chief Bender, Eddie Plank and Jack Coombs, and a fine defensive team. The Tigers' pitching staff was headed by Wild Bill Donovan and George Mullin and two of the longest hitters in baseball, Sam Crawford and Claude Rossman. They were the first of the power teams for which the American League became famous.

Mullin outpitched Bender in the first game of the crucial series and Detroit took the lead by half a game. It rained on September 29 and a doubleheader was scheduled for the following day.

Columbia Park, home of the Athletics at that time, had a seating capacity of 18,000, but 30,000 people jammed into the place to watch the doubleheader. They stood and sat all over the outfield.

Jennings nominated Donovan to pitch the first game and Mack countered with Jimmy Dygert, a spitball expert. He had Eddie Plank ready, but decided to save him for the second game. However, there was no second game. The first one went 17 innings and consumed three hours and 50 minutes of playing time. When it ended it was too dark to start the second game and it was never played.

At the end of five innings, the Athletics were leading, 7 to 1. Jennings would have taken any pitcher other than Donovan out of the game, but Philadelphia was Wild Bill's home town and Jennings let him stay, a sentimental gesture that paid off in the end.

The Tigers had chased Dygert in the second inning and he was relieved by Waddell, who stopped a rally cold by striking out two batters. He was less fortunate in the seventh, when Detroit scored four runs and cut the Athletics' lead to two, but they got one in their half and were ahead, 8 to 5. The Tigers got another in the eighth and were still trailing by two in the ninth.

Cobb came to bat with Crawford on first and none out and hit the ball over the right field fence, tying the score. At this point, Mack took out Waddell and rushed in Plank, who struck out three batters in a row and retired the side.

In the eleventh, Cobb put the Tigers ahead again by hitting a double with Rossman on base, but the Athletics scored in their half and it was 9 to 9. Cobb reached third base in the seventeenth inning, but was left there and after the Athletics took their turn at bat the game was called on account of darkness.

The Tigers left Philadelphia leading the league by half a game. They had two series left, with Washington and St. Louis. The Athletics likewise had two series left, with Cleveland and Washington, but they never got back into the lead. Detroit finished in front.

"I experienced about every thrill that can come in baseball that day," said Cobb years later.

Baseball analysts, telling how a pennant was won, generally point to one series, but you can go deeper in the analysis. You can point to one game as the deciding factor. That game probably had one play on which the outcome depended and the play came on a certain pitch, so that one pitched ball can mean a pennant.

The series that decided the pennant of 1907 was the two-game series in Philadelphia and the game that broke the Athletics was the 17-inning tie.

Victory was snatched from the Athletics in the ninth inning on a home run by Cobb and the home run stood out as the most important hit of the

1907 season. It was made possible because Cobb outguessed Waddell, one of the best lefthanded pitchers of all time, illiterate but cunning, with great physical powers, a remarkable curve ball and speed. Mack used him in relief, sure that he could hold off the Tigers, clinch a victory for the Athletics and return them to the league lead.

I asked Waddell later how Detroit was able to tie the score and he told me: "Up comes this Cobb and I feeds him a fast ball on the inside where he ain't supposed to like to see 'em pitched. I always figured if this fellow had any weakness it was on a ball pitched close in. The way he stood up there made him shift too quick to get a good hold of the ball.

"Well I throws the first one over the inside corner and he don't even look at it. The umpire calls it a strike, but he don't pay no attention. I figure he's lookin' for a certain ball, sure I'll give it to him on the next pitch or the one after that. He got an idea I'm goin' to be workin' on him. I see my chance to cross him up. I says to myself, 'I'll feed this cuckoo one in the same spot an' get him in a hole, then let him guess on what's comin'.

"I throws another for the inside corner an' the second the ball leaves my hand I know I made a bum guess. This Cobb, who didn't seem to have noticed the first one, steps back like he had the catcher's sign, takes a toe hold and swings. I guess the ball's goin' yet.

"After the game I meets this Cobb on the street and I says to him: 'Listen here, it's all over an' everything an' there ain't no hard feelin' or nothin', so tell me why you don't swing on that first one, the fast ball I throws inside to you? You don't give it a look an' yet you're all set for the pitch when I repeats. D'you have the catcher's signal or somethin'?'

"An' he says to me: 'Why, I figures if I lets the first one pass an' make out I don't notice it an' is lookin' for somethin' else, you'll try to cross me up an' shoot the next one over the same spot, feelin' you're double-crossin' me. I feel so sure that when the ball leaves your hand I jump back, take a toe hold an swing. An' sure enough I was right. You hand me the same thing right back.'

"An' I says to this Cobb: 'Kid, you had me doped 100 per cent right.' An' sure enough the lucky stiff did."

The eccentric Waddell pitched one ball wrong in that game. He suspected it was wrong at the time. Cobb verified his suspicions.

CHAPTER 11

Never Tense and Seldom Injured

Cobb played three times as hard as the average big leaguer and lasted four times as long. Players frequently said of him, "He just ain't human."

He went through 24 seasons of the most strenuous competition that any man has known in baseball. He spent six months each year going at top speed, setting a nerve-racking, muscle-tearing, tissue-destroying pace. And 24 years is more than four times as long as even the most optimistic observers said he could last after he had been in the league a few seasons. They did not believe it was physically possible for any human being to continue at Cobb's pace for more than a few years.

College sprinters have brief careers. They burn themselves out. Cobb did more sprinting in one year than a college sprinter does in a lifetime. He played at a clip beyond imagination. He threw himself into the breach, risked his limbs each day in desperate running and sliding. He took long bodily risks and his contemporaries, whom he overshadowed, consoled themselves with the thought that he would not be around long to annoy them. He would burn himself out, break a leg, or an arm, and that would be the end of their troubles. Cobb was hogging the headlines, basking in the spotlight, and they did not like it.

Ty did not burn out. He outlasted his rivals by years. The average major

Opposite: **Jack Quinn (1883–1946) in 1910. In August 1912, New York's spitballer Jack Quinn beaned Ty Cobb just above his right ear, knocking him unconscious. Cobb was hit by opposing pitchers 94 times in his career, but this was the only time he was hit in the head. Salsinger writes that Cobb's batting stance enabled him to duck inside pitches and avoid attempts by opposing pitchers to bean him. Jack Quinn pitched 23 major league seasons with eight different teams, including two seasons with Baltimore in the Federal League. As one of the last pitchers permitted to throw spitballs after they were banned in 1920, he made his final major league appearance in 1933 at the age of 50. He had a career record of 247 wins and 218 losses with a 3.29 ERA. *Courtesy Library of Congress Bain Collection.***

league career spans six seasons. Only the top-notchers go beyond ten. Cobb, who put more into a game than any of them, had one of the longest careers on record and the most brilliant.

He had planned it so. There was method in his baseball madness. His reputed carelessness was by design. He realized the dangers of sliding as well as the next player, but he also knew how to discount the dangers. A man sliding always runs the risk of sprains, dislocations and fractures. Few players ever escaped sprains.

Cobb suffered fewer injuries than any player of his time. Curiously enough his only ankle injury occurred in an exhibition game down south one spring. An improvised diamond was laid out in a corn field. Some of the stubbles had been overlooked. The base lines were of different grades. A player ran downhill to first base, downhill to second and uphill to third. There were also bumps and holes.

Ty had hit a two-bagger and the crowd began yelling, "Steal third, Ty... Steal third!" He tore out for third but as he started his slide his spikes caught in a hidden stubble and his ankle was badly sprained. He was on crutches when the season opened.

Asked why he took such a chance in an exhibition game in a remote hamlet, Cobb said: "Many of those people came miles to see me. It will be the only chance they'll ever have to see me play. They'll always remember me as they saw me that afternoon and I want them to have a proper picture of me in memory."

Early in his career he studied how to escape injury. He started his slide while going at top speed. He hurled his body at an angle. As soon as he left his feet his body went limp. He relaxed completely until he was stretched out on the ground at the finish of his slide. In this way he could throw his body in any direction. He remained partly relaxed. There was no tension and, consequently, no injury.

Cobb learned that the cause of most injuries is failure to relax. Players hesitate a moment before starting their slides. They are uncertain about hitting the dirt. They are tense, their legs are generally stiff. They have not enough speed to carry the body forward. The weight of the body falls on the ankles, causing strains and sprains.

Legs are the most important part of any competitive athlete and when the legs go the athlete goes with them. Few players know how to properly take care of their legs; Cobb did. While he was apparently risking serious injury in hurtling his body over the ground, he was doing it in a manner that insured him against serious injury and his record is the best proof of this.

He was rarely hit by a pitched ball. Only once in his career, in August, 1921, was he hit on the head. John Picus Quinn, one of the last spitball pitchers in the American League, hit him over the right ear and knocked him unconscious. His peculiar stance at the plate enabled him to duck inside pitches.

Few pitchers ever deliberately threw at Cobb and all but one lived to regret it. The exception was a recruit. Hearing that pitchers were afraid to dust Cobb off, he announced that he would not alone dust him off but do it by throwing at his head.

The first time the recruit faced Ty he made good on his promise. He threw at the batter's head and the batter ducked. That first pitch might have been accidental, but when the next one came at Cobb's head, he knew it was intentional. When the recruit came in with the next pitch, Cobb pushed a slow grounder to the right of the first baseman, so placing the ball that there was no chance for the first baseman to make the putout. Cobb trotted toward first, waiting for the pitcher to cover, but the pitcher never moved toward the bag. The first baseman, like Cobb, was waiting for the pitcher to cover. He stood there, holding the ball, having no chance to beat Cobb to the bag. Ty reached first and glared at the pitcher. The recruit was laughing. He yelled:

"Well, I held you to a single, didn't I?"

Whenever Cobb knew that a pitcher was deliberately throwing at him (the times, as I said, were very few), he would contrive to make the first baseman field the ball and force the pitcher to cover, taking the throw, and knock him for a loop. After one such experience, the pitcher abandoned his ambition to dust Cobb off.

For a stretch of eight seasons, Cy Young and Lou Criger, playing with the Boston Red Sox, were one of the famous batteries in baseball. Young would never let any catcher but Criger work with him. After the 1908 season, Boston sold Young to Cleveland and Criger to St. Louis.

Lou's home was in St. Louis and during the winter he gave an interview saying that he could not understand why Cobb was regarded as a great base-runner since most of his running was "boneheaded work." He added: "Cobb has stolen only two bases on me in the last two years and I'll continue to hold him in check."

The interview was widely copied. Someone sent Cobb a clipping. He carried it in his wallet. The Browns opened their first series in Detroit on April 30. As Cobb came up in the first inning he paused outside the batter's box and spoke to Criger.

"So you're all set to show me up, are you?"

"I will if you try any of them monkey shines on me," said Criger.

"Well, this looks like a fine spot to help my base-stealing record."

"Not today you won't."

"Oh, yes, I will. And what's more I'm going to get on base right now and steal on the first pitch."

Ty drew a base on balls. He took a long lead off first and Oscar Graham, the pitcher tried to catch him off, but the runner got back safely. Another lead, another throw. And still another. Tiring of trying to catch Ty off first, the pitcher turned his attention to the batter. As he started his delivery, Cobb broke for second. Criger had called for a pitchout to give him added opportunity to throw to second, but Cobb slid safely into the bag As he got up and dusted himself off, he yelled to Criger:

"That was a better throw than I expected to see an old geezer like you make, but still not good enough."

Criger's pride was broken. He never knew it but he had no chance to throw out Cobb for Ty stole on the pitcher. No catcher in the game could have thrown him out with the lead he got on Graham.

CHAPTER 12

"Cobb Carried Brains in His Feet"

Branch Rickey coached George Sisler at the University of Michigan and when he became manager of the St. Louis Browns he took Sisler with him.

Later, as manager of the St. Louis Cardinals, Rickey helped develop Rogers Hornsby into the star of the National League.

Sisler and Hornsby are two of the game's all-time greats and Rickey deserves a share of the credit for their illustrious careers.

Rickey saw a great deal of Cobb while managing the Browns. He saw a great deal more of Sisler and Hornsby. Asked which of the three was the greatest player, Rickey answered:

"Cobb is easily the greatest. No one can doubt that he is the greatest who ever lived. Why, I believe that Cobb carried brains in his feet. At least he played that way.

"I saw Cobb make one play while I was manager of the Browns that I shall never forget. That one play, if nothing else, would convince me that Cobb was a super player.

"We were playing in Detroit and the score was tied in the ninth. Two were out in the home half of the inning. Carl Weilman, who was a Tiger nemesis all the time he played in the American League, was pitching for us. Two out, bases empty, up came Cobb.

"Weilman began working on him. He was never convinced that Ty was easy, although the records indicate that he was easy for Weilman.

"There was Cobb, shifting around in the batter's box, doing everything he could to disrupt Weilman. He finally managed to get a base on balls.

"As soon as he reached first, he took a long lead off the bag. Weilman threw to Leary, our first baseman, but Cobb easily beat the throw, sliding gracefully into the bag. Leary lobbed the ball back to Weilman and Cobb immediately took another long lead and Weilman made another throw to Leary. Cobb slid back safely and Leary lobbed the ball back to Weilman. The pitcher snatched the ball out of the air and fired it back to Leary, but not in time to catch Cobb.

"Right there I saw a chance to retire the side by catching Cobb off. I stood up in the dugout and yelled to Weilman, "Do it again." Weilman followed instructions, but he had no better luck than with his previous throws.

"This time Leary, disgusted at failing to catch Cobb, lobbed the ball higher than before and Cobb was off in a flash, streaking for second base. Weilman grabbed the ball and threw to Johnny Lavan, our second baseman, but he overhurried the throw and the ball struck the ground at Lavan's feet and caromed off into center field. Cobb bounded up and kept right on going.

"Now, our center fielder had backed up the play perfectly and recovered the ball before Cobb was halfway to third. I figured he was a dead cinch to be tagged out. Jimmy Austin, our third baseman, stood on the line, waiting to take the throw. The ball beat Cobb by yards, but Austin was over-anxious and something happened that convinced me Cobb had brains in his feet; either that or he wasn't human.

"The ball was lying out there between Austin and Cobb for just a fraction of a second. Austin was reaching for the ball, but in that instant Cobb did more thinking than the average player does in an entire season. Instead of sliding for the base, he slid for the ball, feet first, and proved that his foot was quicker than Austin's hand. Before the third baseman could touch the ball, Cobb gave it a kick that sent it rolling into the dugout and he got up and jogged home with the winning run.

"It was a clear case of interference, but I couldn't make the umpires see it that way. The game was over and you aren't going to win any arguments from umpires after they call it a day. On second thought, it would have been a crime to call Cobb out for interference after making a play as brilliant as that.

"Yes, sir, when you're talking about the greatest player of all time you're talking about only one man — Mr. T. Raymond Cobb."

The game the Tigers won on Cobb's kick was one of the few times in which they ever beat Weilman, a forgotten pitcher. He was easy for most other clubs but poison for Detroit and especially Cobb. He won eight games from the Tigers in one season mainly because of his ability to handcuff Ty. He held Cobb to an average of .276 in 25 games.

There was never a harder loser than Cobb. He played to win and he used every ounce of energy to succeed.

There was an illustration of this in a game between the Tigers and the New York Highlanders, managed by Clark Griffith. Jack Chesbro, closing his major league career, was pitching and he had a hard time getting anybody out.

The Tigers were running up an enormous score but for some reason Griffith, now Washington owner, refused to take Chesbro out of the game. Managers do that sometimes.

It seemed that the ninth inning would never end. Cobb, coming up a second time, singled and was prancing around first base when Bill Donovan, coaching there, said to him: "Let 'em tag you out and get this game over. That's the only way they'll be able to get anybody out."

"Yeah, let me tag you out. I'm as tired of this game as you are," said Hal Chase the first baseman.

Chesbro overheard the conversation and threw the ball to Chase. He reached over to tag Cobb. The runner jumped just out of his reach. Hal tried again and Ty jumped again. Chase began running after Cobb and the excitement started. Cobb ran up and down the base line, jockeying between infielders They kept throwing the ball and finally a wide throw was muffed and Cobb slid safely into second. He explained later:

"I just couldn't stand there and let 'em tag me out without at least giving 'em a run for it."

It was never said of Cobb that he laid down. Nearly all players do at times, not meaning that they throw games, but they relax in their efforts. Cobb always played the string out.

In exhibition games, where nearly all players loaf more or less because there is nothing at stake, Cobb played his best. He never learned how to loaf.

CHAPTER 13

A Born Pitcher, He Thought

Cobb was not a perfect player but he came nearer to perfection than any other player before his time, during his time, or since.

His outstanding mechanical fault was a comparatively weak throwing arm and this could have been avoided. Cobb had only himself to blame. He wanted to become a pitcher. As a boy he played on the infield, at shortstop, but the ambition of every boy who plays baseball is to become a great pitcher. Cobb was no exception.

Never during his long career did Cobb doubt that had he pitched, he would have been one of the all-time mound greats. He nursed his ambition for more than two decades. Whenever he could enlist the services of a catcher, Ty would practice pitching. He would work with the catcher for half an hour or more, generally more, and while he worked, he threw twice as many balls as a regular pitcher would throw in the same length of time. He pitched as he played, with a nervous speed.

Players who watched him pitch were never impressed. This hurt his pride and made him more determined than ever to improve and try all the harder.

I remember one bright day at San Antonio, Tex., in the spring of 1909. The Detroit club was training there and Cobb, as usual, had enlisted a catcher and was having his morning workout, pitching. Germany Schaefer, then a veteran and wise in the ways of baseball, walked over to Cobb and told him:

"Listen! Take a piece of advice from me and cut out this monkey business. Forget you're a pitcher. You ain't. You can never be one. You've been pitchin' for four years that I know of and you ain't got no more stuff than a high school kid. There's a lot of good pitchers. There's a couple of thousand that is better than you'll ever be, but there ain't a lot of outfielders with good throwing arms and I'm advising you to try save your arm for the outfield and forget about pitching."

Cobb ignored the advice. He tried all the harder to pitch and prove Schaefer and the others wrong. He never proved them to be anything but right and in the meantime he was weakening his arm. As a fielder, he never matched Tris Speaker, Fielder Jones, Harry Hooper, Hap Felsch and a few more. He lacked their throwing ability.

As a center fielder, Cobb rarely changed his position. He stood in practically the same spot in every game, playing a "dead" center field while other outfielders moved according to the batter and the catcher's signals. A righthanded batter, for instance, will not hit a high fast ball on the outside to the same spot that he will hit a low curve ball, pitched inside. The outfielders began moving when they saw the catcher's signs.

Cobb never did this. He played every batter practically the same way and there was never any objection to this, since Ty depended upon his quick break and speed. He could get to a given point as soon as an outfielder who played position, and sooner than most of them. Because of his lightning break and speed and fine judgment of fly balls, he was an excellent outfielder, although not a great one in the sense that Speaker and Jones were great.

Still, had he played position for batters instead of a stationary outfield, he would have been far less spectacular. A born showman, Cobb dramatized every opportunity. He made all chances look difficult, regardless of how easy they happened to be. Innumerable times he purposely started late after a fly ball or line drive, or slowed down in going after it, enabling him to make a diving or leaping catch of a ball that actually offered an easy and unspectacular fielding chance. He was baseball's master showman.

When Cobb was installed as a Tiger regular, he played right field. Sam Crawford was the center fielder. A few years later they switched positions.

As a right fielder, Cobb revolutionized outfield throwing. When he started to play, outfielders "rainbowed," or "lobbed" the ball to the infield on singles and no player ever attempted to take advantage of the looping, lazy throws. Cobb changed that by turning inside, instead of outside, on hits to the outfield and making a break for second base.

Not alone by base-running, but by his defensive play in right field, did he cause the elimination of lob throws.

It was during a Tiger–Red Sox series that Cobb changed his position in right field. He came in close to the infield, counting on his quick break and speed to go back and get any ball hit over his head.

Harry Hooper, an excellent hitter and smart outfielder, was one of the Boston stars. Hooper undoubtedly remembers the game, because Cobb took two hits from him and when you take two hits from a ball player he does not forget soon.

Hooper was a pull-hitter and rarely hit a ball anywhere but to right field. On his first time at bat, Hooper ran the count to three and two. He hit the next pitch into right field, a smashing line drive that struck the turf and came to Cobb on the first bounce. The Tiger first baseman, Claude Rossman, had been instructed by Cobb to run to the bag and look for a throw if Hooper hit to right and Rossman broke for the bag the instant he saw the ball would land in Cobb's territory. He took Ty's throw and Hooper, a fast man in those days, was out by a step.

The next time Hooper came to bat he grounded out, but on his third appearance he again rifled the ball into right field and Cobb, tearing in, made a quick pickup and threw to Rossman. Hooper was again out by a full step.

Cobb did the same thing to other players. He played the shortest right field of any player covering the position. Even if the runner beat his throw, he had no chance to turn to the inside and take a lead toward second base.

After Cobb continued getting doubles on what were singles for other players, outfielders began changing their methods. Instead of fielding the ball leisurely they would hurry the play and, instead of "rainbowing" the ball back to the infield, they would throw it on a line. The lob throw disappeared from the outfield.

The game changes slowly. During the first few years when Cobb upset infields with his base-running, they said he had the "luck of a lunatic," but when his success not alone continued but mounted, they began paying attention. Other players started copying his methods. This was particularly true of the younger ones since the veterans were too thoroughly drilled in the old methods to change.

No longer did base-runners jog beyond first, turn outside the base line and jog back to the bag; they turned sharply and made a start for second, ready to take advantage of any opportunity. They no longer took things for granted.

As this style became general, the outfielders had to change their methods to meet the new attack. They used to play deep. That gave them a chance to get balls hit far out and they could always come in for short flies and grounders. All outfielders find it easier to come in on a ball than go out on one. That is logical and that is the way they played when Cobb introduced his style of base-running.

The outfielders came in much closer. It gave them a chance to prevent runners from taking an extra base. It gave them a shorter throw and kept the runner from getting an added base on a long throw.

Cobb had noticed, when he began playing in the American League, that base-runners circled the bases by touching the outside corner or stepping on the sacks. He decided that he could gain valuable ground by touching the bags on the inside corner. This would save at least three steps and three steps mean a great deal in a stretch of 90 feet, the distance between bases.

He practiced this. Going from home plate to first base, he tagged the inside corner of the bag as he made a sharp turn, instead of the wide, sweeping turn. He stayed near a direct line between bases and when he touched the next bag it was again on the inside corner. He eliminated yards of waste running and practically lessened the distance between bases. His style was gradually adopted. Today nearly all base runners endeavor to tag the bases on the inside corner of the bag.

CHAPTER 14

A Fine Man, Kind to Umpires

No other player ever knew as many tricks as Cobb or used as many. He studied all the by-play of the game. He knew the turns and twists, all the angles.

On the field, Cobb limped for days when there was nothing wrong with either leg and after the opposing team became convinced that he was injured, he would put on one of his dazzling bursts of speed when the opportunity came to win a game.

He would pretend that his throwing arm was lame, tossing with a decided effort while warming up and lobbing the ball from the outfield during pre-game practice. Opposing players would notice this but when a base runner tried to take advantage of the "discovery," Cobb's arm miraculously recovered.

He often pulled stupid plays, making them appear as stupid as possible to create the impression that he knew no better. Then he took advantage of the impression when the opportunity came.

Cobb became extremely friendly with a player on the Washington team. He would take him to dinner whenever Detroit played Washington and there was always a discussion over the relative merits of their teams.

The player would seek information from Cobb and Ty freely gave it. He would tell his Washington friend that a certain pitcher on the Detroit staff had trouble with his fast ball. Every hit made off him in recent games had been on his fast ball. It no longer carried a hop, was just a practice pitch. The Tigers were wondering how long he would get away with it.

Bobby Veach had a sore arm. His throwing was very weak and the only thing that kept him in the lineup was his hitting.

The Tigers' No. 1 catcher had strained his arm in a wrestling match but Hughie Jennings insisted on using him when he should be out of uniform, nursing his arm. Some team would get wise to the condition of the catcher's arm and start running wild on him. The Washington player would then confide in Cobb. One of the Senators' outfielders had a bad arm but so far no opposing team had found out about it. The arm was very, very bad and the news was bound to leak out sooner or later.

The club's regular catcher had developed some intestinal trouble that affected his throwing. He was slow getting the ball away.

The next day the Washington team would be all set for the Detroit pitcher whose fast ball had lost its hop. Batters were instructed to "lay for the fast one." They waited in vain. Most of what they saw was curve and let-up balls. Once in awhile they looked at a fast one, but it seemed faster than ever before.

When base runners tried to run on the Detroit catcher, whose arm was said to be bad, they found the ball beating them to the bag.

Whenever a player tried to take two bases on a hit to left, because Veach was reported to have trouble throwing to the infield, he discovered Veach rifling the ball ahead of him.

In the meantime the Washington players could not understand why Detroit ran wild whenever a certain outfielder had the ball, the one with the lame arm. Why did they single out that particular outfielder?

They were puzzled why Detroit base runners who never took a chance on any catcher's arm suddenly run on their catcher, the one with intestinal trouble.

Clark Griffith finally suspected what had happened. Stalking into the clubhouse after his team lost another game to the Tigers, he announced:

"The first one of you I catch talking to this Cobb, even to say 'Hello' to him, is going to be fined $300 and the fine will stick. Get me and get me right. What I say goes."

Hot-tempered and pugnacious as he was, Cobb could also be the reverse and he was when it served his ends. He followed a be-kind-to-umpires creed religiously. Until he became manager of the Tigers in 1920 he never had an argument with an umpire, never questioned a decision, never criticized, never argued.

"A great player and fine man," the battle-scarred Timothy Hurst used to say. "Never gives you a bit o' trouble. Always kind an' considerate, over-lookin' yer bad days. A gran' lad indeed."

It was good policy to be kind to umpires. Ty decided that early in his career. A friendly umpire was helpful, an unfriendly one not so good. Umpires are honest; the breath of scandal has never touched them; but they are also human, a fact that most players over-looked. Cobb realized it, but then Cobb was not an ordinary player. He made it a point to treat umpires with respect, kindness and consideration. They were honest, of course, but also human. They could not help becoming prejudiced in his favor. Cobb won them. He never suffered because of his attitude toward umpires. If a play was a toss-up between safe and out, Ty was sure to get the break. He never lost anything by his treatment of umpires and no one can say that he never gained anything. There is no denying that Cobb won a majority of the close decisions and he figured in more plays that were extremely close than any other player.

In those days you never heard an umpire say an unkind thing about Cobb. They were all exuberant in their praise of him and went out of their way to give glowing accounts attesting to his greatness. Why shouldn't they? He was the best friend they had among the players. He understood them.

Cobb, in turn, praised the umpires. One time, in an interview, he extolled the virtues of Tommy Connolly and that would have been very fine if Connolly had not read the nice things that Cobb said about him. A day after the interview was printed, Ty was at bat and the winning run was on second base. The pitcher tried to give Cobb an intentional pass since two were out and the pitcher preferred to take a chance on the next batter.

Overeager to hit, since he had already made three hits off the pitcher, Cobb stepped across the plate and chopped the fourth pitch-out into left field for a single. Ty streaked to first, turned sharply and was ready to advance to second on the left fielder's throw to the plate. Instead, the left fielder threw to second and Cobb slid back to first. He got up, dusted off his uniform, and was startled to hear Connolly's voice. "You're out!" yelled Tommy, who was calling balls and strikes that day.

"I'm what?" asked Ty.

"You're out," reiterated Connolly.

Cobb walked to the plate where the umpire was standing.

"Why am I out? How can I be out? I hit safely, didn't I?"

"That you did, but you hit outside the rules. You stepped across the plate in hitting the ball and the rules don't allow that. When you step across the plate and swing, you're out."

"But I didn't step across the plate."

"Well, you stepped on the plate and you're out."

The decision stood. Ty was out and he lost a base hit. Had Ty not been so exuberant in his praise of Connolly the umpire would likely have been less technical and ignored the fact that Cobb stepped on the plate. Tommy intended to prove that all Ty said about him was correct and richly deserved.

CHAPTER 15

First Batter to Study a Pitcher

Cobb was frequently accused of being a dirty player and intentionally spiking infielders. He always defended himself against these charges, pointing out that the base lines belonged to the runners and that when an infielder blocked the line he did so at his own risk. He said that during his career he intentionally spiked only two players.

Cobb had rows with players on his own team and opposing teams and rows with spectators. He was not an easy man to get along with and he made enemies, but he never set out to "get" a man without first giving him fair warning. If he spiked an infielder or catcher, the injured player had himself to blame.

Few infielders ever blocked the base lines when Cobb was running. They discovered it was unwise. He never took particular care to evade a player and he was within his rights. The rules of the game entitled him to the line and anyone who attempted to block him did so at his own risk.

Infielders went frantic in their efforts to tag Cobb. That is exactly what he tried to make infielders — frantic. But there was one infielder who refused to become frantic, just one who sat down and figured out a way to repulse Cobb on the bases. The exception was Rhoderick Wallace, one of the smartest shortstops of his, or any other, time. He had a long career in the big leagues, turning to umpiring after he retired, but did not like umpiring and quit after a brief trial.

Wallace decided it was sheer folly to try to put the ball on Cobb's body. Base runners could ordinarily be retired that way but Cobb was no ordinary base runner. Infielders tried to tag his body and missed because the body was always going away from them.

Whenever Wallace played against Detroit, he covered second any time Cobb reached first base. When Cobb streaked down the base line toward second, Wallace ran over and took the throw. He straddled the bag, feet far apart, and looked for Cobb's out-stretched feet. Ty always slid with one foot on the ground and the other about a foot above the ground. Wallace would reach out, put the ball under the raised foot, and give a twist. The twist caused Cobb's body to swerve to one side, out of line with the bag. The position of the body left no doubt in the minds of the umpires whether Cobb was safe or out.

Other infielders, noting Wallace's success, tried to copy his trick, but only one ever succeeded in mastering it. That was Charley O'Leary, but Ty did not have to worry about him. O'Leary was his teammate, the Tiger shortstop. He became adept at tagging runners beneath the ankle and giving a quick twist, throwing them out of line.

Jack Sheridan, a great umpire of the period, commented: "If all infielders were like Wallace and O'Leary you wouldn't need no umpires. Them two decides the plays for you. There is never no doubt in your mind when Wallace or O'Leary tags a runner, but Wallace is the cuter of the two by just a little bit.

"A couple of fast steppers, them two. You never see either of 'em take the spikes of a runner. They always manage to get out of the way of 'em."

Umpires on numerous occasions called Cobb safe when he was really out. He had the knack of making a play look different from what it really was. He never missed an opportunity. Whenever possible he got between the umpire and the fielder, hiding the play from the umpire and leaving it up to guess-work. Whenever the umpire had to guess, Tyrus knew he would not get the worst of it.

Before Ty Cobb developed into baseball's leading player, pitchers had always studied batters to discover their strength and weakness, but batters had never studied pitchers. Cobb was the first player to make pitchers a subject for study and no one ever studied them more closely. No man ever found out more about them. He discovered faults of which the pitchers themselves were not aware.

Some of them were puzzled. They could not understand why Cobb was able to hit their best pitches. They never knew that he had discovered some telltale movement of which they were unconscious. Often, when he was given credit for outguessing a pitcher, he did no outguessing; he knew every minute movement the pitcher had and the meaning of each. There was no guesswork; he knew what was coming.

There were few pitchers who continued fooling Cobb through their careers. Sooner or later he would master them. The pitcher who gave him the most trouble in his early years was Doc White, a star of the world's champion Chicago White Sox in 1906. White was a tall, slender left-hander and a very tough pitcher for any club to beat. Many batters had trouble hitting him, but none of them had more trouble than Cobb. In one game White struck out Ty four times and after striking him out three straight times in another game, Freddy Payne, a reserve catcher, was sent to bat for Cobb, the only time in his career that he ever was removed for a pinch batter.

White's curve ball dropped sharply and it was this delivery that handcuffed Ty. He would figuratively break his back trying to get hold of it. The best he could ever do was hit a weak foul off White.

Cobb studied Doc intently. The pitch that he could not hit always broke over the plate. He decided that if he stood far back in the batter's box and swung on the ball after it broke, he might be able to hit it.

The next time that Cobb faced White he stood far back, two feet behind the plate. White's pitch broke as it did before, right over the plate, and Cobb, standing two feet behind the break, connected.

White never again struck out Cobb. The player who had

Addie Joss (1880–1911) in 1910. Cleveland's Addie Joss was one of the few pitchers who held Cobb below a .300 batting average. Cobb faced Joss in 23 games between 1905 and 1910, and batted only .253 against him. Joss's nine-year major league career ended early in 1910 when he was diagnosed with meningitis, resulting in his death at the age of 31 in 1911. Addie Joss had a career win-loss record of 160–97, with an ERA of 1.89. He pitched a perfect game in 1908, winning against Chicago in only 74 pitches, and also bested Chicago with a no-hitter in 1910. He was elected to the Hall of Fame in 1978. *Courtesy Library of Congress Bain Collection.*

not been able to hit a loud foul off him became his nemesis. Ty batted against White in 46 American League games and his lifetime average against White was .335.

The pitcher who had the most success against Cobb was Addie Joss of Cleveland. He was one of the great pitchers who played in the American League. Among his achievements was a perfect game, pitched against the Chicago White Sox on October 2, 1908. Ty batted against Addie in 25 games and his average was .253.

Carl Weilman of St. Louis, who was just as tall as Joss and somewhat thinner, was almost as difficult for Cobb. In the 25 games that Weilman pitched against Detroit, Ty hit .276.

Dusty Rhodes, a teammate of Joss on the Cleveland staff, was just about as big a problem as Weilman. Dusty held Ty to an average of .275 in 20 games.

Weilman probably deserves more credit for "holding down" Cobb's average than any other pitcher. Joss and Rhodes were seasoned big league pitchers when Cobb arrived, but Weilman came on the scene after Ty had established himself as the leading hitter of baseball.

In his first 12 seasons

Bobby Wallace (1873–1960) in 1911. St. Louis Browns shortstop Wallace developed a unique and successful method of tagging Ty Cobb when he tried to steal second base. Wallace would avoid tagging the foot Cobb extended toward the base, and instead reach with ball in hand for Cobb's other foot which was invariably raised as he did his fade-away slide. Wallace would play in the majors for 25 years from 1894 to 1918, 15 years in the American League with the Browns, and ten years in the National League, five each with St. Louis and Cleveland. He was elected to the Hall of Fame in 1953. *Courtesy Library of Congress Bain Collection.*

(1905–16, inclusive), Cobb batted .369, only two points higher than his average for 24 seasons.

Considering only pitchers whom he faced in ten or more games during the first half of his career, Ty hit .400 or better against 13, hit .350 or better against ten and .300 or better against 22 others.

He had an average of .474 against Bullet Joe Bush of Philadelphia, in 11 games, and .471 against Death Valley Scott of the Chicago White Sox, in 20 games. He belted Slim Caldwell of New York for an average of .463 in 20 games, and Tom Hughes of Washington and New York, .458 in 21 games. Hogg of New York, was the victim of a .450 average and Russell Ford, of the same team, was tagged for .442. Joe Boehling of Washington and Cleveland gave up a .435 average and Jack Warhop of New York .411. Hubert (Dutch) Leonard of Boston was hit for .409; Barney Pelty of St. Louis for .411; Eddie Cicotte of Chicago for .408; Fred Blanding of Cleveland for .405, and Jack Chesbro of New York for an even .400.

Among the pitchers against whom Cobb averaged between .350 and .400 were Vean Gregg, Cy Falkenberg, Smoky Joe Wood, Bob Groom, Chief Bender, Jack Coombs, Bob Shawkey, Cy Young, Nick Altrock and Rube Waddell.

He averaged better than .300 against 45 pitchers whom he faced in ten or more games In his .300 to .350 list were such stars as Walter Johnson, Ed Walsh, Eddie Plank and the old jinx, White.

The only great pitcher who ever held him under .300 was Addie Joss, as already mentioned. Frank Smith of Chicago pinned him to an average of .296 in 24 games and against Dolly Gray of Washington he could do no better than .286 in 19 games. His lack of success against Weilman and Rhodes has been previously narrated.

CHAPTER 16

His Weaknesses Became His Strength

To strengthen the muscles of his legs and keep in condition, Cobb had a shoemaker fix lead plates in the soles of his shoes. This was between seasons when he spent his days in the woods and fields.

The idea was original with him, but he was not the first athlete to wear leaded shoes. Alfred Shrubb, England's famous distance runner who at one time held every record from one to ten miles, used the same method to strengthen his legs. When he laced on his light running shoes "they felt light as feathers."

Cobb carried three bats to the plate and swung them while awaiting his turn for the same reason. The bat he used felt so much lighter. Before they realized the value of lugging three bats to the plate, rival players accused Cobb of doing it to show off.

Ty studied himself as thoroughly as he studied his rivals. He realized his various weaknesses when he got into professional baseball and he practiced until he overcame his faults. Not alone that, but what originally was his weakness became his strength.

Other champions of sport reached the top in the same way. Jack Dempsey had a weak left hand. All his punishing punches were delivered with the right. By the time he became a challenger for the heavyweight championship, his left hand was as effective as his right, and possibly even more potent. He developed the left by having someone tie his right hand behind him and using only the left in punching the bag, shadow boxing and sparring. He continued this over a long period until he became almost lefthanded.

Walter J. Travis was one of the great champions of amateur golf. The strongest feature of his play was his putting. And yet Travis was a weak putter in his earlier years.

The size of the average golf cup is 4½ inches. Travis had some cups made that were half size, or just a bit larger than a golf ball. He practiced putting for many hours, trying to roll the ball into the half-size cup. After practicing for long periods with the small cups, Travis returned to the regular cups and they looked about a foot in diameter.

Paavo Nurmi, one of the greatest distance runners, did not develop by running the regulation distances, but running four and five times that far. He ran from 20 to 30 miles daily, sometimes 40 miles. He was developing muscular power and lung power. After running long distances daily, a 10,000 meters event was a mere jog for the Finnish star. That is why he ran so easily and finished so fresh while other contestants fell exhausted.

So with Cobb. He gained his eminence in the same way that other great athletes did. He worked ceaselessly to eradicate his faults

He practiced until he had perfected himself. He was endowed with fewer natural gifts than many of his rivals.

On one occasion he was asked why there were not more great ball players and why he stood out over the field. His answer:

"The trouble with nearly all ball players is that they try to cover their faults instead of correcting them. There is hardly a player who doesn't know his weaknesses. But there hardly ever is a player who tries to correct them. They gloss over them, try to hide them. They're under the impression that they're fooling people, but the only person fooled is the player himself.

"It isn't any fun to go out and practice for hours each day and days each month trying to overcome a fault. There is no joy in concentrating on one thing continuously. It gets awfully monotonous and most men don't care for that kind of monotony. Hiding the fault, or trying to, is so much easier. That's the reason you don't see more good ball players. There are too many lazy ball players."

He made this statement near the end of his career. The game had changed. The lively ball ruined the finesse of the sport, cheapened it. The new generation of players differed from the old.

"There isn't the same love for baseball among the average players today that existed 20 years ago," he observed. "One reason is the dollar. Salaries have gone up tremendous."

He should know. In 1911, he led the American League in batting and base-running for the fifth consecutive season. He hit .420, made 248 hits, scored 147 runs, stole 83 bases and batted in 144 runs, so Frank J. Navin, owner of the Detroit club, magnanimously raised his salary to $9,000 for 1912.

In his last few years in baseball, Cobb saw players who could not have made any big league team in 1912, being paid more than he got for hitting .420, stealing 83 bases, and driving in 144 runs.

"The dollar has cut into the efficiency of players and reduced the quality of baseball," he continued. "When I broke in, players had a love for the game. The salaries were but a fraction of what they are today but money wasn't the magnet that attracted men to baseball, it was the game itself. Now the big attraction is the salary envelope.

"When I entered professional baseball we had ball players, but today we have businessmen. Twenty and 25 years ago we had better players on the whole, but they did not keep in as good condition as the players of today. You used to see men report for spring training in bad physical condition. They had paid absolutely no attention to training or diet during the winter months. By March they were fat, soft and flabby.

"They take better care of themselves now. They pay attention to diet and keep regular hours, at least most of them do. This is not because of any great love for the game, but the knowledge that they have to keep in shape to draw fat salary checks. They have learned that the man who does not keep in condition between seasons doesn't last long and his earning capacity ends abruptly. The longer they last the more money they'll draw and so it is the dollar again that has brought a change in baseball, one for the better.

"There is lacking today that burning desire to win that I sensed when I began playing. The whole game is a business proposition with the average player today. He is paid to play so many games a year and he plays so many and wants to get them over with as quickly as possible. What does he care about the result? He'll get paid anyway, win, lose or tie.

"Many of the recruits that come up now are not quite ready for the big leagues. There is a scarcity of material and the majors need new blood, but the new players are generally still two or three years away. They need more schooling.

"One of the chief troubles with them is that they imagine they're made as soon as they join a major league club. In my day a youngster had to go through a grueling preparatory course in the minor leagues and after he came up to the big leagues he had to sit on the bench for a year or two before he got his chance, but not any more. They pluck them before they're ripe and the pity is that the recruits don't realize that they're still green. You can tell them little, generally nothing.

"Nobody is going to improve them because they know it all already. The result is that their development stops right there. They don't improve one iota. They never get any better and, if anything, they get worse."

What Cobb said 25 years ago is just as true today as it was then.

CHAPTER 17

Climbed to the Top on Confidence

Probably the most valuable asset in batting is confidence. The man who has faith in himself will be able to hit, provided that he has the mechanical ability. A great many players with mechanical ability have been forced out of baseball because their hitting fell off. They got into a slump and never got out and so they passed from the charmed upper crust of the game.

Cobb was a super player because he believed himself to be one. He was convinced that he could play baseball better than any man who ever lived. His faith in himself was unlimited. He said:

"When I step up to the plate I look the pitcher straight in the eye. I let him know that I have confidence in myself, that I'm going to hit the ball. If I convince him of it, I have an advantage over him and put him into a hole.

"Any player who fully believes that he can hit a pitcher is fairly certain to hit him. The reason certain pitchers can beat certain clubs is that the club has become convinced that the pitcher has something on it. Therefore they rarely beat him, if at all."

Weilman, as previously related, beat Detroit eight times in one season. The Tigers were beating far better pitchers then Weilman and weaker clubs were beating Weilman, but the Tigers were totally lacking in confidence when they batted against him and they couldn't beat him. Cobb never had any confidence batting against Weilman, but Weilman was one of the few exceptions and how he managed to remain a Tiger nemesis is a mystery to this day.

"When I stepped up to the plate," said Cobb, speaking generally, "I'd tell myself, 'I'm going to hit the ball.... I'm going to hit.... I can hit it.' I'd keep telling myself I could, and I became convinced I could and often I did."

He had occasional slumps but never extended slumps. He was successful in extricating himself. He was asked several times to analyze a slump and to explain its cause.

"That's difficult," Cobb would say. "I guess nobody knows. They just happen. If you knew what caused them you could avoid them. The trouble is you don't know. You get into them unconsciously. Often it is a matter of psychology; other times it is just plain mechanical. A man may unknowingly change his batting style, he may change his grip or his stance without realizing it."

Trying to pull out of a batting slump, Cobb would appeal to his teammates, ask them to watch him closely, see what he was doing wrong, or what he was doing that he didn't generally do. They would try to help him, but he would also help himself by changing his style at bat. He would start bunting the ball and keep on bunting to get his eye on the ball. He kept this up until he was back in his hitting stride.

After 1920, many batting slumps were caused by the desire to hit home runs. That is still true. Ball players, like golfers, love long drives. When a player hits a home run the thrill of making it will cause him to keep on trying for home runs. He changes his batting style in the hope of driving the ball out of the park. He will get into a slump as a result. He will be unable to get out of the slump. That is how many players end their major league careers.

The effect of the slump is that it destroys confidence. A player goes hitless for several games and becomes disheartened. He loses faith in himself. He believes that luck has deserted him and this mental, rather than the mechanical, state will cause the slump to continue. It may mean the end of his big league career.

It takes courage and complete self-confidence to work out of a slump. There is nothing that will destroy a player's poise more quickly than inability to hit in two or more games. He begins to worry and his fielding deteriorates. He begins making wrong plays and playing wrong positions for batters. He becomes panicky and his usefulness ends.

Batting slumps come to all players. When one came to Cobb he sat down and tried to reason the thing out. He was doing something that he shouldn't do, but just exactly what?

He tried to find out by himself and he tried to find out with the aid of others, but all the while he never lost faith in himself. Ty once told me that he would tell himself, "I was able to hit before and I still can hit," and he believed it.

Cobb won the American League batting championship in 1911 by sending Shoeless Joe Jackson into a slump. It was Joe's first big league season. He was playing with Cleveland and when Detroit and Cleveland opened a six-game series near the end of September, Jackson was leading Cobb in the batting averages.

Ty and Joe had always been friendly. Joe had great admiration for Ty and Ty had great admiration for Joe, whom he still refers to as the greatest natural hitter in the history of the game.

When the aforementioned six-game series opened, Jackson came to the Detroit bench to extend him a friendly greeting. Cobb gave him the cold shoulder, refused his outstretched hand and walked past him as if he didn't exist. Jackson was puzzled and hurt. He couldn't understand Cobb's behavior and began worrying about it.

Ty continued ignoring Joe all through the series and Joe worried himself into a slump.

He didn't get a hit in the series while Ty hit safely in all six games.

As soon as the series ended, Cobb walked up to Jackson, grabbed him by the hand, slapped him on the back, invited him to dinner. That puzzled Joe more than ever and it finally dawned on him that he had been tricked. His slump continued until the end of the season and when the final official averages were announced, Cobb led the league with a percentage of .420 and Jackson was second with .408.

No American League player has hit as high as .408 since 1922, but Jackson's .408 was not good enough to make him champion. Had Cobb not used his applied psychology, Jackson would likely have finished with an average of .430 or better. That is what he was hitting when the six-game series started.

CHAPTER 18

Tips to the Kids from the Gods

Six years ago Cobb wrote an article on the science of batting for the "Famous Sluggers" series, published by the Hillerich & Bradsby Co., of Louisville. In a preface the publishers announced:

"Every word of the original is in Ty Cobb's own handwriting. He is offering here his personal advice to the millions of young Americans who desire to learn how to hit better."

It was a compact article, sufficiently lucid to bring it within the comprehension of every schoolboy.

The author dealt first with the selection of a bat and advised his readers: "For a swing hitter (one who starts his bat from as far back as he can reach and completes his swing with a full follow-through) I suggest using a bat with the feel on the light side; for one who is not a swing hitter the bat should feel slightly heavy."

His own model was never changed in any way during his career except in weight. He wrote: "It was 34½ inches — a length easy to handle — had a medium small barrel with a slight taper to medium large handle, then flared out slightly to a medium shallow knob. My bats weighed 40 ounces right down to the last few seasons during which I went to 36 and finally 35 ounces. As to type, mine was somewhat between the swinger and choke hitter, but nearer the choke."

Boys are inclined to use their favorite major league player as their model and copy his batting stance, but Cobb told them:

"Never copy another batter's position if it should be some exaggerated form of crouch. Take all of your best batters — they stand up and have the look of hitters.

"The space between the feet should be measured by how well balanced you feel. Using a yardstick this space will measure close to 14 inches for players of average height. But I should advise against thinking of a thing of this kind in terms of inches. Just stand so that you can feel balanced on both feet and can step in or out."

Managers and coaches often try to convert pull hitters into free hitters with little or no success. Cobb wrote: "The ability to send the ball into one field or another by design can be developed by practice and the use of the closed, open or square stance.

"For example, a righthanded batter, when attempting to hit to right field (which in his case is the opposite field), should use the closed stance, meaning that his left foot is closer — about four inches — to the line of the plate than his right.

"The same batter should revert to the open stance when trying to pull the ball — that is, hit to left field. His right foot will be about four inches nearer the plate line than his left.

"For hitting straightaway the square stance is the thing, meaning that both feet are an equal distance from the plate line."

Although Cobb's thesis was intended mainly for youngsters it could be read with beneficial results by most of the players in Organized Baseball. For instance: "Never try to guess and get set for a certain kind of ball, for more often than not the pitcher will outguess you and catch you flat-footed with what you're not looking for. In time you will develop the ability to sort of know what is coming in most cases."

In other words, don't be a guess hitter. Cobb never was. He knew what was coming as a rule because he had studied the pitcher closely, knew how he worked, what he threw in certain situations. With him it was knowledge, gained by constant observation, and not guesswork.

A paragraph out of Cobb's own book:

"Never let a defensive thought enter your mind. Make yourself believe that you are better than your opponent and play accordingly."

CHAPTER 19

When Georgians Went to Bat for the Peach

Much has been printed in the newspapers about the reserve clause in recent years and it has been the subject of many discussions in the council chambers of baseball, but Cobb was the first player the clause ever benefited.

After Ty won his fifth straight batting championship by hitting .420 in 1911, Frank J. Navin, then owner of the Detroit club, raised his salary to $9,000 for the 1912 season. That year Cobb won his sixth consecutive batting title with an average of .410 and became the greatest box-office attraction in the history of the game.

The following winter Cobb informed Navin that he wanted $15,000 for the 1913 season. He explained that his future was uncertain. He would probably not last long. From beginning to the end of the season his body was covered with bruises and lacerations. He did not believe his legs would stand up under the punishment to which he subjected them. He might fracture a leg or an arm, ending his career.

"You realize, of course, that I am worth $15,000 a year to you at the box-office, and more besides," he wrote Navin.

The owner's reply was brief and crisp, to-wit:

"I won't pay it."

Cobb retorted, in writing:

"Since you feel that you can't afford to pay me $15,000, wish that you would sell me. The New York club will buy me."

Navin's response was decisive if undiplomatic:

"You'll play for Detroit or you won't play for anybody and you'll take what I offer."

That seemed to end the argument. It ended it as far as Navin was concerned, at least he so believed. When the season opened on Thursday, April 10,

Cobb was at his home in Augusta, Georgia. On Wednesday, April 16, Navin announced to the Associated Press that Cobb was through with baseball unless he played on his (Navin's) terms.

On the day after this ultimatum was published, the Georgia Federation of Labor, holding its annual convention in Augusta, adopted a resolution declaring that a citizen of the Sovereign State of Georgia, Tyrus R. Cobb, was "being restrained in the freedom of his inalienable right to work for whom he may please."

The resolution further charged that the reserve clause in the baseball players contracts was contrary to the law of every state and contravened the Constitution of the United States. The Federation requested that the Georgia delegation in Congress start an immediate investigation.

The union boys were not fooling. Cobb was the idol of his home state and his fellow Georgians were not going to have any Northerner issuing ultimatums and pushing him around.

On Saturday, April 19, Georgia's two Senators, Hoke Smith and Thomas W. Hardwick

Charles "Buck" Herzog (1885–1953) in 1912. Ty Cobb and Herzog fought in 1917 after Cobb cut Herzog while sliding into second base during an exhibition game between the Tigers and the Giants. After a tussle on the infield dirt, Cobb was ejected from the game, but Herzog remained on the field. That evening, Herzog sent word to Cobb, and showed up at his hotel room to fight it out. Although no punches were landed in the wrestling match that followed, Herzog was considerably roughed up by Cobb, who was forty pounds heavier. Herzog played thirteen seasons in the National League with four different teams and played in four World Series with the Giants. *Courtesy Library of Congress Bain Collection.*

announced jointly in Washington that they were going to demand a Congressional probe. "This looks like peonage," they informed the press. Senator Smith wired Cobb:

"Send me a copy of your contract including reserve clause. Wish to see if contract illegal violating Federal laws."

The contents of Senator Smith's wire, along with the joint statements of the two Senators, were published in the Sunday news papers.

Navin had heard about the Georgia Federation of Labor resolution on Saturday. Then he learned of the proposed Congressional investigation promised by the two Senators. He telegraphed Cobb a message that he refused to make public. On Thursday, April 24, two weeks after the season opened, Navin announced that a contract satisfactory to Cobb had been offered and accepted.

When Ty Cobb broke into baseball he had a violent temper and he never fully controlled it during his career. He was involved in many misunderstandings, disputes, arguments and fights. He would become aroused over some minor matter, an imaginary wrong, an unlucky break.

His lack of self-control brought him into embarrassing situations and into the law courts. He had several fist fights with rivals.

In May, 1912, a spectator at the old Hilltop Park in New York kept yelling insults at Cobb. When Ty asked him to discontinue his verbal attack, the heckler became more abusive than ever. Cobb finally went into the grandstand and struck his tormentor. Later it was discovered that the man was a cripple, a fact unknown to Cobb when he assaulted him.

President Ban Johnson of the American League suspended Cobb as a result of the incident. News of the suspension reached Ty in Philadelphia where the Tigers had gone after completing their series in New York. When his teammates learned that Ty had been suspended they rallied to his support. They had witnessed the incident and held Cobb blameless for the assault, believing that he was more than justified in striking the abusive spectator. They demanded that the suspension be lifted and when President Johnson turned down their demand they went on strike.

The strike resulted in one of the weirdest games ever played. It was a Saturday and Hughie Jennings had to recruit a team for the afternoon. He went around town, hiring sand-lot and high school players where he found them.

Cobb in 1913. A 26-year-old Ty Cobb looks pensive as he gazes from the dugout. ***Courtesy Library of Congress Bain Collection.***

Jim McGuire and Joe Sugden, the two Tiger coaches, were also in the lineup. Jim and Joe had been catchers in their day and both had long since retired to managing and coaching. The Athletics had a merry time fattening their batting averages. They won by an overwhelming score.

Frank J. Navin, owner of the Detroit club, President Johnson and other baseball leaders rushed to Philadelphia to settle the strike. This they finally accomplished after a few more days; the players went back to work, and the Detroit club saved its franchise.

In the spring of 1917, the Tigers and New York Giants played a series of exhibition games in the South. The Giants, noted for their "riding" tactics, made Cobb the target for their abuse. The most abusive was Buck Herzog, later a manager. He took Cobb to task for putting on airs in reporting late for spring practice, charged him with being swell-headed, called him a flash-in-the-pan, and so forth. Ty told Buck to save his comedy for the minor leaguers and quit badgering him, but this only stirred Herzog to more violent language. Buck also had the bad judgment to challenge Cobb to a fight and his challenge was accepted with alacrity, if without cheerfulness.

It wasn't much of a fight. Cobb, who out-weighed Herzog, knocked him down with the first punch and Herzog said he had enough.

Cobb likewise had enough. He quit the team the next day and the tour continued without him, both clubs losing heavily at the gate because of Cobb's absence from the line-up. He rejoining the team at Toledo just before the season opened.

Some people have wondered how far Cobb would have gone in baseball without "that terrible temper." The answer is that he would not have gone anywhere. It was his temper, his furious driving compulsion, his burning ambition, his unquenchable desire to excel, that made him the game's greatest player.

He was the greatest competitor that the sport has known and probably the worst loser. His numerous rows, feuds, fights, brought him notoriety but they also increased his gate value. He was the game's greatest box-office magnet until Babe Ruth began wrecking home run records.

Ty knew the value of publicity better than any contemporary, but there were some items that he would rather have done without. Still, his off-the-field activities got the headlines as well as his hitting and base-running.

Cobb never took reverse gracefully. Nothing so hurt him as to lose and often he sat in his room after a losing game and literally wept. His high-strung nature found relief in tears.

Those who gain the peaks are people who cannot endure defeat. Some mask their inner feelings better than others but Cobb, with his fiery disposition, could not wear the mask. He lost complete control over himself. To be beaten meant to be disgraced and he fought all the harder to escape defeat, risked everything to win.

After the New York Yankees lost their second consecutive World's Series to the Giants in 1922, Col. Tillinghast Huston, half-owner of the Yankees at that time, went to the Waldorf-Astoria Hotel, where John J. McGraw had his headquarters, to congratulate him on the Giants' victory. As he was leaving the hotel a friend patted him on the back and said: "Colonel, your team lost but there's one thing they're saying about you that's worth more than winning the Series. They say you're the best loser in the country. I want to congratulate you on that."

Huston thanked him and as the man left, the Colonel turned to an acquaintance, saying:

"That man makes me feel like a rotten hypocrite, an awful four-flusher. 'Good loser!' That's a laugh. Show me the man who is a good loser. All of us are bad losers. We all hate to lose. It hurts us to lose. The difference is that some of us can hide it. We're what is known as 'good losers.' Others cannot hide it. They frankly show it. They're the 'bad losers.' The difference between the good loser and the bad loser is that the good loser is dishonest about it and the bad loser is honest."

According to Col. Huston's definition, Cobb, instead of being criticized for being a bad loser, should have been admired for being honest.

Cobb had his faults, as all mortals have, but he also had his virtues and physical courage was one of them. No one ever doubted his courage, no one ever could.

CHAPTER 20

From Firebrand to Sentimentalist

Dogs are reputed to be keen judges of character. They will shy from certain people, take to others. The attitude of dogs toward a man is believed to indicate the kind of man he is and if this is a true test, then Cobb must be ranked well above the average.

Cobb loves dogs and has always loved them. A noted dog show judge at one time interviewed him, asking his opinion on various breeds of show dogs. Ty told him:

"I know nothing of show dogs or dog shows, but I have studied dogs and I believe them to be among the greatest things in the world. Dogs are little understood but they come closer to being human than any other animal. I honestly believe that dogs have souls. You would agree with me if you had studied them as I have.

"A dog will live with you and he will die with you. Yes, sir, he will die with you. How many dogs have followed their masters to the grave and died there?

"You will find qualities in a dog that you cannot find in human beings. No man ever had a friend as honest or faithful as a dog. There never lived a human being as sincere, frank and honest as a dog. I have gone out hunting with my dogs. Dogs on the hunt don't have the advantage that you have. Your feet are protected by heavy leather and thick soles. The dog has no such protection. He will hunt until he drops, his feet raw from burrs and thistles and underbrush, and then dragging himself home after you, the dog will wait until you yourself are comfortable; then he will come and lie at your side, look up at you and lick your hands. He is tired, exhausted, bruised and sore, but still alert and ready to limp out and serve you."

Cobb, the man who had no sentiment in baseball, who never gave an inch or asked one, who did anything and everything to win, was one of the most sentimental of men in other ways off the field. His love for dogs, his admiration and respect for them, was deep and sincere.

He has remarkable power over dogs. Had he himself trained and handled the pride of his kennel 30 years ago he would have won a national championship.

This dog, Cobb's Hall, was a straight-bred Llewellyn English Setter, by Rigoletto out of Mouna. Rigoletto was by Prince Rodney and Mouna was a litter sister of Momoney. Both Prince Rodney and Momoney were national field trial champions so that Cobb's Hall had almost perfect breeding for field trial competition.

Cobb trained the dog during the winter months, shooting over him, but when he came north in the spring to start another baseball season he turned the dog over to a professional handler.

The field trials were held at Grand Junction, Tennessee, late in autumn and Cobb's Hall and others were pitted against Mary Montrose, the undefeated champion and the greatest field trial performer America ever produced.

Under the professional handler, Cobb's Hall did not behave well. He lacked the polish that he showed when Cobb handled him but even then he finished in a dead heat with Mary Montrose and an extra heat had to be run to decide the championship.

Mary Montrose won the extra heat by a scant margin and it was the closest she ever came to defeat during her brilliant career. The result likely would have been reversed had Ty handled Cobb's Hall.

"Dogs are a great thing for boys," he used to say. "There is no truer companion than a dog, and a boy in the company of a dog is in good company. He will naturally observe the dog and he will learn a great deal by observation that will be helpful to him.

"Dogs are among the world's best instructors. Few of us realize this but if you will study dogs you will find it to be a fact. For one thing, dogs are much more moral than men. They have their own code and it is the only perfect one. In other ways dogs are superior to human beings. If we copied more of their virtues we would all be better off."

Some 30 years ago, W. J. Borland, former psychological examiner of the United States Army, made an examination of Cobb and gave a psychoanalysis of him.

"Cobb has genius without the usual neurotic trend," read Borland's report. Further on he said:

"Cobb never was, is not now, and never can be an egotist. True, the ego, or the psychological equivalent for soul, is highly developed, but the soul of Cobb is never expressed through the medium of egotism. One single trait in his character proves beyond the possibility of doubt that egotism can no more be expressed by Cobb than the Iliad of Homer by the Wild Man of Borneo. That single trait is bashfulness.

"On the emotional side, Cobb has that indefinable quality in personality that infuses others with faith, confidence, enthusiasm and zest for the task at hand, and it is the 'aura' as psychologists call it, that would carry Cobb to the pinnacle of fame as a leader of men in whatever endeavor he chose to follow.

"Extra effort, the drawing upon potential or subconscious reserve, is responsible for outstanding success in any line of human endeavor. It is this quality, whether conscious or not, that has made Cobb the player that he is."

Cobb was never an egotist. He exhibited a bashfulness unusual in men. It was impossible for him to talk in public. He would stutter and stammer. Only when among intimates was he at ease.

He disliked talking about his career. He never discussed baseball unless there was no way out. He gladly discussed any other subject, especially if the man with whom he was talking could increase his fund of knowledge.

When introduced to a stranger he was the most courteous and gracious of men. He always left a favorable impression regardless of the social status of the new acquaintance.

CHAPTER 21

A Man of Many Moods

Cobb lived in moods. At times he was happy and gay, vivaciously alive, and at other times he was gloomy and morose. At times he wondered what it was all about and of what use it could be. On one of these occasions he said:

"If I had my life to live over again I would be a surgeon instead of a ball player. I think I could have done a great deal of good in surgery. I would have been of some help to humanity."

At other times he decided to quit baseball. He intended to settle down, fish, hunt, read and enjoy life.

"Down South we know how to live," he would say. "Down South there isn't the hustle, the bustle, the tear and wear that you find in the North. We get something out of life down there. We know what home is and where. In the North people believe that an apartment of a few rooms is sufficient but we could never think of such a thing in the South. We know food down there and we know how to relax. There is not the battle and the strife for the dollar that there is in the North. Tell me, what do they get out of life — these people that are fighting so hard for fortunes that few ever accumulate? They grow old and helpless long before their time and when they have outlived their usefulness what have they got? What do they get out of life even if they succeed in making a pile of money? By the time they accumulate their fortunes they don't know how to enjoy it."

At other times he would say:

"When I quit baseball, which will be very soon now, I shall depart with one regret and that is that I have done no real good for humanity. I suppose everybody will have forgotten me within a few years' time."

He became tired of baseball. Ty once said: "I am fed up with the continual strain. I'm tired of it all. The ambitions I had when I broke into professional baseball down in Georgia in 1904 have been satisfied. Yes, I have achieved more than I set out to achieve. Now I can go back and settle down and get something really worth while out of life."

Year after year he made up his mind to quit. At the age of 32 he said it was his last season. Then another season and another farewell resolution. He was still playing daily at the age of 42, ten years after he announced his retirement. He had been a millionaire for several years but the lure of the game kept calling him back.

"Thirty-five is the age limit of players in the big leagues," he told me in 1918. "When a man reaches that age he loses his speed and zest for competition. I'm no longer at my top form. I have gradually let down since 1914.

"After a ball player reaches 30 he becomes methodical. I have become methodical and today I find myself doping out each play before I make it with a view to conserving as much energy as possible.

"Most of the success I'm having now is due to psychology. I apply it constantly. For instance, when the Tigers are leading and the opportunity presents itself, I often take chances, making a freak play or stealing a base when there is no necessity for it. I create a series of mental hazards for the opposing team that causes the player to fumble nine times out of ten on a similar play that may follow.

"When I was in the flush of youth I could play all day and all night without ever tiring, but now I find, as the years creep up on me, that I can no longer make the plays that I used to make."

The fires of ambition belong to youth and even with Cobb, in whom the flames burned longer than in any other player, it became more and more difficult to keep the embers smoldering.

"Baseball is a hard, nerve-racking game when you play it for all it's worth," he said. 'There is no rest when you are weary and the travel is tiresome."

He wanted time to read and rest. He liked books as he liked music and pictures. In books he appreciated fine phrasing. The play of words fascinated him.

In reading he preferred biographies. He devoured all the biographies of Napoleon Bonaparte that he could acquire. He regarded him as the greatest character in the world history, with Julius Caesar second. It would be difficult to say that his biographical studies did not have a powerful influence on Cobb's career. He would probably be the last man to say that they did not.

When Cobb became manager, he often thought of the old pennant-winning days and his teammates, the same fellows who badgered and insulted him, rode him and tried to break his spirit, the men who made life miserable for him.

When his team slumped and he failed to arouse it to a fighting pitch, he often said:

"If we only had some of that old gang here now. If we only had a Germany Schaefer, a Claude Rossman, a Charley O'Leary, a Matty McIntyre or Davey Jones. What I'd give to have them on this team right now. Yes and a Charlie Schmidt, a Bill Donovan and a George Mullin.

"Those were the boys, I tell you. They had the real stuff. Their type has vanished They aren't turning out their kind any more. They were the fellows that had the old fight. They were game, those boys. Imagine that crew laying down the way these fellows do! 'Come on at 'em an' tear 'em apart' is what they used to yell. That's just what they did. They battled everybody. You couldn't beat them because they wouldn't let you. They were a rip-roaring lot. If I could only get about six players like them we would have a winning team."

He would add:

"I'm getting old. I'm nearing that stage where it will be the bench for me. The old legs and arms don't respond the way they used to. We all reach that stage sooner or later."

But he never retired to the bench. He remained active until the day he retired. This was after the 1928 season when he finished his career batting .323 for Connie Mack and the Athletics.

CHAPTER 22

"Cobb Did More for the Game Than Any Other Man"

Cobb left baseball a different game than when he entered it. He revolutionized the game, gave it new life, new speed. He brought about a change at a time when baseball had become stagnant. It was in a groove, orthodox, cut and dried to a degree that was monotonous. He brought the game out of its lethargy, gave it gloss, sparkle and sheen. He made more out the game than it had ever been. The rapid development of baseball, its astounding growth and dazzling spread in popularity can be credited to Cobb's vision, to his speed of limb and brain that worked in perfect coordination, and his spirit. He injected into the game a powerful personality that was felt throughout the sport.

"He did more for baseball than any single individual that ever lived," said Byron Bancroft Johnson on one occasion. "The game owes him more than it will ever realize."

As time ran out on Cobb, what did he think of the game? Not as much as in 1905 when he wore a major league uniform for the first time. The lively ball had changed baseball. He never liked the lively ball and opposed if from the start. He never changed his opinion. He said in later years:

"The lively ball has robbed the game of finesse. The art has been taken out of baseball. A premium has been placed upon brawn instead of brain."

He blamed the change on the owners.

"The object of the lively ball is to produce more hits. The club owners believe the public likes hits better than anything else in baseball," declared Ty. "The public does like hits, but I believe that hits can become too common, too cheap. Too much hitting causes an overabundance.

"The lively ball has ruined most of the strategy. Few players know how to bunt and fewer still steal bases. It's not profitable to bunt or try to steal.

The percentage is all against you. Maybe you stand an even chance in trying to steal but it advances you only one base if you're successful. You stand as good a chance to be advanced two bases on a hit and probably score. Stealing third is now pure folly. The outfielders are playing from 30 to 40 feet deeper than they played when I started in the American League. It is a simple matter to take two bases on a hit due to the much longer throw. A runner is almost certain to score on any outfield hit, so why steal third?

"Why take a chance at all in stealing? The thing to do, with the lively ball, is to stay anchored to a base and await for a base hit. There is no percentage in base-running. That's become passé. They now wait for the hit, get runs in clusters. Teams no longer play for one run, they play for runs.

"The best thing to do is play the infield back, aim to get one man, keep the opposing team's run total as low as possible and trust to getting more runs yourself.

"The science of batting has been fairly well lost," continued Cobb. "The main idea now is to stand up there and take a healthy cut at the ball. You don't have to hit it a mile, although you generally do if you connect solidly. But a ball hit on the ground will often do as well. It travels too fast to be handled properly unless hit directly at some infielder.

"A damper has been put on inside baseball since one run is rarely sufficient to win for you. Big rallies are the thing.

"The fast defensive work in which outfielders participated is a thing of the past. They are now out too far to get into the play. How many outfielders do you see throw out runners at the plate on direct throws? In nearly every instance the outfielder shares credit with an infielder who cuts off the throw and relays it to the plate. Two assists are scored where one was scored before.

"Managers don't take many chances. They play a safety-first game, sit back and wait for base hits. They take their cues from the batting averages, showing the percentage is with the batter as against the base-runner. The hit gets you so much more than the steal.

"Baseball moves in cycles. When I broke into the league the craze was pitching. All kinds of freak deliveries were introduced — the shine ball, the emery ball, the licorice ball, the spitball and the rest. Then, suddenly, came reform. All freak deliveries were barred. Baseball went from one extreme to the other. There is never any temperance, either no limit or complete prohibition. This is the day of the slugger. All legislation in the last 30 years has been made with a view to increase hitting. And tomorrow—who knows?"

